Globalization and Educational Rights

An Intercivilizational Analysis

Sociocultual, Political, and Historical Studies in Education
Joel Spring, Editor

Globalization and Educational Rights
An Intercivilizational Analysis

Joel Spring

New School University

LAWRENCE ERLBAUM ASSOCIATES, PUBLISHERS

2001   Mahwah, New Jersey   London

Lawrence Erlbaum Associates, Inc., Publishers
10 Industrial Avenue
Mahwah, NJ 07430

Cover design by Kathryn Houghtaling Lacey

Library of Congress Cataloging-in-Publication Data

Spring, Joel H.
Globalization and educational rights :
an intercivilizational analysis / Joel Spring.

   p. cm.–(Sociocultural, political, and historical studies in education)

Includes bibliographical references and index.
ISBN 0-8058-3881-3 (cloth : alk. paper)
ISBN 0-8058-3882-1 (pbk. : alk. paper)
1. Right to education–Cross-cultural studies.
2. Comparative education. I. Title. II. Series.
LC213 .S66 2001
379.2'6—dc21
                                                2001018942
                                                        CIP

Books published by Lawrence Erlbaum Associates are printed on acid-free paper, and their bindings are chosen for strength and durability.

Printed in the United States of America
10 9 8 7 6 5 4 3 2 1

Contents

Preface

I became interested in an intercivilizational approach to educational rights while reading the reaction of Asian scholars to Western concerns about human rights violations. As these scholars pointed out, Western history is filled with horror stories of inquisitions, genocide, and the rape of colonial lands. The West is hardly a model for the safeguarding of human rights. Then I began to think about the 1948 Universal Declaration of Human Rights as an international project and not simply a Western project. The "natural rights" tradition of the West considered rights to have originated from a lost state of nature. On the other hand, "human rights" are considered the necessary conditions for promoting human welfare. Focusing on human welfare broadens the scope of rights doctrines from "natural rights" to rights that are considered essential for human existence. The Western natural rights tradition never made education a right. In contrast, education in the 20th century is considered by most national constitutions a necessary condition for the promotion of human welfare and, therefore, is identified as a right. As a global idea, the meaning of educational rights varies between civilizations. In this book, my intercivilizational analysis of educational rights includes some of the world's major civilizations, namely Confucian, Islamic, Western, and Hindu.

Educational rights are included in national constitutions written since the global spread of human rights ideas after World War II. Most European constitutions now include an article on educational rights in contrast with the continued neglect of educational rights in the United States constitution. The constitutions of China, India, and all Islamic countries contain statements on educational rights. International human rights statements, including the Universal Islamic Declaration of Human Rights, include educational rights.

However, there are civilizational differences over the meaning of educational rights. In the book's first chapter, I consider educational rights as part of the global flow of ideas and the global culture of schooling, and the tension this creates with different civilizational traditions. In chapter 2, I examine the meaning of educational rights in the Confucian tradition, the recent history of China, and in the Chinese Constitution. In chapter 3, I look at educational rights in the context of Islamic civilization and as presented in the constitutions of Islamic countries. There is a sharp contrast between the religious orientation of Islamic educational rights and those of China and the West. In chapter 4, I explore the problems created by the Western natural rights tradition and the eventual acceptance of educational rights as represented in European constitutions. One focus in this chapter is the development and prominence given in the West to the relationship between schooling and equality of opportunity. In chapter 5, I investigate the effect of global culture on India and the blend of Western and Hindu ideas in the Indian Constitution. I highlight the problems created by centuries of discrimination against women and lower castes for the fulfillment of educational rights. And finally, in chapter 6, I present an educational rights statement based on my intercivilizational analysis and on my examination of constitutions. It is my intention that my statement of educational rights will serve as a model for the inclusion of educational rights in national constitutions.

—*Joel Spring*

1

Global Education
and an Intercivilizational
Analysis

What is the goal of the 1948 Universal Declaration of Human Rights declaration that "Everyone has a right to education"? What is the meaning of equality and freedom as related to this goal? Do human rights, equality, and freedom have the same meaning in all civilizations? Is there an evolving global purpose for education?

In answering these questions, I examine differing civilizational concepts of education, equality, and freedom. Also, I study the educational rights provisions in a representative sampling of national constitutions. Based on these analyses, I propose constitutional amendments to ensure the implementation of a right to education that affirms equality and freedom of education.

My analysis includes Confucian, Islamic, Western, and Hindu civilizations. These represent the majority of the world's people; I did not include, for reasons of time and space, the world's indigenous civilizations. For my purposes, civilization refers to "religions, languages, ethics, and customs that influence thoughts and behavior of people transcending national boundaries."[1] Within this meaning, Confucian civilization refers to those Asian people who are influenced in their thinking by centuries of Confucian teachings. Islamic civilization is held together by the teachings of the Qur'an and the use of Qur'anic Arabic. Western civilization is a product of Judaic-Christian ideas, and the legacy of the Greek and Roman cultures. I selected Hindu civilization, which rests on ancient Hindu laws, because the current constitution of India is a product of the clash between Western and Hindu civilizations. Besides being a product of intercivilizational exchanges, the Indian constitution provides important insights into the problems of establishing standards for the implementation of the universal right to education.

ILLUSTRATING THE GROWING UNIFORMITY OF GLOBAL EDUCATION: "NOT ONE LESS"

Amidst these civilizational differences, there is a growing uniformity of global education. This uniformity is a reflection of global economics. Throughout this book, I discuss the interaction between the uniformity of global education and differing civilizational concerns about education. Also, I want to consider my opening questions on equality and freedom of education in the context of global educational trends. This discussion will sharpen the differences between civilizational concepts of education and global trends.

The Chinese movie "Not One Less" provides a good illustration of the use of equality and freedom in global patterns of education. In the movie a 13-year-old substitute teacher in a poor and desolate village in rural China excites her charges with the arithmetic problem of determining how many bricks must be moved in a nearby factory to earn enough money for the teacher to travel to the city in search of a missing student. After moving 1,000 bricks, the pupils and teacher stop at a store to buy something to drink. Being poor and growing up in rural isolation, the teacher and students don't know what can be bought to quench their thirsts. The shopkeeper acts as an instructor in modern consumption. She points to a shelf of Coca-Cola®. The teacher and students then engage in another arithmetic exercise and determine that they can afford two cans of the liquid refreshment. The teacher and students experience their first taste of Coca-Cola®. Later in the film, after the teacher has slept on city streets and on a train station floor in search of her missing student, a local television studio decides to use her to highlight problems facing rural education in China. Appearing on the program "China Today," the frightened girl stares speechless into a video camera marked with the Sony Corporation logo. A Sony brand television conveys her image to the lost student who is in a street restaurant having been helped by its compassionate owner.

The film's concluding credits thank the financial support received from the Coca-Cola Corporation, the Ford Motor Company, and the Sony Corporation followed by a general request for donations to help support education in rural China. Obviously, these three multinational corporations would love to change the lives of rural peasants so that they could earn enough money to buy their products. In the film's final scenes, "China Today's" film crew arrives in the village with the teacher and lost student accompanied by a truck full of educational materials. The students use colored chalk from the new supplies to write messages of appreciation on the classroom chalkboard.

"Not One Less" suggests that the universal right to education means learning to be modern workers who are able to purchase products of multinational corporations. Of course, at one level, there is nothing wrong with this goal. The movie's impoverished villagers do seem to lack adequate nutrition and health care. Certainly, education and economic development could help solve these problems. On the other hand, will the villagers be happier if they are educated so that they can work to purchase canned soda drinks, televisions, and cars? Furthermore, it is through education that the teacher and students acquire a taste for these products. They learn to want and need these commodities!

The film's overall message is that educational and economic development will provide equality of opportunity in the labor and consumer markets. Rather than being lost and begging in the city's work and consumer world, educated students will have an equal chance to compete for jobs and money, and the freedom to buy. Education will save the rural peasantry!

As reflected in "Not One Less," equality and freedom in education are frequently thought of as preparing students for equality of opportunity in the competition for jobs and income and the freedom to consume. However, I do not feel that these definitions should represent all the goals implied in Article 26 of the 1948 Universal Declaration of Human Rights. Equality of opportunity and freedom of consumption, I believe, fail to adequately express the full range of meaning of equality and freedom existing within the world's civilizations.

AN INTERCIVILIZATIONAL APPROACH TO DEFINING EQUALITY AND FREEDOM OF EDUCATION: CONFUCIAN, ISLAMIC, WESTERN, AND HINDU

Do all civilizations share a common meaning regarding "human rights," "education," "equality," and "freedom?" To answer this question, I will apply an intercivilizational method suggested by Onuma Yasuaki, a Professor of International Law at the University of Tokyo. He argues for an intercivilizational approach because the people of Western countries assume that they are the reason for the global presence of human rights doctrines. Onuma Yasuaki argues that Asian countries that are denounced for violation of human rights "were once under colonial rule and the victims of military intervention and economic exploitation by developed countries."[2] Onuma charges Western nations with hypocrisy when charging nations such as China with human rights violations. He stresses that, "For those who have experienced colonial rule and interventions under such beautiful slogans as 'humanity' and 'civilization', the term 'human rights' looks like nothing more than another beautiful slogan by which great powers rationalize their interventionist policies."[3] Onuma contends that finding a human rights tradition in Western societies is very difficult because of the West's long history of feudalism, colonialism, enslavement of other populations, genocide of indigenous peoples, and discrimination against women. Certainly, the very existence of Hitler and the Jewish Holocaust raises doubts about the superiority of Western societies over others in the arena of human rights. Human rights, meaning rights provided to all human beings including women and children, is not part of the natural rights movements in Western societies as they originated in the 18th and 19th centuries.

Westerners, Onuma contends, assume only non-Western religions and cultures have to be examined to discover human rights traditions. For instance, Westerners do not attempt to "find" human rights in Christianity or Western cultures because they assume that they are a distinct part of those traditions. Westerners write books and articles that attempt to identify human rights traditions in such religious and cultural traditions as Buddhism, Confucianism, Muslimism, and Hinduism.[4]

Representing what he feels are the doubts held by many East Asians about the West's claim to superiority in human rights, Onuma writes, "Prior to the twentieth century, the history of human rights is the history of qualifications. The male-dominated French National Assembly of 1792 denied the Declaration of the Rights of Women, and the West-centric Versailles Conference of 1919 rejected the Japanese proposal for including a racial equality clause in the Covenant of the League of Nations. The century and a half following the American Declaration of Independence and the French Declaration of the Rights of Man and Citizens ... witnessed the peak of colonization by Western powers."[5]

For instance, when it was proclaimed in the 1776 American Declaration of Independence that "All men are created equal" the White citizens of these sparsely populated and relatively unknown group of British colonies owned slaves, and they were engaged in wars of genocide against a local native population.[6] The previous year, colonist Patrick Henry, ignoring the plight of slaves and Native Americans, declared, "I know not what course others may take, but as for me, give me liberty or give me death!"[7] The words were intended for the ears of fellow slave-holding Virginians who were debating resistance to the British crown and not those of enslaved Africans and Native Americans.

In reality, the human rights movement of the 20th century resulted from interaction between civilizations. In fact, the 1948 Declaration of Human Rights was a product of a dialogue between members of the United Nations. Of course, Western nations participated in the dialogue and exerted influence. But, given the painful history of Western violations of human rights, it would be difficult to maintain the argument that the West is the sole source of ideas about human rights and of concern about protecting the welfare of all human beings.

Consequently, I take an intercivilizational approach to defining equality and freedom in education. As I will demonstrate, every civilization has given different meanings to these concepts. From this intercivilizational approach I extract universal concepts of equality and freedom in education and I demonstrate the problems and prospects for their applicability in differing civilizations.

THE UNIVERSAL DECLARATION OF HUMAN RIGHTS AS AN INTERCIVILIZATIONAL DOCUMENT

The intercivilizational nature of equality, freedom, and human rights was exemplified by a symposium hosted by the United Nations Educational, Scientific and Cultural Organization (UNESCO) just prior to the issuance of the 1948 Declaration.[8] The purpose of the symposium was to find a common ground among various intellectual traditions for the support of human rights. China was represented by Chung-Shu Lo, who in his symposium essay demonstrated the difference between Chinese and Western concepts of rights. He observed that "the problem of human rights [as conceived by Westerners] were seldom discussed by Chinese thinkers ... There was no open declaration of human rights in China ... until this conception was introduced from the West."[9] In fact, according to Chung-Shu, there was no Chinese equivalent for the word rights. The Chinese translation of rights includes two words *Chuan Li*, meaning "power and interest." Lo claimed this translation was done by an unnamed Japanese writer on Western public law in 1868 because Japan also lacked any equivalent words for the Western idea of rights.

However, despite the lack of any clearly identifiable human rights tradition, Chung-Shu suggested that some traditional Chinese ideas could be considered close to Western ideas. For instance, he quoted the Chinese classic, *Book of History*: "Heaven sees as our people see; Heaven hears as our people hear. Heaven is compassionate towards the people ... Heaven loves the people; and the Sovereign must obey Heaven."[10] Based on this quote, Chung-Shu argued that the Chinese people believed in the right to revolt against rulers who did not serve the welfare of the people. Chung-Shu stated that the Chinese relationship of the ruler to the ruled paralleled some European traditions. He claimed that "human" rights doctrines could be supported by Chinese traditions. Chung-Shu observed, "The sovereign as well as the officials were taught to regard themselves as the parents or guardians of the people, and to protect their people as they would their own children."[11]

Other essayists to the UNESCO volume objected to the Western natural rights traditions. S.V. Puntambekar presented a Hindu concept of human rights that emphasizes the spiritual nature of humans. He criticized the Western stress on reason and science that marked the emergence European rights doctrines. In criticizing the Western tradition for suppressing the spiritual nature of life, Puntambekar wrote, "We shall have to give up some of the superstitions of material science and limited reason, which make man too much this-worldly, and introduce higher spiritual aims and values for [human]kind."[12]

Puntambekar derived a set of human rights from Hindu traditions. He identified five social freedoms and five individual possessions or virtues necessary for achieving the good spiritual life. Each social freedom was linked to an individual possession or virtue. Puntambekar provided a list of social freedoms and individual virtues; this is presented in Table 1.1.

Also concerned about Western claims to originating human rights ideals, Islamic leaders are divided between those who worry that the human rights movement is an attempt to impose Western values on them and those advocating an Islamic basis for universal human rights. International legal scholar Ann Mayer writes, "One finds Muslims who disparage human rights as reflecting alien, Western values. In

TABLE 1.1

Hindu Concept of Human Rights[13]

Social Freedoms	Individual Possessions or Virtues
1. Freedom from violence	1. Absence of intolerance
2. Freedom from want	2. Compassion or fellow freedom
3. Freedom from exploitation	3. Knowledge
4. Freedom from violation or dishonor	4. Freedom of thought and conscience
5. Freedom from early death and diesease	5. Freedom from fear and frustration or despair

their view, international human rights are incompatible with Islam, Muslims must reject them."[14]

However, Islamic scholars do identify traditional ideas that are designed to protect the rights and welfare of Muslim people. For instance, a number of Muslim countries participated in the writing of the 1981 Universal Islamic Declaration of Human Rights. This declaration recognizes the benevolent and protective aspects of Moslem traditions.[15] The 1990 Cairo Declaration on Human Rights in Islam declares, "Fundamental rights and Universal freedoms in Islam are an integral part of the Islamic religion and that no one as a matter of principle has the right to suspend them in whole or in part or violate or ignore them ... "[16]

Some Westerners recognize the intercivilizational character of human rights ideas. For instance, Paul Gordon Lauren equates human rights with a regard for the general welfare of people. In other words, human rights are those ideas in each civilization designed to promote the welfare of all. Lauren uses this approach in his book *The Evolution of International Human Rights*. For example, Lauren finds in both Christian and Hindu civilizations prohibitions against hurting others. He states that "the first and foremost principle of Hinduism ... is noninjury to others. The edict is stated directly and universally: 'Noninjury ... is not causing pain to any living being at any time through the actions of one's mind, speech, or body.'"[17] Initiating the spread of Buddhism almost 2,500 years ago, Lauren argues, Siddhartha Gautama criticized the existence of social inequalities and urged followers to become a fraternity of equals dedicated to compassion and charity. Lauren also states that Confucianism emphasizes the responsibility of each person to promote harmony, maintain the welfare of others, and recognize that all people are of equal worth. In addition, Lauren considers human rights to be a concern of 10th century Islamic scholar Al-Farabi, who envisioned a moral society "in which all societies individuals were endowed with rights and lived in love and charity with their neighbors."[18]

In using an intercivilizational approach, I equate concerns about human welfare with concerns about human rights. Each of the major civilizations discussed in this book have traditions that speak to the issue of human welfare. However, as I discuss, all of these traditions contain certain ideas that hinder the full development of humans. All civilizations also have educational traditions, but these traditions contain ideas that have sometimes limited equality of educational opportunity and freedom.

HUMAN RIGHTS IN THE GLOBAL FLOW AND THE GLOBAL CULTURE

Along with the intercivilizational approach used in this book, I use Arjun Appadurai's concept of ideoscapes in the global cultural flow.[19]

Trained as an anthropologist, Appadurai substitutes the expression *global cultural flow* for the term *global culture*. However, I believe that the term *global culture* remains useful in denoting the growing uniformity and homogenization of the world's cultures.

I think of the global flow as a conglomeration of ideas, technology, media, and money that envelopes the world. Inside the global flow is a loosely coherent thread of global culture that sometimes is clearly defined and at other times is diffuse and opaque. The global culture is a magnet attracting people to a particular ideology regarding economic opportunity and consumption.

Global culture denotes the standardization and homogenization of cultures that is occurring with the spread of mass consumer goods and economic development. I imagine the thread of global culture winding its way through the confusion of the global flow. Unlike the global flow, this identifiable thread of global culture appears uniform and standardized, drawing people and resources to it while creating a sameness and uniformity to worldwide economic growth.

I have heard travelers comment of the growing sameness of consumer goods and popular culture. In my own country, I see similar-looking malls with identical stores selling identical products. No matter what campus I visit, college students melt into the same image. I find this increasing uniformity wherever I travel. Visiting Taiwan, I heard the same rhetoric about schooling as I do in the United States. Walking the streets of Taipei I passed Starbucks coffee shops, McDonald's fast-food hamburger emporiums, and Seven Eleven convenience stores. The same hotel and clothing chains are everywhere. I could find only a Kentucky Fried Chicken open on a Sunday afternoon while driving around the Carribean Island of St. Lucia. At the time, I thought of lines of people around the world all waiting to eat chicken cooked according to the same formula.

Resisting the pull of global culture, some people reach into the global flow seeking social and economic alternatives, or they try to remain rooted in their local culture and language. Other people, particularly those in underdeveloped countries, try to grab hold of the thread of the global culture only to find it outside their grasp because of economic deprivation or political oppression. Whatever their circumstances or desires, the world's people feel the attraction of the global culture as they try to define their place in the stream of worldwide events.

In coining the term *global flow*, Appadurai's purpose is to denote constant change and to indicate that the meaning of ideas is dependent on historical, linguistic, and political contexts.[20] He purposely uses the suffix *-scape* in identifying ideoscapes, ethnoscapes, mediascapes, technoscapes, and financescapes as major parts of the cultural flow because -*scape* implies the fluid and irregular shape of a landscape. Also, -*scape* is meant to signify the varying perspectives of the world's peoples. For instance, ethnoscapes refers to the movement of people as tourists, immigrants, refugees, and others. The meaning of these ethnoscapes depends on the perspective of the viewer. Certainly, tourists and immigrants view local people differently than local people view the tourist and the immigrant. Television, movies, and other conveyances of fiction and advertising move across the global landscape having different effects on the imaginations of the world's peoples. Technoscapes and financescapes, as their names imply, represent the uneven effects of rapid technological development, multinational corporations, and global capital.

Ideas of equality and freedom are part of the global flow. Appadurai considers them master terms in the "political narratives that govern communication between elites and followers in different parts of the world."[21] However, they have differing meanings within different civilizations. The confusion over the meaning of equality and freedom, and the current tendency to emphasize equality of opportunity and freedom of markets (or consumption), should not obscure the importance of these concepts in the global flow of ideas. The words have an emotional aura that promise all things to all people. Using the words *equality* and *freedom* as they exist in the global flow of ideas meaning different things in different contexts, people demand social change ranging from simple improvement of living conditions to revolution.

As emotional symbols in the global flow, equality and freedom can be invoked to defend a wide range of political and economic actions. Their meaning depends on the user and his or her goals. Ignoring their historical and varied usages, people can attend to the words equality and *freedom* in the global flow and use them to serve their own interests. Today, political leaders can declare the goal of equality while only planning for the equality of a few. Freedom of economic markets can result in restricted freedom for the poor and workers. Ironically, the words *equality* and *freedom* can be invoked to create their opposites: inequality and oppression.

Unfortunately, Appadurai makes the very mistake warned about by Onuma Yasuaki. Appadurai claims that the West introduced concepts of human rights, equality, and freedom into the global flow. Ideoscapes, according to Appadurai, "are composed of elements of the [Western] Enlightenment world view … [where] the diaspora of these terms and images across the world, especially in the nineteenth century, has loosened the internal coherence that held them together in … [the] Euro-American master narrative."[22] According to his argument, ideas such as equality and freedom originated in the Western Enlightenment of the 18th and 19th centuries and flowed around the world with the expansion of European and U.S. colonialism and the creation of international organizations and multinational corporations during the post-colonial period.

While the West cannot claim responsibility for introducing human rights concepts into the global flow, European and U.S. colonialists did have a major influence on speeding ideas through the global flow by attempting to force Western languages and ideas onto other countries and by causing the diaspora of large numbers of the world's peoples. Western colonialism will be a theme throughout this book because of its effect on the global flow of ideas and the reaction to it by Confucian, Islamic, and Hindu civilizations.

THE INTERCIVILIZATIONAL CHARACTER OF GLOBAL EDUCATION

The global culture of education is a uniform thread in the global flow. There is a tendency for the world's school systems to embrace an educational model that emphasizes human capital accounting and economic development. This global model is a result of colonialism, global contacts, and international economic planning. It envisions schools educating workers for jobs created by economic development. Because economic and technological development and change are occurring at a swift pace, it assumes that students must have life-long learning skills. Within the human capital model, life-long learning refers to the ability to constantly learn new skills as job requirements change. Life-long learning should not be confused with dreams of scholars lying under trees reading great literature and philosophy. Life-long learning is an economic concept.[23]

From Korea to Japan to China to Singapore to India to the European Union and to North and South America, schools are evaluated by politicians as suppliers of human capital for economic development. Using business concepts, the outcomes of investment in education are measured by test scores, on-the-job performance, and the congruence of instruction with labor market needs. In this global model, the "knowledge society" is one where the level and quality of education is matched with personal income. Parents struggle to ensure that their children do well on high-stakes tests by providing special tutors and sending their children to cram schools. Test results determine the prestige of the school the child will attend which, in turn, affects the child's future income. The overall quality of the school system determines, it is argued, the prosperity of the nation.

However, there are dissenters to this model, particularly among those wedded to indigenous educational practices. As I discuss later in this book, many Islamic schools follow traditional methods of instruction. In addition, indigenous groups are struggling to restore their traditional educational practices after experiencing years of cultural genocide. In a 1996 meeting of representatives of the world's indigenous peoples, alternatives to the global human capital model were proposed. They are described in *Indigenous Educational Models for Contemporary Practice: In Our Mother's Voice*. The volume's preface expresses a clear alternative vision to global corporate education:

> Indeed, Native peoples, like the individual flowers entwined lovingly into a fragrant lei, must value our interconnectedness and work collectively to assure that our unique histories, languages and traditions are not lost. This book is an offering to that personal responsibility and commitment each of us has to look with and teach out.[24]

In addition, scattered throughout this book are discussions of repeated attempts to protect local moral teachings from what were considered the decadent influences of outside cultures.

The global culture of education is a result of a complex interaction between nations and international economic organizations. It is an ongoing intercivilizational process. The World Bank and the Organization for Economic Development and Cooperation are major advocates of human capital approaches to educational planning. I have described these developments in detail in *Education and the Rise of the Global Economy*.[25] Therefore, rather than rehashing that study, which would divert attention from the goal of this book, I will provide a few brief examples of the interplay of the world's educational systems.

In 1983, the United States government published *A Nation at Risk*, which blamed the country's public schools for falling behind in economic competition with Japan and Germany. The report declared, "If only to keep and improve on the slim competitive edge we still retain in world markets, we must rededicate ourselves to the reform of the educational system for the benefit of all."[26] Corporate and educational leaders declared the Japanese school system to be superior to that of the United States. As a result, U.S. schools began to model the test-driven Japanese schools including the development of cram schools to prepare for high-stakes tests.[27] Ironically, which American leaders often failed to note, the current Japanese school system was forcefully modeled after the U.S. educational system by the occupational government following Japan's defeat after World War II. Japanese education had been influenced by European imperialism. However, during the 1960s, a conservative Japanese government reinstituted central control of a national curriculum through national testing, as opposed to the U.S. model of local school boards and local control. This Japanese examination tradition and the use of schools as a system of moral control was, in part, a result of Confucian traditions resulting from past influences from China. In chapter 2, I explain this Confucian tradition. Also, it must be pointed out here that the Japanese model of education illustrates that the global culture of education is not a one-way flow. Japanese education was not only shaped in important ways by global influences, but also has influenced the educational systems of other nations. Prior to its defeat during World War II, Japanese imperialistic policies included the introduction of Japanese education throughout Asia.[28]

Other examples abound around the globe. Singapore's Prime Minister Lee Kuan Yee declared himself a Confucian. His government and moral instruction in Singapore's schools were modeled on Confucian principles. At the same time, Lee adopted a human capital approach by linking education directly to economic development. Singapore's 1997 Master plan for Informational Technology, designed to capture a large part of the international computer software market, directly coordinated changes in the school system's curriculum with the needs of this new industry. Slogans such as, "Future Wealth Will Depend on Capacity to Learn" slip easily off the tongues of educational leaders. Reflecting the cross-cultural nature of Singapore's endeavors, its government's outside models are Japanese and U.S. schools. In addition, British colonialism left the legacy of English as the language of higher education.[29]

Equality of opportunity is an important concept in human capital education. Equality of opportunity means that everyone should have a chance to compete for positions in the labor market. Supposedly, schools will be the instrument for ensuring equality of opportunity. It is my contention that the growing uniformity of global culture involves an acceptance of definitions of equality and freedom that are, respectively, focused on equality of opportunity and freedom to consume. These concepts are basic to the human capital model. The concept of equality of opportunity breeds uniformity because it requires uniformity of character and actions. The assumption is that all people will be motivated to compete for wealth. The phrase "equality of opportunity" means equal opportunity to accumulate wealth. Of course, this version of equality results in a society with economic inequality. The rules of the game are the only thing equal about equality of opportunity. Consequently, the concept of equality of opportunity requires the individual to have a character structure committed to the life goal of competing for wealth. Implied in this global concept of opportunity is that the competitors will use their wealth for the consumption of products. Therefore, hard work, pursuit of wealth, and consumption are the uniform and principle human values accompanying spread of global culture.

Education, as reflected in the movie "Not One Less," is considered by many people to be the means for instilling the character structure required for participation in equality of opportunity. Political theorist C. Douglas Lummis concludes that world economic development is driven by the idea "that everyone in the world is or ought to be playing the same game."[30] He argues that this requires a transformation of culture and personal values: "For the peoples of the world to play the development game, they must first be made over into players."[31]

Global planners speak openly of the necessity of a particular character structure required for economic development. An advocate of economic development, Lucian Pye, states "Part of the process of modernization involves the learning of new skills ... the acceptance of new ideas ... new values and the changing of preferences. A still deeper dimension of the process calls for a fundamental change in motivations and in the direction in which it is felt the human energies can properly be directed."[32] In contrast to Pye, Loomis bemoans the current situation where the "whole teeming multiplicity of the world's cultures, developed through the labor and imagination of all human history, is now to be placed under a single standard of value."[33]

The idea of "freedom of consumption" also contributes to global homogenization. Equality of opportunity is premised on the idea that the wealth gained under the rules of equal economic competition will be used to exercise freedom of consumption. Important economic values are implicit in the concept of freedom of consumption. The economic goal is *not* simply adequate nutrition, housing, medical care, and physical comfort for the world's population. If this were the goal, then conceivably at some distant future there would be an end to world economic development. The steady desire for and purchase of consumer goods is the motivating force behind equality of opportunity and freedom of consumption. This motivation is based on two important economic requirements.

The first requirement is that people learn to need new products. In the movie "Not One Less," the children learned to drink Coca-Cola. Coca-Cola became a learned need for these rural students. In recent years, the world's population has learned to need computers and wireless telephones. The assumption is that economic growth is driven by the constant development of new products. Consequently, the industrial and financial systems will be sustained only if these new products are purchased. This means the constant learning of new needs. This, in turn, requires that the hard working consumer continually exist in a state of dissatisfaction waiting to purchase new products. If consumers were completely satisfied with existing goods, the system might collapse.

The second requirement is that consumers are motivated by what Thorstein Veblen called *conspicuous consumption*. As the term implies, conspicuous consumption means the purchase of consumer products that serve as public displays of one's wealth and status. The brand and model of automobile a person owns usually serves as a public symbol of their social class.

Conspicuous consumption and equality of opportunity are interlinked. The goal of equality of opportunity is to enable individuals to amass wealth in an economic system that requires constant consumption. Being more successful at amassing wealth means winning the game. But how is anyone going to know that a person is a winner? In the global culture, the symbols of achievement are consumer products. The bigger the winner, the bigger the consumer. Conspicuous consumption is the public reward!

Multinational corporations foster uniformity bred by personal commitment to hard work, competition, learning new needs, and conspicuous consumption. Their products drive the whole system of work and consumption. Multinational corporations desire uniformity in market and labor values. Multicultural education for international corporations can simply mean learning to market goods in different cultural settings. In this context, cultures are treated as instrumental for the marketing of a product. Local cultural icons might be added to an advertisement to appeal to local populations. However, no matter what the message, the medium and product are the same. Advertising attempts to convey consumer values related to a particular product. If advertising has an effect, then markets, despite original cultural differences, begin to look the same. Also, multinational corporations look for similar values among their workers. The purpose of multicultural education in this situation is to teach different cultural groups how to work cooperatively. The sharing of work values, similar to the sharing of consumer values, adds another dimension to the growing homogenization and sameness of global culture.

HUMAN RIGHTS STATEMENTS ON EQUALITY, FREEDOM, AND THE RIGHT TO EDUCATION

There is a tension between the global culture of education and human rights statements on education. In the global ideoscape, formal schooling has existed in various forms. Today, the association of education with economic development, such as plans promoted by the World Bank, frequently conflicts with educational rights provided in human rights documents. It is important to note the formal statements on educational rights before proceeding to an intercivilizational analysis. These formal statements of educational rights provide a framework for reflecting on the meaning of equality and freedom in education. They will also provide another lens for looking at the conclusions of my intercivilizational analysis.

There is not only tension between human rights statements and the global direction of education, but there are unresolved conflicts within the human rights documents themselves. The idea of educational freedom generates the most troubling conflicts as it rubs against differing civilizational concepts of education and collides with the issue of religious freedom. Most cultural, political, and religious groups have difficulty with the educational freedom granted to children under the Convention on the Rights of the Child adopted by the United Nations in 1989. Articles 13 and 14 of the Convention provide for freedom of thought, expression, and access to information. These Articles define a child as a person under the age of 18.

Article 13

1. The child shall have the right to freedom of expression; this right shall include freedom to seek, receive and impart information and ideas of all kinds, regardless of frontiers, either orally, in writing or in print, in the form of art, or through any other media of the child's choice.

Article 14

1. State Parties shall respect the right of the child to freedom of thought, conscience and religion.[34]

Obviously, religious leaders, parents, and governments often object to these rights because they want to control the information and ideas received by the child. But how will this control be exercised without violating the spirit of these educational freedom rights? For instance, in the United States there exists a religiously based movement to exclude theories of evolution from the public school curriculum. There are also attempts, sometimes successful, to remove discussions of birth control from sex education courses.[35] Would these actions violate the statement of rights in Articles 13 and 14 of the Convention of the Rights of the Child? Or would they be in keeping with the following qualifications added to these two articles that provide for censorship by governments and parents?

Article 13

2. The exercise of this right may be subject to certain restrictions, but these shall only be such as are provided by law and are necessary:

(A) For respect of the rights or reputations of others; or

(B) For the protection of national security or of public order (order public), or of public health or morals.

Article 14

2. States Parties shall respect the rights and duties of the parents and, when applicable, legal guardians, to provide direction to the child in the exercise of his or her right in a manner consistent with the evolving capacities of the child.

3. Freedom to manifest one's religion or beliefs may be subject only to such limitations as are prescribed by law and are necessary to protect public safety, order, health or morals, or the fundamental rights and freedoms of others.[36]

Do the above qualifications to freedom of expression, thought, and access to information mean that a government can institute a highly nationalistic and propagandistic form of education in order to ensure "protection of national security or of public order?" Do they allow parents to restrict a child's knowledge of evolutionary theory? Can Islamic countries restrict the religious education of children in the name of "public safety, order, health or morals?"

How does the concept of the right to freedom of expression, thought, and access to information compare with global trends in education? Human capital and accounting approaches do not consider the issue of intellectual freedom. Government examinations control the content of the public school curriculum. There is little room for exercising intellectual freedom when you are cramming for high-stakes tests that will determine your place in the economic structure. Whoever controls the content of the government examinations exercises major influence over the content of students' minds.

Can there be intellectual freedom in religious societies? Or, stated another way, should the right to intellectual freedom exist in religious societies? Is there a basic conflict between the right to freedom of expression, thought, and access to information, and religious rights?

Clearly, educational freedom is a very contentious right both in the context of human rights and, as I will discuss, in the context of intercivilizational analysis. Educational equality, on the other hand, is supported by human rights doctrines. The problem for educational equality is one of definition and positive government action. Basically, educational equality means that everyone has an equal chance to receive an equal education. This is called *equality of educational opportunity.*

However, the meaning of equality of educational opportunity is complicated by the necessity of specifying what is an "equal chance" and what is an "equal education." One way of defining "equal chance" is to specify that race, gender, language, religion, and social class can not pose barriers to receiving an education. This I call the "access to education" part of giving everyone an equal chance to receive an education. Equal access to education is clearly delineated in the United Nations' 1960 Convention Against Discrimination in Education. The Convention states:

Article 1

1. For the purposes of this Convention, the term "discrimination" includes any distinction, exclusion, limitation or preference which, being based on race, color, sex, language, religion, political or other opinion, national or social origin, economic condition or birth, has the purpose or effect of nullifying or impairing equality of treatment in education and in particular:

   (A) Of depriving any person or group of persons of access to education of any type or at any level;

   (B) Of limiting any person or group of persons to education of an inferior standard....

2. For the purposes of this convention, the term "education" refers to all types and levels of education, and includes access to education, the standard and quality of education, and the conditions under which it is given.[37]

Article 1 of the Convention Against Discrimination in Education provides a very clear and forceful statement about equality of access to education. As I will discuss, a major international problem is discrimination against women in education.

There is another aspect of "an equal chance" to receive an education which is related to the idea of an "equal education." First, I must point out the difficulties in defining an "equal education." Does an equal education mean that everyone receives the same education? Or does it mean everyone receives an education that reflects their abilities, interests, and life-goals? For instance, might students with special needs require an education that is different from others? Some students might want to go into trades while others might want to go to college. What does an equal education mean in this context?

An "equal chance" and an "equal education" are dependent on the distribution of educational resources. The equal distribution of resources is complicated by the possibility that some students might require more educational resources than other students. Article 4 of the Convention Against Discrimination In Education attempts to resolve this problem:

> The States parties to this Convention undertake ...
>
> (B) To ensure that the standards of education are equivalent in all public educational institutions of the same level, and that the conditions relating to the quality of education provided are also equivalent.[38]

Article 4 leaves unanswered the problem of providing additional resources for previously neglected populations, such as African Americans in the United States. In many parts of the world, women have suffered from centuries of educational neglect. Adult female illiteracy rates are high compared with those of men. In India, as I will discuss, lower castes, both men and women, were traditionally excluded from schools. These populations require additional financial resources if they are to overcome centuries of educational neglect. Will additional funds for these groups be considered as providing unequal educational opportunity?

Another important aspect of "equal education" is the language of the classroom. Is there an equal education when a minority language student is taught in the dominant language of the country? For instance, is a Spanish-speaking student being taught math in English receiving an equal education as compared to an English-speaking student in the same classroom? Another problem is a language-minority student's being denied instruction in the dominant language. The Convention Against Discrimination in Education addresses this issue by protecting minority language rights and providing for the right to learn the dominant language:

> Article 5
>
> (C) it is essential to recognize the right of members of national minorities to carry on their own educational activities, including the maintenance of schools and, depending on the educational policy of each State, the use or the teaching of their own language, provided however:
>
> (i) That this right is not exercised in a manner which prevents the members of these minorities from understanding the culture and language of the community as a whole and from participating in its activities, or which prejudices national sovereignty;
>
> (ii) That the standard of education is not lower than the general standard laid down or approved by the competent authorities; and
>
> (iii) That attendance at such schools is optional.[39]

CONCLUSION

Equality, freedom, and human rights are powerful emotional symbols in the global flow, symbols that promise relief from oppression and poverty. The world's peoples can use these symbols to demand political and economic justice. However, the emotional power of the concepts can often obscure the twists and turns in logic and meaning that have allowed some people to use these symbols to justify exploitation and tyranny. Concepts of equality of opportunity and freedom to consume heighten the uniformity and the homogeneity of the thread of global culture running through the global flow. Acting as a magnet attracting world resources, the global culture standardizes human life while destroying the environment and creating more economic inequality.

Education is being standardized along the thread of global culture. The goals of equality of opportunity and freedom to consume are producing similar educational systems around the world. Embedded in the global culture, the proliferating language of schools around the world is human capital, life-long learning, and the learning society. This is the language of equality of opportunity in a technological society where the major goal is the production and consumption of new products. In this framework, education is treated as an economic investment which will provide students (human capital) with equality of opportunity.

In the following chapters I will be analyzing historical and contemporary Confucian, Islamic, Western, and Hindu ideas regarding educational rights. I am considering these ideas as part of the global flow. These educational ideas live alongside the global flow, in the thread of global education that incorporates the idea of human capital. Also in the global flow are human rights documents. These human rights declarations are often in conflict with civilizational ideas in the global flow and with the educational ideas woven into the thread of global culture. It is from this global flow and global culture that I extract my ideas on the right to education and the meaning of equality and freedom of education. To accomplish this goal, I use human rights documents, civilizational perspectives on education, and concepts of global culture of schooling.

2

China: Confucius, Mao Zedong, and Socialist Modernization

I met Mian Tao Sun at an education conference in Taiwan in December, 1999. At the time, he was studying Taiwan's private schools while on leave from his post as Dean of the School of Education at Chung Cheng University in central China. In my ignorance about the evolution of socialism in China I assumed that he would be opposed to private schooling, particularly since he was a member of the Communist Party and had participated in the Cultural Revolution during the late 1960s and early 1970s. Under the leadership of Mao Zedong, the Cultural Revolution uprooted teachers and students, sending them into the fields and factories to learn from workers and peasants. The ideological goal was to stop the growth of what Mao Zedong considered counter-revolutionary thought and to ensure a relationship between theory and practice. Dean Sun believed that he had wasted several years of his life by forced participation in the Cultural Revolution.

During our early morning breakfasts of rice soup, black eggs, and vegetables in the student center at the National Taiwan Normal University, I learned that while attending Harvard University Mian made a special trip to Burlington, Vermont to visit the grave of the American philosopher and educator John Dewey. At first I was not surprised by his graveside visit, because I knew that Dewey had visited China in 1919 for a 2-year lecture tour. During that time, frequent comparisons were made between Dewey and China's great intellectual leader Confucius.[1] At one university, Dewey actually received a citation that named him the "Second Confucius." When the Communists gained power, however, Dewey's writings were heavily criticized.[2]

Given the initial Communist rejection of Dewey, I was surprised to learn that Dr. Sun, along with his job as dean, operated a private school based on Deweyan principles. I was informed by a Taiwanese professor who visited Dr. Sun's school that banners hanging in the classrooms proclaimed "Learning By Doing" and "Education Through Experience."

After returning to the United States, I sent Professor Sun an e-mail containing what I thought was a warning about the global development of private schooling.* In particular, I thought my defense of public schools against private greed would appeal to a member of the Communist Party. I wrote:

January 10, 2000

Dear Professor Sun,

I thought a great deal about our conversations. I am interested in the development of private schools in China. Certainly, in the United States, conservative ideology is undermining the concept of public schooling and replacing it with private schools operated by corporations for a profit. Some of these for-profit educational corporations are already international in scope. What you see happening in China is only the beginning of the "capitalist" or "free market" evolution in education. I can envision global corporations operating for-profit schools to educate obedient workers who will work for low wages.

Best,

Joel Spring

To my surprise, Professor Sun responded with an e-mail supporting private schooling in opposition to public schooling. Rather than translating my comments as an objection to private schooling, he interpreted them as support:

January 11, 2000

Dear Professor Spring,

I do agree with your ideas about private schools. To set private school is not only to get profit, but also to motivate the educators who working in private schools to work just according to their own educational ideas. You

---

*In reproducing this e-mail correspondence with Dr. Sun, I have retained his original wording and spelling. The reader will appreciate that English is a second language for Dr. Sun

see, if you work in the public schools, it is very hard for you to teach in the way that you think is right, you just work according to the administrative officer. In the private schools, you can make the educational experiment in your assumption of education, just like Dewey made educational experiment in Chicago University. I have run a private school from kindergarten to senior high school, although I feel little tired everyday, I live very happy.

Sincerely,

Mian Tao Sun

Surprised by his defense of private schooling, I responded with another warning about possible corporate domination:

January 12, 2000

Dear Professor Sun,

I agree that private schools can provide greater freedom for teaching similar to John Dewey's school at the University of Chicago. However, the latest trend in the United States is for corporations to franchise schools similar to McDonald's Hamburger franchises. Consequently, these corporate private schools are more controlling than government schools. I envision a future where elementary and secondary schools will be operated by large international corporations such as Sony or Disney. This will create greater standardization than in the past and it will focus education on the training of good workers.

Best,

Joel Spring

I knew that there was something seriously deficient in my understanding of China and Chinese Communism when Professor Sun replied with a positive response about corporate control of schools by Sony and Disney:

January 18, 2000

Dear Professor Spring,

Sony and Disney are great corporations, absolutely that they set the schools should be for their own benefits. Just [as] you pointed [out] , they always focus education on the training of good workers. In order to realize this purpose, they prefer to control the schools by themselves rather than by government. This atmosphere is not only popular in United States but also in China or even everywhere in the world. I think, this atmosphere is a good thing not [a] bad thing. Government has no right to control these schools because government does not support money to these schools.

Sincerely,

Mian Tao Sun

While Professor Sun's arguments might not fit traditional notions of Marxist rhetoric, they are congruent with Article 19 of the 1982 Constitution of the People's Republic of China. Besides outlining the state's support of compulsory education, Article 19 declares, "The state encourages the collective economic organizations, state enterprises and institutions and *other sectors* of society to establish educational institutions of various types in accordance with the law [my emphasis]."[3]

Does Article 19 encourage freedom of ideas in establishing private schools such as the school established by Professor Sun? What does the establishment of private schools mean for equality of educational opportunity in China? When I asked Professor Sun, "Who sends their children to privates schools?" His answer was simply, "The rich."

I believe that understanding the concept of freedom and equality as applied to education in the People's Republic of China requires an examination of the interweaving of traditional and contemporary Confucianism with Mao Zedong's educational ideas, current socialist modernization programs, and Chinese nationalism. In the context of the global flow, the real threat of European and Japanese colonialism had affected China more than abstract Western Enlightenment ideas of equality and freedom. Until the late 19th century, the Chinese government tried to isolate itself from Western influence. When isolationism failed and Western and Japanese colonization seemed imminent, Mao Zedong and others turned to Marxism. But their brand of Marxism was a product of assimilation to Chinese thought. "In its Maoist incarnation," philosophers David Hall and Roger Ames wrote, "Chinese Marxism has redefined a doctrine which ... [turned] universalistic aspirations into a kind of 'neo' neo-Confucianism." A similar thing occurred with the socialist modernization movement after the death of Mao. While privatization, for example in education, is occurring it is taking place within the framework of Chinese Nationalism and Confucianism. I will first examine Confucian educational ideals and then the impact of Chinese nationalism.

THE CONFUCIAN TRADITION

There is a wide-ranging debate about the continuing effect of Confucianism in China and other Asian nations. Mao Zedong, as the country's leader from 1949 to 1976, tried to purge the country of Confucian educational traditions. During Mao's reign there was little formal instruction in Confucianism. However, after Mao's death his successor, Deng Xiaoping, and the current government leader Jiang Zemin, resurrected Confucian traditions. As an example of this Confucian revival, the China Confucius Center was opened in Beijing in 1984. At a Confucian Conference, Jiang Zemin recalled that after regular school hours his father had him read Confucian texts.[4]

Of even greater significance considering the Communist Party's initial equating of Confucianism with feudalism was the opening in 2000 of the Confucius Culture University in the philosopher's hometown of Qufu. In language that would have shocked Mao Zedong, the *People's Daily*, the official newspaper of the People's Republic of China, accompanied the announcement of the university's opening with the statement, "Confucius, who lived about 2,500 years ago, has been respected for generations as China's 'Great perfection, ultimate sage, and foremost scholar.' His teachings promote the concepts of benevolence and traditional rites."[5] Also, the *People's Daily* reported on March 19, 2000 that a website "devoted to Confucius, one of China's greatest thinkers and educators, has been listed among the most popular Chinese websites with over 360,000 visitors." The article asserted that, "Confucius's doctrines have been passed down through the ages and continue to influence the Chinese community."[6]

Confucian influences continue outside of China, according to writer Tu Wei-Ming. He contends that in places such as Singapore and Korea, "The central government is expected to have a holistic vision of the well-being of the nation ... [and] the political leader [is expected] to be a teacher as well as an exemplary public servant ... The Confucian scholar-official mentality still functions in the psychocultural construct of East Asian societies."[7] Others see the Confucian tradition enduring in Japan, Korea, and Taiwan as reflected in the close relationship between scholars and the government, and in the belief that the government has the responsibility for the total welfare of all people. For example, in 2000, the recently elected President of Taiwan, Chen Shui-bian, quoted Confucius regarding the ongoing issue of its independence from mainland China: "A benevolent government will please those near and appeal to those from afar [and] when those afar will not submit, then one must practice kindness and virtue to attract them."[8]

EQUALITY IN CONFUCIAN EDUCATION

Any discussion of equality and freedom in Chinese education must begin with an analysis of the educational ideals of Confucius (circa

551–479 B.C.E.). Regarding equality, Confucius states in *The Analects*, "Men are close to one another by nature. They diverge as a result of practice."[9] Another translation of this passage from *The Analects* is "By nature close together, through practice set apart."[10] This natural equality refers to equality in moral capacity. All humans, according to Confucius, are born with the ability to be moral. A primary goal of education is to develop that morality. Therefore, according to Confucius, education should be for all people. Confucius said, "In education there should be no class distinctions."[11]

The Confucian concept of morality, consequently equality, is based on a naturalistic and secular interpretation of what it means to be human. In contrast to monotheistic religions, such as Christianity and Islam, Confucian morality is not derived from the dictates of a supernatural being. There is no God in Confucianism. It is a system of ethics designed to promote harmony and peace between human beings. Consequently, unlike the Judaic-Christian emphasis on guilt, Confucianism stresses public shame. It is one's reputation in relationship to others that is important and not the judgement of a supernatural god.

Unlike Hinduism where, according to the *Dharmasutras*, caste determines access to education, Confucius made it clear that no group of people should be denied an equal opportunity for education. Confucius says, "I have never denied instruction to anyone who, of his own accord, has given me so much as a bundle of dried meat as a present."[12]

For Confucius, learning morality is learning the "Way." Everyone is born not only with the ability to be moral but also with the potential to learn the "Way." In Confucianism, the "Way" or "Tao" is a complex concept that includes "the right Way of life, the Way of governing, the ideal Way of human existence, the Way of the Cosmos, the generative-normative Way (pattern, path, course) of existence."[13] The Way is also applied to the state. In fact, it is the responsibility of rulers, according to Confucius, to ensure that the government follows the Way. After reviewing the many aspects of the meaning of the Way, Confucian scholar D. C. Lau concludes, "The Way, then, is a highly emotive term and comes very close to the term 'Truth' as found in philosophical and religious writings in the West."[14]

For Confucius, inequality refers to the unequal learning and practice of morality. Social duty is another term for the practice of morality. Therefore, inequality can be defined as the unequal effort by people to learn and fulfill their social duties. For instance, some people will not seek instruction and others will lead a life without virtue. Many Confucian teachings emphasize the moral superiority of the poor person who follows the Way as opposed to the rich person who does not follow the Way. Confucius said:

> Wealth and honor are what people desire, but one should not abide in them if it cannot be done in accordance with the Way. Poverty and lowliness are what people dislike, but one should not depart from them if it cannot be done in accordance with the Way. If the noble person were to depart from humaneness, how could he fulfill that name? The noble person does not abandon humaneness for so long as the space of a meal. Even when hard pressed he is bound to this, even in times of danger he is bound to this.[15]

This naturalistic and secular approach to morality was most clearly stated by Mencius (circa 371–288 B.C.E.), who was a leading exponent of Confucian teachings. Mencius argued that the "four sprouts" or "four beginnings" of morality are present in all people. These basic human characteristics are "compassion, shame, modesty, and the sense of right and wrong."[16] Compassion, for instance, Mencius contended is a natural attribute of being human. He stated, "if anyone were suddenly to see a child about to fall into a well, his mind would always be filled with alarm, distress, pity, and compassion. That he would react accordingly is not because he would use the opportunity to ingratiate himself with the child's parents, nor because he would seek commendation from neighbors and friends, nor because he would hate the adverse reputation."[17]

Mencius related each of these "four sprouts" to particular moral capacities. Humanness grows from the sprout of compassion, rightness from the sprout of shame, ritual and decorum from modesty, and wisdom from the sense of right and wrong. Everyone has the ability to achieve these moral capacities. In reference to the moral equality of humans, Mencius stated:

> "As far as the natural tendencies are concerned, it is possible for one to do good, this is what I mean by being good. If one does what is not good, that is not the fault of one's capacities. The mind of pity and commiseration is possessed by all human beings; the mind of shame and aversion is possessed by all human beings; the mind of respectfulness and reverence is possessed by all human beings; and the mind that knows right and wrong is possessed by all human beings."[18]

And, again in Confucian terms, inequality is a result of the practice or neglect of these moral qualities. Regarding these moral capacities, Mencius stated, "Seek and you will get it, let go and you will lose it."[19]

Of course, the development of moral capacities requires social interaction. In contrast to Christianity's concern with the inner self, Confucianism is primarily worried about the outer self. Herbert Fingarette summarizes, "The virtues that Confucius stresses are indeed all "dynamic" and social. For example, *shu* (mutuality in human relations), *chung* (loyalty) and *hsin* (good trust toward others) all inherently involve a dynamic relation to other persons. On the other hand, such "static" and "inner" virtues as purity or innocence play no role in the *Analects*."[20]

To ensure harmony in social relations, according to Confucius, requires the exercise of rites as opposed to the imposition of laws. Rites are the norms to be used in social interactions. In one sense they are a form of social etiquette. Social interactions are governed by *li*, which is related to traditional patterns of social conduct, and *jen*, which refers to a person that pursues proper social conduct and human relationships.[21]

THE LITIGIOUS VERSUS
THE SELF-REGULATED SOCIETY

The assumption of equality of moral capacities supports a belief that the best means of maintaining social order is through self-regulation as opposed to legal restraints. Rites rather than laws are, according to Confucianism, the best means for creating a peaceful society that follows the Way. Rather than law, Confucianism relies on education, personal morality, and benevolent rulers to ensure adherence to social norms. Consequently, rites serve as the mechanism for ensuring the peaceful working out of social problems. The great American Confucian scholar, Wm. Theodore DeBary states, "Confucius saw ... ritual decorum as an essential form of civility, fundamental to human governance and preferable to the attempted enforcement of laws."[22] Regarding the difference between a society based on law and one based on rites, Confucius said:

> Guide them by edicts [laws and regulations], keep them in line with punishments, and the common people will stay out of trouble but will have no sense of shame. Guide them by virtue, keep them in line with the rites, and they will, besides having a sense of shame, reform themselves.[23]

Some scholars argue that Confucian emphasis on rites and shame, as opposed to law, still plays an important part in many Asian societies. In his introduction to a volume of essays on *Confucian Traditions in East Asian Modernity*, Tu Wei-Ming asserts that East Asian societies have difficulty in developing legal systems because of a lack of a juridical tradition and a reliance on social interactions for settling disputes. As examples, he gives, "consensus as a preferred way of decision making, negotiation as a conventional method of resolving conflict, informal arbitration as a frequent substitute for formal legal procedures ... and mediation through third parties."[24]

Some East Asians argue that the "social diseases" existing in Western societies are a result of reliance on laws to maintain social order. This argument is used to counter complaints by Western nations that East Asian countries violate human rights doctrines. Onuma Yasuaki is particularly critical of Western emphasis on legal means for protecting human rights. Referring to the "social diseases" of crime, drugs, and lack of family and community values, he contends that East Asians feel that "these diseases may well be a consequence of excessive legalism and individual-centrism."[25] The Western reliance on legalism is, for me, exemplified by highway speed limits. In the United States, speeders will often slow down when seeing a police car and then speed up when the police car passes out of sight. In this situation, the speeder is governed by law and not by a sense of social responsibility to protect others by driving at safe speeds. Consequently, speeding laws provide only limited highway safety. However, according Onuma's perspective, if speeding laws were replaced by a concern about others and a sense of shame at the idea of endangering other drivers, then highways would be safer.

Therefore, from Onuma's viewpoint, the Confucian reliance on self-regulation through moral education and self-reflection produces a safer and more harmonious society than reliance on social regulation through laws. Accordingly, universal Confucian education is the key to the good and peaceful society.

CONFUCIAN EDUCATIONAL IDEAL

For over 2,000 years, Confucian scholars argued for the necessity of universal education as a means of achieving a harmonious and peaceful society.[26] Despite the fact that this ideal was never achieved under Confucian leadership, the goal predated by many centuries any similar suggestion in Western countries. Likewise, the implementation of a civil service examination to create a government meritocracy predated by many centuries comparable efforts in the United States and Europe.

The goal of universal education was based on the assumed equality of moral capacities. However, there was a recognition of unequal abilities in developing moral capacities. But all people could develop them by applying varying degrees of effort. In the *Doctrine of the Mean*, Confucius makes a distinction between the sage "who, without an effort hits what is right, and apprehends, without the exercise of thought who naturally and easily embodies the right way"[27] and those who must work hard at achieving the same level of understanding. In reference to those requiring extra effort to achieve knowledge and understanding, Confucius said, "if another man succeed by one effort, he will use a hundred efforts. If another man succeed by ten efforts, he will use a thousand. Let a man proceed in this way, and, though dull, he will surely become intelligent; though weak, he will surely become strong."[28]

The ideal of moral equality was mirrored in the uniformity of primary education that existed for centuries not only in China but also in Korea and Japan. Besides the learning of reading and writing, this education included the study of basic Confucian texts. The Confucian curriculum began with the *Three Character Classic* which was written in the 11th century as a guide to Confucian ideas for young children. This was followed by a series of other Confucian texts including the *Analects*, the *Great Learning*, the *Doctrine of the Mean*, and the *Works of Mencius*.[29] The first lesson in the *Three Character Classic* presented the ideal of moral equality:

Men at their birth are by nature radically good,
In this, all approximate, but in practice widely diverge.[30]

The interrelationship between education and the good society is explained in the *Great Learning*. This *Great Learning* focuses on an organic relationship between individual education, the family, and the state. Ideally, the virtuous person will maintain a harmonious family which will be the basis for a peaceful society that follows the Way. The key concept in individual education is "ching-shih" which is composed of "the ethics of virtue, intellectualism, ritualism, meditative practices, and asceticism."[31] The *Great Learning* states:

The ancients who wished to manifest their clear character to the world would first bring order to their states. Those who wished to bring order to their states would first regulate their families. Those who wished to regulate their families would first cultivate their personal lives. Those who wished to cultivate their personal lives would first rectify their minds. Those who wished to rectify their minds would first make their wills sincere. Those who wished to make their wills sincere would first extend their knowledge. The extension of knowledge consists in the investigation of things. When things are investigated, knowledge is extended; when knowledge is extended, the will becomes sincere; when the will is sincere, the mind is rectified; when the mind is rectified, the personal life is cultivated; when the personal life is cultivated, the family will be regulated; when the family is regulated, the state will be in order; and when the state is in order, there will be peace throughout the world. From the son of Heaven down to the common people, all must regard cultivation of the personal life as the root or foundation.[32]

One important element of ching-shih that would remain a theme in Mao Zedong's educational proposals was meditative practices. In Confucianism, meditative practices do not have the same meaning as they do in Hinduism. In Hinduism, meditative practices imply an attempt to escape the temporal world of desires. In Confucianism, meditative practices mean self-reflection and self-criticism regarding one's interaction with the social world. Mao Zedong made self-criticism as central piece of political education. Citizens would be required to meditate on their political and social actions, and then offer self-criticism as part of the process of personal self-education.

FREEDOM OF SPEECH, SCHOLARS, AND THE GOOD SOCIETY

While the ideal was universal education, the reality was the unwillingness of the government to provide the funds. Consequently, Confucian scholars assumed the role of providing moral guidance to society. Confucian scholars recognized that most people did not have the time to devote to the arduous task of achieving moral perfection. Consequently, as Chang Hao wrote, "Out of the assumption that only a minority with the requisite moral qualities could govern, there grew the vocational ideal that it is the nobleman's privileged responsibility to set the world in order by assuming a position of leadership and rendering public service to society."[33]

The Confucian ideal of universal education was compromised by the existence of inequalities in the exercise of power. While all humans were equal in their moral capacities, they were unequal in the exercise of power. A major problem was how to maintain virtue in a society where power could be used to exploit others. Mencius provided the following guidelines for human interactions based on inequality of power and social status:

Between parent and child there is to be affection

Between ruler and minister, rightness

Between husband and wife, [gender] distinctions

Between older and younger [siblings] an order of precedence

Between friends, trustworthiness.[34]

Included in Mencius's guidelines were two important relationships affecting equality and freedom in education. The first was the relationship between ruler and minister which, as I will explain, involved the social role of the scholar, civil service examinations, and freedom of speech. The second was the relationship between husband and wife which involved inequality between genders.

"Rightness" in the relationship between ruler and minister was exemplified by the story of Qian Tang, who in the 14th century exercised the Confucian duty to speak the truth and provide moral direction to rulers. The Emperor Taizu (1513–1587) ordered Qian Tang to remove material written by Mencius from the civil service examination. The Emperor thought Mencius insulted his imperial position. In addition, he ordered the removal of Mencius's tablet from the Confucian temple. His ministers refused to obey. Taizu ordered the death of any who refused to obey. Immediately after the death threat, minister Qian Tang brought a coffin to court and announced "It would be an honor to die for Mencius."[35]

Qian Tang represented the ideal role of the Confucian scholar as a minister providing moral guidance to government leaders. However, this ideal could be used to justify an authoritarian government. Reasoning that all people are born with equal moral capacities but only a few have the time to develop those capacities, Mencius argued, "Some labor with their minds and some labor with their strength. Those who labor with their minds govern others; those who labor with their strength are governed by others. Those who are governed by others support them; those who govern others are supported by them."[36]

The role of the civil service examination was to select the best people to be government ministers. Based on Confucianism, the examinations were initiated in the 2nd century B.C.E. and were used as a means of selecting government officials until the early 20th century. Of course, the dream of the examinations identifying scholars of virtue to advice rulers was eventually compromised. Some Confucians objected to the examination system because it was simply used as a stepping stone to the government bureaucracy. Present-day Confucian scholar Chang Hao wrote, "For many Confucian literati bureaucracy as a meritocracy was burdened with a civil service examination system oriented toward a careerism that undermined the moral fervor of Confucian officials."[37]

Therefore, despite careerism, the ideal was to help the government follow the Way by educating a group of Confucian scholars who would be selected by merit (the examination system) to act as ministerial advisers. Freedom of speech was implicit in the role of scholar. It was the duty of the scholar to speak out against injustice. It was also the duty of the scholar to exercise freedom of speech in trying to improve society.

DeBary stated, "Confucius insists on the following of the Way as a higher duty than simply taking office, and ... acting on behalf of the Way to reform an imperfect human society."[38]

For Confucius, freedom of speech was the freedom to speak about the good. Confucius said:

> If what he [the ruler] says is good and no one goes against him, good. But if what he says is not good and no one goes against him, then is this not almost a case of leading the state to ruin?[39]

Mencius insisted on the duty of the scholar-ministers to criticize the ruler:

> "If the prince made serious mistakes, they [scholar-ministers] would remonstrate him."[40]

The duty of scholars to speak out was not limited to their role as state ministers. Confucius and Mencius were not state officials. They were scholar-teachers. For instance, Mencius believed the Yang and Mo school of thought existing during his time was destructive of public morality and harmony. In expressing the view that people, particularly scholar-teachers, were obligated to speak out against what they believed was wrong, Mencius said:

> I am not fond of disputation. I have no alternative. Whoever can, with words, combat Yang and Mo is a true disciple of the sages.[41]

Combined with the Confucian plea for universal education, the duty to speak out against immorality is the basis for a self-regulating society in contrast to a society regulated by laws. Ideally, all citizens assume the responsibility for reflecting on their own actions and criticizing the actions of others. The good society is the product of individual responsibility. As I stated in the previous section, some East Asians criticize Western nations for an overemphasis on social control by legal measures. From their perspective, laws cannot produce the harmonious and peaceful society. This can only be accomplished by individuals and society learning the Way and speaking out for the Way.

INEQUALITY AND THE OPPRESSION OF WOMEN

Mencius states that the guiding principle of gender relationships is "Between husband and wife, [gender] distinctions." However, this is only one of a few statements made by Confucius or Mencius about the status of women. Present-day Confucian scholar Chenyang Li argues

that there is little to support the idea that early Confucian scholars provided any justification for the oppression of women. He contends,
"Confucianism became oppressive to women only at a later stage, since
Confucianism had existed before it became so, one can say that op-
pressing women is not an essential characteristic of Confucianism."[42]
In fact, Li demonstrates a close parallel between original Confucianist
thought and the care ethics advocated by American feminists Nel
Noddings and Carol Gilligan. In a very interesting cross-cultural comparison, Li argues that the concern with human relationships and the
duty to protect the welfare of others that Noddings and Gilligan associ-
ate with female concepts of justice in the United States closely parallel
the ethical positions advocated by Confucius and Mencius.

However, Confucianism does become oppressive toward women
after Mencius's death with the introduction of Yin–yang school of philosophy between 255 B.C. E. and 23 C. E. Yin and yang are two com-
plementary forces that were originally associated with nature. Yang is
considered the superior and dominant force, whereas yin is the sub-
missive. Applied to gender relationships, the male is the yang and the
female is the yin. In marriage, the female goal is to serve the husband
and the sons. Female virtue, under the Yin–yang association, is
judged primarily in terms of obedience to the husband. For the wife,
"to die of starvation is a small matter, but to lose integrity is a large
matter."[43]

Dong Zhongshu (179–104 B.C.E) played a major role in incorporat-
ing Yin–yang into Confucianism. He believed that the major human relationships of ruler and subject, father and son, and husband and wife
were based on the principles of Yin–yang. He stated, "The ruler is the
yang, the subject yin; the father is yang, the son yin; the husband is
yang, the wife yin ... The yang acts as the husband, who procreates [the
son]. The yin acts as the wife, who gives assistance [to the husband]."[44]

Even from the standpoint of 19th century male Europeans, the
Yin–yang philosophy had produced a particularly oppressive situation
for Chinese women. A French Catholic missionary traveling in China in
the 1840s wrote, "The condition of Chinese women is most pitiable;
suffering, privation, contempt, all kinds of misery and degradation,
seize on her in the cradle, and accompany her pitilessly to the tomb."[45]
Reflecting the woman's yin status in gender relations, he wrote, "Her
very birth is commonly regarded as a humiliation and a disgrace to the
family—an evident sign of the malediction of Heaven. If she be not immediately suffocated ... she is regarded and treated as a creature radically despicable and scarcely belonging to the human race."[46]

Waves of feminist criticisms of Confucianism occurred in the early
20th century. Wm. Theodore DeBary quotes a Chinese feminist of the
time, "The learning of Confucianism has tended to be oppressive and

to promote male selfishness ... We can see that the Confucian insistence on propriety is nothing more than a tool for murdering women ... Keeping women at home allowed men to pursue education while women were trapped in ignorance. Isn't this the greatest of injustices?"[47] The revolution of 1911, which overthrew the imperial system and resulted in a republican government under the leadership of Sun Yat-sen, opened the door to major changes in the education and status of women.

CHINESE NATIONALISM: "WESTERN FUNCTION, CHINESE ESSENCE"

While Western ideas about politics and technology influenced China, the more important impact of the West was its role in sparking the growth of nationalism and creating a sense of shame that continued into the 21st century. Feelings of nationalism resulting from a reaction to Western imperialism are evident in the current Constitution of the People's Republic of China adopted in 1982, which opens with a historical summary of China's place in the global flow of Western colonialism. Compared to other countries, China suffered minor losses to European powers. But these minor losses still bother Chinese leaders. Nationalism appears in the opening sentences of the Constitution's Preamble: "China is one of the countries with the longest histories in the world. The people of all nationalities in China have jointly created a splendid culture and have a glorious revolutionary tradition."[48] This opening is immediately followed by recognition of the effects of colonialism: "Feudal China was gradually reduced after 1840 to a semi-colonial and semi-feudal country. The Chinese people waged wave upon wave of heroic struggles for national independence and liberation and for democracy and freedom."[49]

The reference to "after 1840" is to the Opium Wars when the Chinese government tried to stop British merchants from selling drugs to the Chinese people. In response, the British sent warships up Chinese rivers and forced the government to sign the Treaty of Nanking, which made Hong Kong into a warehousing area for opium and created treaty ports at Canton and Shanghai. At the time, this was a major defeat of the Chinese government's efforts at self-protection from Western influence.

Reflecting this continuing sense of outrage about Western colonialism, Deng Xiaoping, Chinese government leader after Mao Zedong's death in 1976, explained to a visiting Japanese delegation in 1984, "For more than a century after the Opium War, China was subjected to aggression and humiliation."[50] Release from Western oppression, according to Deng

Xiaoping, "is because the Chinese people embraced Marxism and kept to the road leading from new-democracy to socialism."[51]

China's revolutionary fervor was fueled by the haunting memories of foreign incursions. Born on December 26, 1893 in Hunan Province, Mao Zedong grew up surrounded by anti-foreign feelings. Two years before Mao's birth, Griffith John, an English missionary visiting Changsa, the capital of Hunan, wrote, "it is one of the few places left in the whole world which no foreigner may presume to enter. It is perhaps the most intensely anti-foreign city in the whole of China, a feeling kept up by the literati with the full sympathy of the officials."[52] Growing up in this anti-foreigner atmosphere, Mao developed a fear of possible takeover by the West or Japan, both economically more powerful and aggressive. He later remembered reading at the age of 14 a pamphlet predicting Japanese takeover of the Chinese island of Taiwan and of Korea, and the loss of Chinese power over Indochina and Burma. "After I read this," he recalled, "I felt depressed about the future of my country and began to realize it was the duty of all the people to help save it."[53]

While fearing the power of the West and Japan, Mao was aware of the importance of Western technological development. He claimed that at an early age he was influenced by Zheng Guanying's *Words of Warning to an Affluent Age*. The book urged the introduction of Western technology into China. It described technological developments, such as electricity, telephones, steamships, and railways. In addition, it called for introducing Western education and parliamentary democracy. Mao claimed that the book persuaded him to give up farm life to devote himself to a life of learning.[54]

The attraction of Western technology created a dilemma for both the Chinese and Japanese, but their responses differed. Leaders of both countries believed in the superiority of their traditional Confucian cultures over Western cultures but recognized that Western technological development opened the door to possible European conquest of their countries. The obvious solution was to learn Western science and technological methods. The problem was how to introduce a foreign science and technology without diminishing the power of Confucian ethical culture.

Before Chinese leaders attempted to resolve this dilemma, Japanese officials under the slogans of *Western Science, Eastern Morals* and *Japanese Spirit, Western Skills* began to introduce Western science and education. One Japanese advocate of learning Western technology, Sakuma Shozan, argued in 1855, "In order to master the barbarians ... there is not a better first step than to be familiar with barbarian tongues [which would create a] clearer understanding of the conditions among the enemy nations."[55] It was Sakuma who declared the goal of "Western Science, Eastern Morals." In 1868, the Japanese government created an Education Department which issued a declaration that, "Knowledge shall be sought from throughout the world."[56]

The relatively early introduction of Western science and technology into Japan provided that country with an initial military advantage over China and other Asian countries that would continue until the defeat of Japanese forces at the end of World War II. In 1895, Japan defeated China and took over Korea and Taiwan. In 1905, Japan defeated the Russians and took over control of Manchuria. Japanese defeat of Russia stoked the flames of Asian anti-European feelings and provided an example of the ability of Asians to stop Western imperialism. "At that time," Mao recalled, "I knew and felt the beauty of Japan, and felt something of her pride and might ... of her victory over Russia."[57]

In the 1870s, the Chinese government responded to Western aggression with a "self-strengthening movement." In the words of Mao's biographer Philip Short, "Under the slogan, 'Western function, Chinese essence,' reformers argued that if the country had access to modern weapons, it could repel the invaders and preserve unchanged its Confucian way of life."[58]

In the 1890s, Chinese flocked to Japan to learn about Western science and technology. This resulted in a flow of Western ideas between Japan and China. This flow was illustrated for me during my visit to Taiwan where government buildings constructed during the Japanese occupation are still being used. The buildings were designed by Japanese architects who were trained in Europe. Their facades are supported by a jumble of Roman and Greek columns with some buildings looking like transplants from Vienna or Berlin.

One of the results of nationalism as a response to colonial aggression, and the impact of global ideoscapes, was the development in the 1890s of a "constitutionalist" movement. Constitutional government was a Western idea. There was no precedent for constitutional government in Chinese traditions. Indeed, Confucian traditions opposed rule by law. However, Chinese scholars quickly adapted the idea of constitutional government to Confucian traditions. Out of these efforts grew a revolutionary movement that eventually overthrew the imperial government and led the country down the path to what was called Mao Zedong thought, Marxism-Leninism, and the 1982 Constitution.

CHINESE CONSTITUTIONALISM: EQUALITY OF PLEASURE AND PAIN

Liu Shipei (1884–1919) and Liang Qichao (1873–1929) were the two leading Chinese scholars who tried to reconcile Confucianism with constitutional guarantees of equality and freedom. Liu adapted the ideas of Jean Jacques Rousseau to Confucian traditions in *The Essence of the Chinese Social Contract.* He envisioned a past when Chinese people were equal and without rulers. Eventually, he argued, a greedy group took over power and created a society of unequal power and wealth. Liu was influenced by Western anarchist thought, particularly that of Prince Kropotkin, and dreamt of a future society with economic equality and equality of political power.[59]

Interestingly, Liu added a new dimension to the concept of equality by relating it to equality of work experience. In his utopian vision, everyone over the course of their lives would have an opportunity to participate in every form of work from farming to teaching to factory work. Equality of work was directly related to his concept of equality of outcomes. All people would experience the pleasures and pains resulting from differing work conditions.

Following Confucian traditions, Liu was not interested in abstract concepts of rights, such as equality and liberty, but in rights as conditions that fostered positive social relationships. He felt that abstract concepts of rights were meaningless as long as social inequalities existed. Social inequality, he contended, was directly related to person's social duties, which included work. Peter Zarrow, an Australian professor of Chinese history, summarizes Liu's thinking: "As long as 'duties' (yiwu) remained unequal, or in other words as long as people were forced to perform different kinds of labor so that their suffering and pleasure remained unequal, any abstract equality of rights merely masked injustice."[60]

Equality of social duties, in Liu's thinking, was a necessary condition for independence and liberty. Liu made a distinction between the conditions of independence and liberty. His concept of freedom incorporated the Confucian ideal of self-regulation. "I believe," Liu wrote, "that humans possess three great rights (*sandquan*); the right of equality (pingdengquan), the right of independence (*duliquan*), and the right of liberty (*ziyouquan*)."[61] He defined independence as not depending on others and as not controlling others. Liberty, he stated, resulted from not being controlled by others. However, he argued, limitation of liberty might be required to obtain equality. Liu insisted that, "The right of independence is a means of maintaining the right of equality. Only when the right of liberty is used excessively and conflicts with the liberty of others, will it contradict the goal of equality of humanity. Therefore, if we want to maintain humanity's right to equality, we should rather limit the individual's right to liberty."[62]

It is interesting to see how Liu took the ideas of equality and freedom as represented by Rousseau and Western anarchism from the global flow and fused them with the Confucian concept of social duties. Personally, I have not encountered a Western writer who defines equality as equality of social duties. As a Westerner, I found this definition unique and appealing. I have not encountered a Western argument that recognizes that social duties carry with them varieties of pleasure and pain, and that true equality requires an equal exposure to this broad range of human experiences.

Gender equality was of particular importance for Liu and his wife, He Zehn. Writing extensively on women's rights, they unleashed over a century of criticism and reform designed to overcome traditional oppression of Chinese women. However, they believed that equality between men and women could not be achieved until equality reigned throughout society. This would include, of course, equality of social duties between men and women.[63]

Liu's vision requires universal equal education to prepare both men and women for equality of social duties including being a teacher. Like the Confucian tradition, he views equal education as necessary for independence and liberty.

In a similar fashion, Liang Qichao, the most influential reformer prior to the 1911 revolution, linked equality of educational opportunity to self-government and citizenship. Arguing that Western imperialism and Japanese power were aided by a sense of nationalism, he proposed popular education and revival of traditions as the key to Chinese nationalism. The title of his journal, *Renewing the People*, conveyed the goal of using traditional Chinese education as a means of introducing a nationalistic spirit. Liang wrote, revealing his own nationalistic feelings and disdain of the "barbarian" other:

> The world of today is not the world of yesterday. In ancient times, we CHINESE were people of villages instead of citizens ... Since China majestically used to be predominant in the East, surrounded as we were by small barbarian groups and lacking any contact with other huge states, we Chinese generally considered our state to encompass the whole world.[64]

In agreement with the goal of "Western Function, Chinese Essence," Liang proposed a new form of public morality that would be based on a study of other nations but at the same time reflect the traditional Confucian goal of social harmony and self-regulation. Liang wrote:

> Hence, we who live in the present group should observe the main trends of the world, study what will suit our nation, and create a new morality in order to solidify, benefit, and develop our group. We should not impose upon ourselves a limit and refrain from going into what our sages had not prescribed. Search for public morality and there will appear a new morality, there will appear "a people renewed."[65]

Similar to Liu Shipei, Liang does not adopt the Western concept of abstract rights but, within the Confucian tradition, he considers rights as products of social interaction. Liang wrote:

> The rights of the state are composed of the rights of individuals. There-
> fore, the thoughts, feelings and actions of a citizenry will never be obtain-
> able without the thoughts, feelings and actions of each individual
> member ....That the people possesses rights means that the state pos-
> sesses rights; and that the people is without shame means that the state
> is without shame.[66]

In summary, the "constitutionalists" prepared the way for the 1911 revolution and the later attempts to create equality and freedom. How-ever, concepts of equality and freedom were fused with the traditional Confucian commitment to social morality and self-regulation. Impor-tant to this movement was the advocacy of equal rights for women. Here too, equality of gender was placed within traditional Chinese con-cerns with social responsibility. Equality of gender meant equality of social responsibilities. Combined with the Confucian belief in equality of moral capacities, this brand of gender equality meant that men and women have an equal capacity to be moral and to fulfill their duties to society. And, underlying these arguments, was a commitment to equal educational opportunity. The constitutionalists argued that equal edu-cational opportunities were necessary for the creation of a free and equal society. Education, they believed, would develop equal moral ca-pacities, strengthen the Chinese people with nationalism, and prepare for equality of social duties.

MAO ZEDONG: THINKING EQUALITY
AND FREELY EXPRESSING TRUTH

Confucian principles, including equality of moral capacities and the social duty to speak out against injustice, continued in various forms after the 1949 founding of the People's Republic of China. In fact, Mao Zedong extended the concept of equality to include the moral obliga-tion for all people to think of others as equal. Referring to the Confu-cian concept of freedom of speech, Merle Goldman provided the following explanation for the pro-democracy and free-speech move-ment in China in the 1990s:

> The intellectuals in the People's Republic regarded themselves as the in-
> termediaries between the rulers and the ruled, informing the leadership
> of the effect of their policies on society and urging reforms if the effect
> was deleterious and evoked resistance. Similarly like the literati [Confu-
> cian], they thought of themselves as an elite, charged with guiding the

people and even the leaders toward a more humane and just society. It is not surprising, therefore, that China's modern intellectuals emphasized freedom of the press and expression in their definition of democracy, because *these freedoms made it possible for them to fulfill their responsibility as intellectuals* [my emphasis][67]

These Confucian traditions were blended into what became officially known as Mao Zedong Thought and Marxism-Leninism. As stated in the in the Preamble to the 1982 Constitution, "Under the leadership of the Communist Party of China and the guidance of Marxism-Leninism and Mao Zedong Thought, the Chinese people ... will ... follow the socialist road."[68] In this quote it is tempting to equate the Confucian "Way" with the "socialist road." Marxism-Leninism was adapted to Chinese traditions. For example, while studying Marxist texts in 1930, Mao stated, "We must study Marxist 'books,' but they must be integrated with our actual situation."[69]

My primary interest is Mao's ideas regarding equality and freedom, not the details of his rise to power or the political intrigues of his reign. But I do feel the reader needs some sense of chronology of Mao's life to understand the development of his ideas. Born on December 26, 1893, he was a teenager at the time of the 1911 revolution and in his 50s when he proclaimed the founding of the People's Republic of China in 1949. The major cultural and economic events of his regime, which I discuss later, were the *Hundred Flowers* (1957), the *Great Leap Forward* (1958), and the *Cultural Revolution* (1963). Mao died in 1976. The following is the official history of Mao's rise to power as stated in the 1982 Constitution of the People's Republic of China:

The Revolution of 1911, led by Dr. Sun Yat-sen, abolished the feudal monarchy and gave birth to the Republic of China. But the historic mission of the Chinese people to overthrow imperialism and feudalism remained unaccomplished.

After waging protracted and arduous struggles, armed and otherwise, along a zigzag course, the Chinese people of all nationalities led by the Communist Party of China with Chairman Mao Zedong as its leader ultimately, in 1949, overthrew the rule of imperialism, feudalism and bureaucrat-capitalism ... and founded the People's Republic of China.[70]

Mao Zedong's ideas were formed in the crucible of Confucianism and anti-foreign nationalism. While Mao Zedong would later in life try to disown his Confucian education and heritage by linking it to feudalism, Confucian traditions continued to play a major role, particularly during the Hundred Flowers campaign and the Cultural Revolution.

Mao received a classical Confucian education. As previously mentioned, Mao's education began at the age of 6 by learning about moral equality from the *Three Character Classic*.

Mao's biographer, Philip Short, hypothesizes that 6-year-old Mao had difficulty understanding the explanation of moral equality provided by a 15th century commentator in the *Three Character Classic*. However, the commentary does illustrate the importance given to the concept of equality of moral capacities, and from this we can infer possible influence on Mao. The 15th-century commentary in the *Three Character Classic* explains the first lines of the book, "This refers to man at his birth. The wise and the simple, the upright and the vicious, all agree in their nature, radically resembling each other, without any difference. But when their knowledge has expanded their dispositions and endowments all vary ... thus perverting the correct principles of their virtuous nature."[71]

As a young man, Mao joined others in nationalistic protest against the actions of foreign powers. Mao's classmate wrote in a letter to his family in 1918, "You should know that the foreigners want to take China's land, they want to take China's money and they want to harm China's people ... Our aim is to look forward to the day of China's resurrection."[72] During the same period, Mao made the following declaration of Chinese nationalism and belief in the superiority of Chinese civilization:

> Our Chinese people possess great inherent capacities! The more profound the oppression, the more powerful its reaction, and since this has been accumulating for a long time, it will surely burst forth quickly. I venture to make a singular assertion: one day the reform of the Chinese people will be more profound than that of any other people, and society of the Chinese people will be more radiant than that of any other people ... [and] it will be achieved earlier than that of any other place or people ... Our golden age, our age of glory and splendor, lies before us![73]

Mao later recalled that during his 20s, "My mind was a curious mixture of ideas of liberalism, democratic reformism, and utopian socialism." Similar to Liu Shipei and other Chinese political activists, Mao was strongly attracted to anarchism and the works of Kropotkin. Anarchism provided the Confucian ideal of a society governed by self-regulation as opposed to laws. At the same time, he continued to be interested in Confucius. In 1920, Mao visited Confucius's grave and wrote, "I stopped at Qufu, and visited Confucius's grave. I saw the small stream where Confucius' disciples bathed their feet, and the little town where the sage lived as a child ... I saw the birthplace of Mencius."[74]

A year after visiting Confucius's grave, Mao and his fellow 17 members of the New People's study group voted on which "-ism" to follow with anarchism and Bolshevism being the most favored. It does seem peculiar, the idea of a group of young men voting on their ideological path. Twelve members voted for Bolshevism, three voted against, and three remained undecided. This ideological vote shaped the future direction of Chinese history.[75]

During this period, Mao became committed to the principle of equality for women. Two years prior to the vote on Bolshevism, he took on the role of a woman to explain the plight of females in China. Assuming the role of a woman, he wrote, "Gentlemen, we are women! ... We are also human beings ... [yet] we are not even allowed to go outside the front gate. The shameless men, the villainous men, make us into their playthings ... We want to sweep away all those devils who rape us and destroy the liberty of our minds and our bodies!"[76] Later, he argued that women's equality and freedom from the marriage system was dependent on gaining economic independence.

By the 1930s, Mao advocated sexual liberation as the key to breaking the traditional marriage system. He encouraged extra-marital affairs by women. Equality of rights in marriage and divorce were the first laws enacted in the temporary Chinese Soviet Republic of the 1930s and by the later People's Republic of China. Mao proudly proclaimed, "This democratic marriage system has burst the feudal shackles that have bound human beings, especially women, for thousands of years, and established a new pattern consistent with human nature."[77]

Mao's ideas on equality and freedom were tested and refined during the Hundred Flowers and the Great Leap Forward. He never rejected the Confucian idea of equality of moral capacities. During the Hundred Flowers and the Cultural Revolution he insisted on the capacity of the common people to correct the actions of the leadership. However, as I will explain, there were important boundaries placed on the right of the people to speak out against government authority.

In 1958, Mao outlined his concept of equality in a draft resolution written for the Chinese Communist Party. This statement on equality must be understood in the context of the Hundred Flowers campaign which, in part, was based on the criticism that a new class of government bureaucrats were acting as if they were better than the common people. For Mao, overcoming this form of inequality required a change in attitudes. In other words, equality required that people think and act toward others as equals.

"[We] must," Mao wrote, "adopt an *attitude of genuine equality* towards cadres and the masses and make people feel that relationships among men are truly equal [my emphasis]."[78] Embedded in this concept of equality was the idea of equality of social duties. All social duties were to be considered of equal value. Mao wrote, "People do different work and hold different jobs. No matter how high one's position is, one must appear among people as an ordinary worker. One must not assume airs; one must get rid of bureaucratism."[79]

Mao's thinking on equality of social duties was similar to that of Liu Shipei. This was one reason for sending intellectuals into the fields and factories during the Cultural Revolution. Besides wanting to connect theoretical education with workers' needs and destroy the elitist feelings of intellectuals, Mao also argued for the social value of experiencing differing occupations. In 1968, he wrote in the *Peking Review*, "The majority or vast majority of the students trained in the old schools and colleges can integrate themselves with the workers ... [and] be re-educated by the workers, peasants and soldiers under the guidance of the correct line, and thoroughly change their old ideology. Such intellectuals will be welcomed by the workers, peasants and soldiers."[80]

When applied to the educational process, equality of social duties became equality of educational experience. In this, Mao rejected the ideal of scholars, whom he categorized as "bourgeois intellectuals," devoting their days to theoretical studies. In 1967, during the cultural revolution, Mao wrote, "workers should, in addition to their main industrial work, learn military affairs, politics, and culture, and take part in the socialist educational movement."[81] In turn, he argued, "students are in a similar position. Their studies are their chief work; they must also learn other things. In other words, they ought to learn industrial, agricultural, and military work in addition to class work. The school years should be shortened, education should be revolutionized, and the domination of our schools by bourgeois intellectuals should by no means be allowed to continue."[82]

I don't want to stretch the connection between Mao Zedong Thought and Confucianism, particularly since Mao denounced the traditional intellectual leadership of Confucian scholars as bourgeois and he let the Red Guard destroy Confucian relics at Qufu. However, there are parallels between Mao's principle of thinking of others as equal and the pronouncements by Confucius in *The Doctrine of the Mean*. Confucius said, in reference to the "superior" human,

> In a high situation, he does not treat with contempt his inferiors. In a low situation, he does not court the favor of his superiors.[83]

Mao stressed the equality of moral capacities, the first lesson of his childhood, in his attacks against bourgeois intellectuals. He argued that intellectuals had become a special class with feelings of superiority to the common population. He justified the Cultural Revolution as a necessary struggle to eliminate the sense of superiority among intellectuals and provide an opportunity for the people to exercise their equal moral sensibilities. This meant that the educational system had to be changed to ensure the replacement of bourgeois thinking with the natural capacities of the common people. Using socialist rhetoric, these ideas were stressed in the 1966 "Decision of the Central Committee of the Chinese Communist Party Concerning the Great Proletarian Revolution." This document stressed the importance of an educational revolution:

> In the great proletarian cultural revolution a most important task is to transform the old educational system and the old principles and methods of teaching.

> In this great proletarian cultural revolution, the phenomenon of our schools dominated by bourgeois intellectuals must be changed.

> In every kind of school we must apply throughly the policy advanced by Comrade Mao Zedong, of education serving proletarian politics and education being combined with productive labor, so as to enable those receiving an education to develop morally, intellectually and physically and to become laborers with socialist consciousness and culture.[84]

Mao's attack on so-called bourgeois intellectuals highlights the problem of freedom of speech imbedded in Confucianism and Mao Zedong Thought. As previously discussed, the Confucian scholar had the duty to speak out against injustice and immorality. This duty carried with it the responsibility to not advocate injustice and immorality. This was freedom of speech to advocate and protect the Way.

But, who should determine whether speech advocates justice or injustice? Confucians might respond that this is to be determined by people in their search for the Way. But in Confucianism individual actions cannot be abstracted from their social context. An individual's concept of justice and morality is directly related to its social consequences. If freedom of speech is limited to advocating justice and morality, then freedom of speech can be denied to those preaching the opposite. Based on this concept of freedom of speech, when is free speech allowed or denied?

This was the dilemma faced by Mao in the Hundred Flowers movement. Mao envisioned the Hundred Flowers movement as allowing freedom for the people to speak out against the government. This freedom was to act as a check against the development of an unjust government bureaucracy. In the Hundred Flowers campaign, Mao replaced the Confucian ideal of intellectuals checking the actions of government through free speech with the masses of common people exercising that power. Of course, this meant limiting free speech to statements of justice and morality. But how would this limitation be determined?

Initially, Mao advocated complete freedom of speech in a statement with the descriptive title, "On the Correct Handling of Contradictions Among the People." Reflecting his poetic side, Mao made the distinction between 'fragrant flowers' and 'poisonous weeds.' Mao stated, "[The slogan of] 'Let a hundred flowers bloom, a hundred schools of thought contend' … was put forward in recognition of the various different contradictions in society … If you want to grow only [fragrant flowers] and not weeds, it can't be done … To ban all weeds and stop them growing, is that possible? The reality is that it is not … They will still grow … It is difficult to distinguish fragrant flowers from poisonous weeds."[85]

Mao believed that the practice of freedom of speech would result in the "true" ideas winning out. "If they have something to fart about, let them fart!," he declared, "If it's out, then one can decide whether it smells bad or good … If the people think their farts stink, they will be isolated."[86] In less colorful language, he contended, "Truth stands in contrast to falsehood and is developed out of the struggle against it. Beauty stands in contrast to ugliness and is developed out of the struggle against it."[87]

Of course, according to Philip Short, what others thought were fragrant flowers, truth, and beauty were not necessarily in line with Mao's thinking. After only a few months of letting a "hundred flowers bloom," Mao was disturbed by the intense criticism of the government and the party. Consequently, he decided to use the call for freedom of speech as a means of identifying enemies of the regime. In a secret memorandum entitled "Things are turning into their opposites," Mao plotted, "We shall let the Rightists run amuck for a time and let them reach their climax … Some say they are afraid of being hooked like a fish … Now that large numbers of fish have come to the surface of themselves, there is no need to bait the hook."[88] And then, he warned, "There are two alternatives for the Rightists. One is to … mend their ways. The other is to go making trouble and court ruin. Gentlemen Rightist, the choice is yours, the initiative (for a short time) is in your hands."[89]

The limits of the Confucian concept of free speech are illustrated by the quick reversal of the goal of using free speech to check government actions to using it as a means of catching so-called right-wing thinkers. The assumption that the purpose of free speech is the freedom to advocate moral and just ideas opens the door to allowing government authorities to limit free speech based on their ideas of morality and justice.

The same issue was presented during the Cultural Revolution. The Red Guard was given free reign to criticize public officials for anti-Mao Zedong Thought. The Red Guards could be considered as operating within the Confucian tradition of exercising a social duty to speak out against injustice. However, historians and the present Chinese Communist Party have argued that the Cultural Revolution primarily focused on promoting ideas that supported those in power and not ideas of justice.

Shortly after Mao's death in 1976, the government arrested the so-called "Gang of Four" who were alleged to be responsible for the policies of the Cultural Revolution that had undermined the educational system and had sent many to prison for supposedly voicing anti-Mao Zedong ideas. In the end, Mao's policies demonstrated the limitations of Confucian ideas of freedom of speech. However, he did raise the Confucian idea of equality of moral capacities to a new level by stressing the importance of thinking of others as equals. Incorporated into Mao's educational goals were the ideals of equality of social duties and equality of thinking about others. The next and current stage of the evolution of Chinese communism, "Socialist Modernization," continues to be entwined with the evolution of basic Confucian beliefs.

SOCIALIST MODERNIZATION AND HUMAN RIGHTS

There has been widespread Western criticism of Chinese violations of human rights regarding the incarceration of intellectual dissenters, the 1989 killing of demonstrators in Tiananmen square, and repressive actions towards religious groups. Westerners were particularly critical of the Tiananmen square killings because the demonstrations were labeled a pro-democracy movement. However, when American social theorist Craig Calhoun took a poll of the participants he found that they were not demonstrating in support of electoral politics. They were demonstrating for free speech, or in Confucian terms, the right to be heard. Writing about the political repression in Tiananmen Square in the context of Confucian influence on intellectuals in the People's Republic of China, Merle Goldman argues, "Their [the demonstrators] use of petitions and articles in the party press and the Democracy Wall activist's use of wall posters and unofficial journals to advise and criticize resembled the [Confucian] literati's use of memorials offering advice and criticism to higher officials or the emperor."[90]

While the Tiananmen Square demonstrators could be portrayed as exercising the traditional obligation of the Confucian scholar, the actions of the government could be described as exercising the traditional Confucian responsibility to maintain public harmony. Of course, this argument can be dismissed simply as an excuse for maintaining political power by claiming that any political demonstration threatens public order. It would be difficult to dispute claims that the arrest of political dissidents is anything other than political oppression and a method for those in control to maintain existing power.

On the other hand, the censorship of advertising in China could be viewed as an example of Confucian abridgement of free speech for the purpose of maintaining social harmony. Westerners often think of free-speech rights as extending to advertising. The Chinese government insists that advertisements must not "jeopardize the social order."[91] For instance, the Western mega-advertising firm of Saatchi and Saatchi found that in China they could not use a commercial for an athlete's foot medication that depicted an actual afflicted foot. The Chinese government prohibits the advertising display of patients or medical symptoms because these images might disrupt social harmony.[92]

China can also be accused of denying the rights of cultural minorities, particularly the people of Tibet. Currently, the Dalai Lama, the leader of Tibetan Buddhism, is in exile in India. There is a worldwide protest to free Tibet from China and restore the Dalai Lama to religious and political power. The restoration of the Dalai Lama directly threatens China's political control of Tibet.

The Chinese government's defense of their actions in Tibet follow a typical Confucian line of thinking. Buddhism has always suffered in China because of the tendency of many Chinese to dismiss religions that are directed towards some form of afterlife. Within Confucianism, Heaven, Nirvana or any other afterlife causes people not to focus on improving the quality of temporal life on earth. In addition, from the Chinese government's perspective, the restoration of the Dalai Lama will mean that Tibet will be ruled by a theocracy. From a socialist and Confucian point of view, a theocracy is one of the worst forms of government. These views were expressed in an official Chinese government White Paper on "Tibet [sic] Culture Extinction" issued in 2000. The White Paper refers to the Dalai Lama's complaints about the extinction of Tibetan culture as a "demand that modern Tibetan people keep the life styles and cultural values of old Tibet's feudal serfdom wholly intact."[93] The government claims to be protecting Tibetan culture by adapting it to the modern world. There has been, the White Paper argues, "a substantive shift ... from the self-enclosed, stagnating and shrinking situation to a new stance—the stance of opening up and development oriented to modernization and the outside world. While developing and promoting its traditional culture, Tibet is also developing modern scientific and technological education and news dissemination at an unprecedented rate."[94] This stance on cultural rights was reiterated by Li Ruihuan, chairman of the National Committee of the Chinese People's Political Consultative Conference during a 2000 visit to Canada. *The People's Daily* reported, "Li urged that people must adopt a scientific attitude toward the traditional culture of their nationality. They should not be pedantic and cherish the outmoded and preserve the outworn.... "[95] Rejecting the idea of preserving traditional cultures and the necessity of updating cultural practices, Li emphasized, "It is only possible for traditional culture to be boosted up to a new glory after it has been intertwined together with the contemporary world and broken through boldly the out-of-date thoughts so that it can absorb nutrition from vivid social practices."[96]

Although it is not hard to see how these limitations on free speech and cultural rights can be justified in the framework of Confucian thought, at the same time it can be argued that their primary purpose is to maintain the political power of the present Chinese government. Chinese President Jiang Zemin's comments on human rights at the United Nations Millennium Summit could be interpreted as just a ploy to allow his government to violate human rights or as a statement reflecting traditional fears of outside influence and a desire to protect a Chinese interpretation of human rights. At the Millennium Summit, Jiang argued that the two fundamental principles of the United Nations were the protection of national sovereignty and human rights. He stated that the existence of human rights depends on the protection of national sovereignty. He also emphasized the importance of each country maintaining its own social system: "The people of a country are entitled to independently choosing [sic] their own social system and development model in the light of their national conditions and *to shaping their own way of life* [my emphasis]."[97] Is this statement purely self-serving, or does it reflect traditional Chinese thought?

EQUALITY, FREEDOM, AND SOCIALIST MODERNIZATION

The point I am making is that concepts of equality and freedom in the present Constitution of the People's Republic of China reflect, among other influences, the long history of Confucian ideas as modified by Mao and adapted to Marxist-Leninist thought under the current leadership's goal of "socialist modernization." Clearly stated in the Constitution are concepts of equality linked to social duties, professions of free speech limited by the requirement to speak out for morality and justice, and the treatment of intellectuals as a special group.

In this context, universal education is still promoted as the key to the good and moral society. Operating under the goal of creating and maintaining a "socialist spiritual civilization," education, not laws, is considered the key to creating a self-regulated and harmonious society. In addition, as part of the socialist modernization movement, schools are called upon to train workers. Adopting the rhetoric of equality of opportunity, the schools help find and train people for an occupation suited to their talents. Work is considered a social duty. In the 1950s, the Chinese adopted the phrase "red and expert" to describe the educational goal of creating and maintaining a harmonious and moral society, while training for specific jobs. "Red and expert" captures the idea of equality of moral capacities in learning to be "red" while living in a society of unequal occupations.

As I discussed regarding Professor Sun's private Deweyan school, China's constitution encourages public and private organizations to start their own schools. The promotion of these independent schools reflects traditional Confucian objections to detailed control by central governments as opposed to self-regulation by local community structures and individuals. This self-regulation is now referred to as the "market."

Article 15 of China's constitution explains how privately owned and controlled schooling can be allowed in a country that professes allegiance to Marxist-Leninist traditions. Article 15 reflects the idea of "Chinese essence" being integrated into Marxist-Leninist thought. Mao frequently voiced the opinion that the Chinese brand of Communism would eventually triumph over all other types of government and economic systems. The Chinese form of socialism combines central planning and control with economic self-regulation or, in modern economic language, the market principles. Article 15 declares:

> The state practices planned economy on the basis of socialist public ownership. It ensures the proportionate and coordinated growth of the national economy though overall balancing by economic planning and the supplementary role of regulation by the market.[98]

In keeping with Confucian traditions, applying market or self-regulatory principles to the development of schools does not mean freedom of instruction. The assumption is that schools produced by the actions of the market and that are self-governed will teach socialist principles of morality and justice as defined by the government. Article 15 forcefully qualifies the action of the market with the authoritarian statement, "Disturbance of socioeconomic order or disruption of the state economic plan by an organization or individual is prohibited."

Article 19, which includes the previously quoted statement supporting the development of private education, ensures that private schools will teach a common socialist ideology. Article 19 declares, "The state undertakes the development of socialist education and works to raise the scientific and cultural level of the whole nation."[99] Article 23 links socialism to the educational ideal of "red and expert":

> The state trains specialized personnel in all fields who serve socialism, expands the ranks of intellectuals and creates conditions to give full scope to their role in socialist modernization.[100]

The training of "specialized personnel" is part of socialist modernization or the "expert" part of "red and expert." For instance, Donald Tsang, Financial Secretary of the Hong Kong Special Administrative Region, announced on June 4, 2000 the success of the region's efforts in promoting education in information technology (IT). Stating that it is important to "nurture a technically savvy workforce to safeguard our economic future," Tsang declared the goal of having all Hong Kong school children master the general application of information technology within the next 5 years.[101]

While training to meet the needs of economic development (the "expert" part of education), the "red" part of education (socialist morality) continues to be essential. Article 24 of China's constitution identifies the socialist values that will promote the Confucian ideal of education as the basis for a self-regulated society. Article 24 places emphasis on "high ideals," "morality," "rules of conduct," "civic virtues," and "love of motherland" in the context of a "socialist spiritual civilization":

Article 24

The state strengthens the building of socialist spiritual civilization through spreading education in high ideals and morality, general education and education in discipline and the legal system, and through promoting the formulation and observance of rules of conduct and common pledges by different sections of the people in urban and rural areas.

The state advocates the civic virtues of love for the motherland, for the people, for labor, for science and for socialism; it educates the people in patriotism, collectivism, internationalism and communism and in dialectical and historical materialism; it combats capitalist, feudalist and other decadent ideas.[102]

The goal of "socialist spiritual civilization" could be considered a fusion of Confucian values with socialist development. The educational goal of building civic morality is considered an important part of socialist modernization. Using the language of following the Way, or in this case the "socialist road," the Constitution's Preamble states:

Chinese people of all nationalities will continue to adhere to the people's democratic dictatorship and the socialist road, steadily improve socialist institutions, develop socialist democracy, improve the socialist legal system, and work hard and self-reliantly to modernize industry, agriculture, national defense and science and technology step by step to turn China into a socialist country with a high level of culture and democracy.[103]

The limitation of freedom of speech in public and private schools, and in the broader society, to teaching and statements supporting the "socialist road" and socialist spiritual civilization is explicitly enunciated in Article 28. Again, a parallel can easily be made between the Confucian limitations on free speech and Article 28's authoritarian pronouncement, "The state maintains public order and suppresses treasonable and other counter-revolutionary activities; it penalizes criminal activities that endanger public security and disrupt the socialist economy as well as other criminal activities; and it punishes and reforms criminals."[104]

In general, freedom in China's constitution is limited by the requirements of harmony and public order. Article 51 states:

> Citizens of the People's Republic of China, in exercising their freedoms and rights, may not infringe upon the interests of the state, of society or of the collective, or upon the lawful freedoms and rights of other citizens.[105]

Limitations on freedom of religious expression, including religious activities in public and private schools, are justified by the government's duty to maintain public order. Article 36 demonstrates how a declaration of freedom, "Citizens of the People's Republic of China enjoy freedom of religious belief," can be restricted by concerns with social harmony:

> The state protects normal religious activities. No one may make use of religion to engage in activities that disrupt public order, impair the health of citizens or interfere with the *educational system of the state* [my emphasis].[106]

The Confucian concept of the right and duty to exercise free speech to check government actions is specifically stated in the Constitution's Article 41. Similar to Mao's distinction between "fragrant flowers" and "poisonous weeds," Article 41 seeks to control public criticism by prohibiting "distortion of facts" and "false incrimination." I believe that Article 41 expresses the traditional Confucian ideal of public criticism of government and highlights the potential danger of severe restrictions on free speech. Article 41 states:

> Citizens of the People's Republic of China have the right to criticize and make suggestions regarding any state organ or functionary. Citizens have the right to make to relevant state organs complaints or charges against, or exposures of, any state organ or functionary for violation of the law or dereliction of duty, but fabrication or distortion of facts for purposes of libel or false incrimination is prohibited.[107]

The combination of right and duty is also applied to education. Rights, in this context, only have meaning in the context of social relationships. And, of course, social relationships involve social duties that contribute to the maintenance of an orderly and peaceful society. For example, China's constitution provides for the right to work along with the duty to work. "Citizens," declares Article 42, "Have the right as well as duty to work."[108]

Very seldom do Western thinkers link such ideas as "the right to education" with a duty to be educated. "Citizens of the People's Republic of China," Article 45 states, "have the right as well as the duty to receive an education."[109]

GENDER EQUALITY AND INEQUALITY

Equality for women is declared in Article 48. Again, the reader should keep in mind that rights are associated with social duties. Article 49 reflects Mao's concern with forced marriages and his belief that equality for women depends on freedom from marriage contracts. Article 49 also stresses traditional family relationships by making it a duty for grown children to support their parents:

Article 48

Women in the People's Republic of China enjoy equal rights with men in all spheres of life, in political economic, cultural, social and family life.

The state protects the rights and interests of women, applies the principle of equal pay for equal work to men and women alike and trains and selects cadres from among women.

Article 49

Marriage, the family and mother and child are protected by the state.

Both husband and wife have the duty to practice family planning.

Parents have the duty to rear and educate their children who are minors, and *children who have come of age have the duty to support and assist their parents.*

Violation of the freedom of marriage is prohibited. Maltreatment of old people, women and children is prohibited [my emphasis].[110]

Despite the Constitution's guarantee of gender equality, the continuing influence of the Yin–yang school of philosophy results in women retaining a subordinate position in Chinese society. Amartya Sen estimates over 50 million statistically missing women in China as a result of the aborting of female fetuses, infanticide, and the neglect of the health and nutritional needs of female children.[111] On a global scale, there are statistically 5% more boys born than girls. However, if boys and girls are given equal care more girls survive because they are physically hardier. Consequently, despite the higher birth rate for males, the ratio of women to men exceeds 1.05 in United States, the United Kingdom, and France. For sub-Saharan Africa the ratio is 1.022. The ratio for China is 0.94.[112]

On the other hand, China has made greater attempts than India, as I discuss in chapter 5, to achieve equality of education for women. According to the UNICEF report, *The State of the World's Children 2000*, the adult literacy rate for females as a percentage of the male literacy rate in China is 80%, whereas in India it is only 55%. Comparisons of female school enrollments also indicate a greater effort on the part of the Chinese government, as compared to the Indian government, to provide equal educational opportunity. In China, the female enrollment rate as a percentage of male enrollment rate for primary school is 99%. This figure indicates almost full equality of educational opportunity for women in attending primary school. The figure for secondary school is 91%. These percentages are much higher than those reported for India, which are 87% for primary school and 66% for secondary school.[11] Of all these statistics, the number of missing women is the most horrifying. It is possible that the Confucian belief in moral equality can provide a quicker road to gender equality.

CONCLUSION: THE CONTRIBUTION OF CONFUCIUS, MENCIUS, MAO ZEDONG THOUGHT, AND SOCIALIST MODERNIZATION TO IDEAS OF EQUALITY AND FREEDOM IN THE GLOBAL FLOW

China, like the rest of the world, is being influenced by global culture of schooling with its emphasis on equality of opportunity and equality of educational opportunity as a key to economic development. Under the doctrines of socialist modernization, as in most other countries influenced by global culture, equality of opportunity and education promises economic efficiency by providing a labor pool of well-schooled workers. The "expert" part of the socialist educational dictum to educate all to be "red and expert" is central to the educational aspects of the global culture.

"Black July," the dreaded time of the college admission examinations in China, resembles similar educational contests throughout the global culture resulting from the increased importance of schooling in determining the economic outcomes of human lives. The People's Republic of China utilizes one examination to determine who will go on to college. There is an obvious temptation to compare this examination to the civil service examinations of Imperial times. However, the civil service examinations were supposed to select the best scholars to help guide the ship-of-state. The "Black July" examination determines an individual's future education and employment.

For example, on July 9, 2000, parents gathered anxiously outside examination centers waiting for their children. Many of these parents were denied a higher education during the period of the Cultural Revolution. One parent, Zhang Mei, whose 19-year-old daughter was inside the Beijing center taking the exam, told *New York Times* reporter Erik Eckholm, "In our time [referring to the Cultural Revolution], young people had to go work in the countryside."[114] Representing the hopes of parents everywhere who are affected by the global culture of schooling and school examinations, Ms. Zhang commented, "We weren't well educated. But to make it in society these days you just have to go to college."[115] Referring to the importance of examination in determining their daughter's future, she said, "This is a really big event in her life."[116] Another parent, Yan Yanan, worried, "I'm more nervous than my daughter. I'm worried that she might fail, or have to go to a second-rate university, but college has become a must these days."[117]

Similar to tests faced by students around the world, the Chinese test determines both entrance to college and the social ranking of the college the student will attend. It is assumed that the more prestigious the college, the better the financial and occupational life outcome for the student. The author of a Chinese book on the social impact of the examination, He Janming, told Erik Eckholm, "If you get over the top, you'll see a bright future, the pot of gold. If you fail, your life seems to be at an end."[118]

English as the global language receives support by being a required subject on the examination. This provides clear evidence of the intention of the educational system to prepare students for the global economy. All students are tested on Chinese, English, and mathematics. In addition, students choose between sets of examinations for entrance into a science or a liberal arts program.

The examination system serves the human capital role of selecting talent for the economic system. What sets Chinese civilization apart is the "red" part of "red and expert" in education. This represents the moral education element of the Confucian tradition, which is also found in schools in other countries like Japan and Singapore.[119] The source of morality in Western and Hindu traditions is religion with its claims of representing the moral requirements of a spiritual being. In these traditions, guilt is the method of social control. In Confucian traditions, and under the doctrines of socialist modernization, morality is derived from real social interactions. Shame is the method of social control.

Consequently, in Chinese civilization, morality is studied in relation to the human condition. Morality is not fixed but is derived from changing social needs. Therefore, constant study is required to determine the moral standards that will best contribute to a well-ordered society. In other traditions, morality is a set of rules for social conduct that are memorized. Values, particularly those derived from religion, are not studied and judged according to their contribution to social harmony. In some cases, particularly in fundamentalist movements, religious dogma is considered ordained for all time and not to be changed with the evolution of social practices and needs.

This difference is illustrated by my confused reaction to a Japanese student studying in the United States who wondered how Americans became moral since they did not study morality in school. In Japan, moral education is an important part of the curriculum. I quickly responded to the student by pointing to the role of the family and religious institutions. Later, I realized my lack of understanding of the student's question. The student was perplexed about the American situation because in her mind morality was something to study and to reflect upon with regard to its social value. I had thought, in Western fashion, of morality as a series of moral maxims to be memorized and reinforced by punishments.

These different approaches to moral education help to explain why John Dewey was hailed as a "Second Confucius" and why his educational ideas are incorporated into Mian Tao Sun's private school. Rejecting morality as a religious ideal, Dewey also argued that morality was a product of social interactions and that it needed to be constantly improved and adapted to changing social situations. "Learning By Doing" and "Education Through Experience" are Deweyan slogans that attest to this pragmatic approach to morality. In addition, Dewey emphasized the importance of human interaction as the source of knowledge. Similar to the Confucian tradition, Dewey advocated the study of morality as a means of increasing our understanding of how to improve social conditions.

U.S. philosophers David Hall and Roger Ames believe that Deweyan pragmatism can close the gap between Western and Far Eastern concepts of society. They argue that the Western reliance on an abstract set of "natural rights" has little meaning in a tradition governed by "rites" or the search for the best means of achieving social harmony. Referring to Dewey's emphasis on the community as the source of knowledge and human progress, Hall and Ames contend, "John Dewey's vision of a democratic society demonstrates surprising affinities with the traditional Chinese understanding of social organization ... Confucianism and pragmatism share a number of important philosophical assumptions, and may thus serve as resources for intercultural conversations."[120]

China's traditional commitment to universal education is premised on a belief in equality of moral capacities and social duties. Thinking of others as equal is an important part of developing one's moral capacities. This evolving morality requires self-reflection and self-criticism. In addition, everyone has an equal social duty to speak out against corrupt governments and social injustice. However, this freedom is seriously compromised by concerns about free speech disrupting the social order.

The existence of Mian Tao Sun's private Deweyan school is now understandable against the background of Confucian traditions. Translated into a Chinese ideoscape, Western concepts of privatization and a market economy take on a different meaning. Rejecting legalism as a mechanism of social control, Confucian traditions support privatization and market economies as long as *private actions support social harmony and the social good*, whereas in the West, privatization and markets are associated with the pursuit of profit without any obligation on the part of the profiteers to show concern for others.

Because the Deweyan aspects of Mian Tao Sun's school are meant to instill in students a desire to search for the best means of promoting the social good, it can be concluded that his school embodies a commitment to a society governed by a belief in equality of moral capacities and the equality of social duties. Confucius, Mencius, and John Dewey would probably all approve of Professor Sun's school and his comment that, "I have run a private school from kindergarten to senior high school, although I feel little tired everyday, I live very happy." Certainly, the Confucian ideal is to create a world where we can all "live very happy."

3

Equality and Freedom in Islamic Education

The boys sat in an airless room at the Haqqania madrasa in Pakistan memorizing the *Qur'an* and the *Hadith*.[1] These texts have formed Islamic civilization for over 1,000 years. Across the globe from the Americas to Europe, Africa, the Middle East, Pakistan, and Indonesia, children attending Islamic schools read the same books. Similar to the power of Confucian texts, these readings have influenced the minds of countless generations.

Pakistan's approximately 10,000 madrasas train future religious and political leaders. The Haqqania has graduated leaders of the Taliban, Afghanistan's ruling group. The Taliban are known for their strict enforcement of Islamic law. At Haqqania, the students, ranging in age from 8 to 30, spend 6 months to 3 years memorizing the *Qur'an* in the original Arabic. This is difficult for many of the students since they only speak Pashto, the dialect of this region of Pakistan. The *Qur'an* is the uncreated Word of God as revealed to Mohamed (570–632 C.E.). As the actual Word of God, its true meaning can only be understood in Arabic. The *Hadith* is a collection of the sayings of Mohamed. The *Hadith* is an important source of religious teachings but, unlike the *Qur'an*, it is not the uncreated Word of God.

The following passages from the *Qur'an* underscore the importance of reading the original Arabic version, "We have sent it [the *Qur'an*] down as a clear discourse that you may understand (12:2)."[2] Another translation of this passage is: "We have sent it down as an Arabic *Qur'an*, in order that ye may learn wisdom."[3] Also, the *Qur'an* states, "We have sent down this Exposition and We will guard it [from corruption]" (15:9).[4]

QUR'ANIC ARABIC: THE LANGUAGE OF ISLAM

By studying the *Qur'an* in the original Arabic, Haqqania's students and students studying in Islamic schools around the world are learning a language shared by almost 1 billion Moslems. Not only does this tighten the cultural ties between Islamic nations and communities, but it also highlights the importance of language rights in countries where Moslems are a minority community. For instance, Moslems residing in the United States are demanding equal treatment for Qur'anic Arabic in public schools and colleges. Akhtar Emon, a major advocate of offering Qur'anic Arabic as a second language in U.S. public schools, asks, "If Spanish, Latin, German, French, Italian, Hebrew, Russian, etc. are taught as a second language in public places of learning, then why not Qur'anic Arabic?"[5] He identifies the Institute of Arabic and Islamic Studies and the As-Sunnah Foundation of America as major organizations that could help plan the introduction of Qur'anic Arabic into U.S. public schools. Also, Emon supports the use of educational vouchers in the United States that would allow Moslem parents to use public money to select Islamic schools for their children.

To bolster his argument for the teaching of Qur'anic Arabic as a second language in the United States, Emon cites the case of Malaysia, where the language has been taught in schools since 1915. In the first 6 years of primary school, Qur'anic Arabic is taught along with the Malay language. In the first 3 years of secondary school, Qur'anic Arabic is a required second language. In the last 2 years of high school, when students are divided into different vocational tracks, Qur'anic Arabic remains a common course of study.

Emon hopes that similar programs in other countries will make Qur'anic Arabic a truly international language. He argues, "When you visit Malaysia, you can easily get by even if you do not know the Malay language, as long as you know some Arabic. Malaysian model would be an excellent one to emulate for other countries, including Pakistan, Iran, Afghanistan, Indonesia, Bangladesh, Turkey, Bosnia, etc."[6]

Emon sidesteps the issue that Qur'anic Arabic is learned primarily for religious reasons and, therefore, raises in some countries—such as the United States and France—the potential violation of the principle of separation of church and state. He does admit that in the 21 Arabic-speaking nations, natives speak different forms of Arabic and that they have to consult special reference works to fully understand the *Qur'an*. For instance, a Syrian might not fully understand a Moroccan because of their particular forms of colloquial Arabic.

Should Moslems have a right to learn Qur'anic Arabic at government expense? Should Qur'anic Arabic be considered a minority language? Or should Qur'anic Arabic be considered a religious language and treated under human rights doctrine regarding the free practice of religion? I return to these questions at the end of the chapter.

ISLAM AND THE WEST

When reporter Jeffery Goldberg visited the Haqqania madrasa in the year 2000, he found classes being conducted in the centuries-old style of a white-bearded teacher reading from the text while students listened. Missing were the wide-ranging discussions and suggestions of differing interpretations of the *Hadith* that often provides the intellectual spark in Islamic education. However, during one visit, the class erupted in discussion over the meaning of a Jihad. Initially, the class was studying passages on Zakat or Charity. According to my English translation of the *Hadith*, they might have been reading the following passages which form the basis for Islamic responsibility for the welfare of others. Undoubtedly, these passages provide the religious basis for welfare benefits, including health care and housing, found in the constitutions of Islamic countries. The *Hadith* states:

> The *Qur'an* teaches that the poor and needy have a right to a share of other people's wealth.

> Avoid Hell by giving charity, even if it means sharing your last date, and, if you have nothing at all, by speaking a kind word.

> God will have no sympathy for the person who showed no sympathy for men.[7]

Interrupting the discussion of the *Hadith*, a student asked Goldberg what he thought of Osama bin Laden who was accused by the U.S. government of being an international terrorist. The *Qur'an* specifically supports a jihad or holy war against an oppressor. It promises entrance into paradise for those killed. The *Qur'an* states:

> Fight those in the way of God who fight you, but do not be aggressive: God does not like aggressors (2:190).[8]

> Fight them till sedition come to end, and the law of God (prevails). If they desist, then cease to be hostile, except against those who oppress (2:193).[9]

> And those ... who fought and were killed, I shall blot out their sins and admit them indeed into gardens with rippling streams (3:195).[10]

> Those who barter the life of this world for the next should fight in the way of God. And we shall bestow on him who fights in the way of God whether he is killed or is victorious, a glorious reward (4:74).[11]

In response to the question about Osama bin Laden, Goldberg quoted from the *Hadith* a passage which forbids the killing of innocent people: "It is narrated by Ibn Umar that a woman was found killed in one of these battles, so the Messenger of Allah, may peace be upon him, forbade the killing of women and children."[12] This passage suggests that God does not approve of terrorism directed at civilian targets such as airplane and car bombs. Students responded to Goldberg by asking for proof that women and children were killed by Osama bin Laden. One student said, "Osama wants to keep Islam pure from the pollution of the infidels. He believes Islam is the way for all the world. He wants to bring Islam to all the world."[13]

The reporter responded by saying that the *Qur'an* forbids compulsion in religion. I believe Goldberg was referring to the following passage from the *Qur'an:*

> There is no compulsion in matter of faith. Distinct is the way of guidance now from error. He who turns away from the forces of evil and believes in God, will surely hold fast to a handle that is strong and unbreakable, for God hears all and knows everything (2:256).[14]

A student replied to Goldberg that there was no compulsion in religion but that the West was forcing Moslems to live under the rule of infidels. This response highlights the Islamic view of the world as being divided between believers and nonbelievers, with the nonbelievers condemned to Hell.

This division of the world is clearly stated in the *Qur'an* and serves as an important limitation on concepts of equality in the Islamic world. The *Qur'an* states:

> God is the friend of those who believe, and leads them out of darkness into light; but the patrons of infidels are idols and devils who lead them from light into darkness. They are the residents of Hell, and will there forever abide (2:257).[15]

Besides affecting the boundaries of equality between believers and nonbelievers, this division has important implications for the meaning of religious freedom under constitutions of Islamic countries. Many of these constitutions discriminate against religious minorities.

Besides religious dogma, history is another source of suspicion about the intentions of non-Moslems, particularly the Christian West. Similar to China, Islamic countries still feel the humiliation of Western imperialism. Islamic history and Islamic jurisprudence complete the studies of students at Haqqania. The course in Islamic history provides strong reminders of Western imperialism. Islamic conflict with the West is much older than that experienced in Asia. The starting point of current tensions can be dated from 1095, when European crusaders launched a holy war to capture the city of Jerusalem. Their invasion was greeted by an Islamic jihad that continues to this day.

Similar to Asia, Islamic populations wonder about Western claims that they are the progenitors and protectors of human rights in the global flow. Taught from an Islamic perspective, the history of relations with the West is one of invasions and colonialism. Consequently, conservative Islamic leaders simply dismiss human rights as a Western or Zionist plot. Legal scholar Ann Mayer quotes Iranian religious leader Ayatollah Khomeini: "What they call human rights is nothing but a collection of corrupt rules worked out by Zionists to destroy all true religions."[16] The president of Iran, Ali Khamene'i commented, "When we want to find out what is right and what is wrong, we do not go to the United Nations; we go to the Holy Koran [Qur'an]. For us, the Universal Declaration of Human rights is nothing but a collection of mumbo-jumbo by disciples of Satan."[17]

ISLAMIC HISTORY AND THE WEST

What are the roots of this historical antipathy with the West? What perspective on the past do students learn when studying Islamic history? One place to begin this inquiry is Amin Maalouf's *The Crusades Through Arab Eyes.* For centuries, students in the West have learned about the Crusades as an heroic venture by knights in shining armor marching off to rescue the Holy Land from pagan Moslems. From the historical documents stitched together by Maalouf, the Moslem perspective is that of an unexpected invasion by a barbarous and heathen army dressed in white sheets with red crosses followed by a rag-tag crowd of religious fanatics and prostitutes. At the siege of Antioch in 1097, the Crusaders were described as roasting Moslem spies on spits and eating them as crowds watched in horror from the city walls. Once inside the walls, the Crusaders purportedly raped and killed women and slaughtered all the men.[18]

It is easy to draw parallels between the atrocities supposedly committed by the Crusaders and those supposedly committed by Yugoslavian troops against Moslem inhabitants of Kosovo and Bosnia in the 1990s. The Yugoslavian troops represented a population that was primarily Eastern Orthodox Christians who had a long-standing hatred of the resident Moslem population. The Crusaders also received encouragement from the Eastern Orthodox church as they raped and pillaged their way to Jerusalem.

In 1098, the Crusaders attacked Ma'arra, where the population surrendered when promised that their lives would be spared. Breaking their promise, the Crusaders slaughtered the population and purportedly "boiled pagan adults in cooking-pots ... [and] impaled children on spits and devoured them grilled."[19] A supposed official letter from the Crusaders to the Pope stated, "A terrible famine racked the army in Ma'arra, and placed it in the cruel necessity of feeding itself upon the bodies of the Saracens."[20] The Crusaders pillaged and raped their way south until reaching the walls of Jerusalem in 1099, where they marched around the city throwing themselves against the walls as priests prayed and chanted. In July, the Crusaders breached the wall.

The resulting sack of Jerusalem was burned into the pages of Islamic history. After Mecca and Medina, Jerusalem was declared the third holy city of Islam after the Prophet Mohamed was led by God to the city for a miraculous meeting with Moses and Jesus. The Qur'an recognizes Moses and Jesus as prophets of God who were betrayed by their followers. The meeting of Mohamed, Jesus, and Moses represents the continuity of the divine message of Moslem faith. The loss of Jerusalem was a heavy blow to the followers of Islam.

Islamic history provides sharp contrasts between the actions of Moslem and Christian conquerors of Jerusalem. In 638, 'Umar Ibn al-Kattab captured the city and was greeted by the Christian Greek Patriarch. 'Umar asked to visited the Christian shrines. Prayer time arrived while 'Umar was in the Church of the Holy Sepulcher. He asked permission to roll out his prayer rug but the Patriarch worried that Moslems would appropriate the spot because it would become known as the site where 'Umar prayed. Respecting the Patriarch's wishes, 'Umar took his prayer rug outside and on that place was built a mosque. When the Crusaders entered in 1099, an Islamic chronicler wrote, "The population of the holy city was put to the sword, and the Franj [Crusaders] spent a week massacring Moslems. They killed more than seventy thousand people in al-Aqsa mosque."[21] Another chronicler recorded, "The Jews had gathered in their synagogue and the Franj burned them alive. They also destroyed the monuments of saints and the tomb of Abraham, may peace be upon him!"[22]

In Islamic history, the success of the Crusaders was a result of the disunity among the Arab peoples. There were many failed attempts to bring the armies of separate Islamic principalities together to fight the Europeans. Out of fear, some Islamic leaders greeted the Crusaders with food and other provisions, hoping they would be spared the horrors of cannibalism and slaughter. Consequently, the success of the Europeans in conquering Jerusalem became a symbol for the necessity of Islamic unity.

The Islamic hero who was able to achieve unity and defeat the Europeans was Saladin (1138–1193). Like all great historical heros, Saladin is portrayed as a wise and noble leader. Between 1164 and

1169, he helped Egyptian rulers turn back attacks by Crusaders. In 1169, he became vizier of Egypt and commander of the Syrian army. By 1187, he had united enough Moslem nations to make it possible to recapture Jerusalem from the Christians.

There exist numerous stories that contrast the honor of Saladin with the treachery of the Crusaders. The most important was the re-taking of Jerusalem. When entering the city, he ordered his troops to not engage in any pillage or massacre of the citizens. He posted guards to protect Christian places of worship and he announced the right of Christians to conduct pilgrimages to them whenever they wanted. Christians were allowed to leave the city after paying a trib-ute. Old people, widows, children, and former prisoners were al-lowed to leave without paying the tribute. In Islamic history, Saladin is the true follower of God while the Crusaders are portrayed as the followers of Satan.[23]

Amin Maalouf provides the following summary of Moslem senti-ments regarding Saladin's capture of Jerusalem: "His prime objective [in conquering Jerusalem], as he himself explained, was to do his duty before his God and his faith. His victory was to have liberated the holy city from the yoke of the invaders—without a bloodbath, destruction, or hatred. His reward was to be able to bow down and pray in places where no Moslem would been able to pray had it not been for him."[24]

From the Moslem perspective, the next wave of Crusaders were mo-tivated by an extreme religious fanaticism that resulted in the partici-pation of the Philip Augustus, king of France and the famous Richard the Lionheart, king of England. They arrived with the blessing of the Pope in 1191 to recapture Jerusalem. Saladin and Richard the Lionheart exchanged messages, with each claiming the importance of Jerusalem for their religion. A truce was reached the following year, al-lowing Saladin to retain control of Jerusalem and the Europeans to re-tain control of a small sector along the coast. Christians were guaranteed safe passage to visit holy sites in Jerusalem. For the next 100 years, the West persisted in its attempts to recapture the city. Finally, in 1291 they were expelled from the area. A Moslem chronicler of the time, Abul'l-fida' commented on their expulsion, "God grant that they never set foot there again!"[25]

From the Moslem perspective, Saladin conducted a jihad against an infidel aggressor who acted as an instrument of Satan and engaged in acts of terrorism and cannibalism. From the Western perspective, the knights in shining armor were making noble sacrifices in a holy war to capture lands that should be under Christian control. In the year 2000, a similar scenario was replayed as peace talks broke down between Israel and Palestine over the control of Jerusalem and the President of the United States announced the moving of the U.S. Embassy to the city. For those learning history from an Islamic perspective, the struggle over Palestine and Jerusalem was part of a jihad with the West that had lasted more than 1,000 years. The only difference in 2000 was the existence of Israel, whose creation was backed by Western countries. Consequently, many Islamic constitutions combine concerns with imperialism with concerns with Zionism. From the standpoint of the Qur'an, Jews represent the greatest threat. The Qur'an states, "You will find the Jews and idolaters most excessive in hatred of those who believe; and the closest in love to the faithful are the people who say:'We are the followers of Christ,' because there are priests and monks among them, and they are not arrogant (5:82)."

Amin Maalouf suggests that the Crusades were the beginning of the rise of the importance of the West and of the decline of the Arab world. The Arab world at the time of the Crusades extended from Iraq to Spain. From Maalouf's viewpoint, the Arab world at the time was "the intellectual and material repository of the planet's most advanced civilization."[26] This claim, while supporting Arab nationalism, needs some historical perspective. At this time, the Mayan and Inca civilizations were thriving in the Americas, and China would certainly be considered a contender for the most advanced civilization. However, Maalouf's view is limited by his focus on the rivalry between Arab nations and the West. Consequently, even though Moslem Turks created the Ottoman Empire after capturing Constantinople in 1453 and sending troops to the walls of Vienna in 1529, he feels the best of Arab civilization in the form of mathematics, science, medicine, astronomy, and architecture was imitated, absorbed, and surpassed by Europeans after the Crusades. Exemplifying Arab nationalism, Maalouf concludes, "The Franj learned much in the Arab school, in Syria as in Spain and Sicily. What they learned from the Arabs was indispensable in their subsequent expansion."[27]

Mathematics is an example of what the West learned from Arab nations. There is a long history of intellectual exchange between regions that is exemplified by the history of the trigonometry term "sine." The story of the "sine" demonstrates the antiquity of global ideoscapes. In this example of ancient intellectual exchange, the great 5th-century Indian mathematician Aryabhata discussed the concept of "sine" and in Sanskrit called it *jyabha-jya*, which was then shortened to *jya*. From this term, Arab scholars phonetically derived to the meaningless word *jiba*. Later Arab writers substituted *jaib* for this meaningless word. In Arabic, *jaib* also means "cove" or "bay." When Western Latin scholars learned trigonometry from Arabs, they translated *jaib* into the Latin word meaning a cove or bay which is *sinus*. From this usage comes the term *sine*.[28]

EDUCATION, PAN ISLAM, ARAB NATIONALISM, AND THE ISLAMIC STATE

One result of the breakup of the Ottoman Empire in the 19th and 20th centuries was a call for national education to foster loyalty to an Islamic state and, for some Moslem leaders, to foster a pan-Islamic movement. As one of the largest empires in world history, the Ottoman government claimed to represent all the Islamic peoples. At its height, the Ottoman Empire extended east from Istanbul across northern India and south into present-day Indonesia, and west across northern Africa. It included Arabian Peninsula and most of the east coast of Africa. Its power continued from roughly the 13th century to 1922, when Turkey was declared a republic.

Ottoman sultans declared themselves to be legitimate heirs to the caliphate, which made them the religious leaders of all of Islam. The caliph was considered the successor to the Prophet Mohamed. Claiming to be part of this religious succession, Ottoman sultans could demand loyalty from their Moslem subjects. Also, based on the model Moslem state organized by Mohamed, the caliph's government was to be a theocracy using the *Shari'ah*, the religious and moral principles of Islam, as the law of the land.[29]

Today, many Islamic nations continue the tradition of Mohamed by declaring the *Shari'ah* to be the law of the land. Most militant Islamic fundamentalist movements proclaim a desire to create a theocracy governed by the *Shari'ah*. This has important implications for education and concepts of equality and freedom.

It was European imperialism that led to the breakup of the Ottoman Empire and, in the mind of some Moslems, the destruction of a pan-Islamic theocracy. In the words of Arab-born historian Bassam Tibi, "The combination of the European colonial penetration, the decay of the Ottoman Empire, and the extension of the techno-scientifically more advanced European civilization all over the world was perceived by the Islamic peoples as signifying an external real threat. The first reaction was the mobilization of Islam against the West."[30]

Similar to China and Japan, Western imperialism resulted in an attempt to utilize Western advances in science and military technology while maintaining Islamic values. The collapse of the Ottoman Empire was blamed in part on its failure to keep pace with the development of knowledge in Western countries. For instance, after Napoleon's invasion of Egypt in 1798 and his departure in 1801, the new ruler Muhammad 'Ali decided to seek independence from the Ottoman Empire by building a modern army with the assistance of the French government. His plan for modernization included the building of a new educational system. As part of this effort, he sent a group of Egyptian students to study in France. While in France, one of the students, Rifa'a Rafi' al-Tahtawi, kept a diary. The diary was published and considered so important that it became required reading for Egyptian civil servants. As a result, al-Tahtawi had a major influence on Egyptian thinking about the process of Westernization.

In his diary, al-Tahtawi points out that at the height of their civilization Arabs were superior to Europeans and provided them with their knowledge of mathematics and natural sciences. He wrote that Europeans "even admit to us that we have been their teachers in many branches of knowledge, and they acknowledge that we came before them. And it is obvious that the one who is the first to achieve deserves merit."[31] However, he argues, the Islamic peoples had fallen into a sleep of "indifference" which allowed Europeans to advance on knowledge that Arab civilization had initiated. What was now required, al-Tahtawi maintained, was that Islamic peoples needed to use knowledge from "foreign countries to obtain from them the things of which it is ignorant."[32] Al-Tahtawi emphasized that he respected Europeans "in their capacity as men and because of their knowledge, and not because they are Christians."[33]

The idea of using the best of the West while maintaining Islamic values was most clearly articulated by two 19th-century Moslem scholars, Jamal al-Din al-Afghani and Muhammad 'Abduh. Facing the realities of British and French colonization of Egypt and North Africa, they articulated an anticolonialist position for Islam, and they argued for a pan-Islamic movement. They argued that Moslems should utilize those parts of European civilization that would strengthen Islam, while at the same time revitalizing Islamic civilization. They rejected the notion then popular in Europe that only Europeans could produce culture and civilization. German historian Walther Braun concluded about al-Afghani that he "never lost sight of his central purpose, to awaken the Islamic peoples to resistance against Europe, and to stir up opposition among them to those of their number who paralyzed this resistance."[34]

Rejection of natural law and rights theories proposed by Europeans was an important area of agreement among these three scholars. While European science and mathematics might strengthen Islamic countries, natural rights theories were considered a threat to a theocratic government based on the *Shari'ah*. This ideological position continues to today, and it is an important issue regarding human rights doctrines.

In addition, Muhammad 'Abduh argued that national education systems should include religious education. Today, most Islamic nations include religion in their national education plans. This presents an important issue regarding freedom of thought in education. Regarding

Egyptian national education, 'Abduh wrote, "If one seeks to educate and improve the Egyptian nation without religion, it is as if a farmer would try to sow seed in unsuitable soil ... his efforts will be in vain."[35]

In contrast to pan-Islamism, Sati' al-Husri called for Arab nationalism and Arab unity through national education and a revitalization of the Arabic language. Born into a Syrian family in Yemen in 1882, he studied education in Paris, Switzerland, and Belgium. During World War I, he was appointed Ottoman Director of Education in Syria. After the War, he became responsible for Education and Archaeology at the University of Baghdad. After a number of other education posts, he moved to Egypt where he joined the Cultural Department of the Arab League in 1947 and founded the Institute for Advanced Arab Studies in 1953. Eventually, he became chair of Arab Nationalism at the Institute. His writings became compulsory readings in nationalist school systems throughout the Arab world. He died in December 1968, leaving behind a vast collection of writings on Arab nationalism. His ideas are included in many of the constitutions of the Arab world.

Al-Husri believed national education was the key to revitalizing the Arab world and awakening the oppressed people of the Islamic world. He argued that the teaching of history should emphasize the "glorious past in order to provide a basis for the national awakening."[36] He contended that national education was the key to Arab unity. He wrote, "The struggle for the national awakening requires much more effort and hardship to spread belief in the nation, and all available means must be used to strengthen this belief."[37]

Attracted to German romantic notions of nationalism, Al-Husri argued that history was the consciousness of a nation, and language was its soul. The foremost means of maintaining Arab culture and saving it from European domination was the preservation of the Arab language. He wrote, "A common language and a common history [are] the basis of nation formation and nationalism. The union of these two spheres lead[s] to a union of emotions, aims, sufferings, hopes, and culture."[38] In addition, Al-Husri was attracted to the militaristic aspects of German nationalism and considered military service a means for achieving a national education. He declared, "The barracks are as much institutes for national education as national schools."[39]

"Arab socialism" adds another dimension to nationalistic impulses and to educational ideals. Today, socialism is frequently referred to in the constitutions of Arab nations. This form of socialism should not be confused with Marxism. The leading advocate of Arab socialism, Michel 'Aflaq, explicitly states:

> When I am asked to give a definition of socialism, I can say that it is not to be found in the works of Marx and Lenin. I say: socialism is the religion of

life, and of its victory over death. By giving work to everyone and helping them to develop their talents it keeps the patrimony of life for life, and leaves for death only dried up flesh and scorched bones.[40]

Arab socialism embodies the teachings on charity expressed in the Qur'an along with the concept of *umma* (community). In Islamic thought the *umma* stands above the individual. In fact, traditional Moslems object to the Western emphasis on the individual. The individual in Islam is an organic part of the *umma*. This concept of the relationship to the community reinforces nationalistic ideals. Within Arab socialism and nationalism, the state is the organic community in which the person is an organic part. The goal of nationalistic education is to wed the individual to the *umma* as represented by the state.[41]

Today, Arab nationalism, socialism, pan-Islamic ideas, and the tradition of a theocratic state based on the *Shari'ah* continue to influence Islamic systems of education. All of these influential ideas and movements are problematic regarding the concept of freedom in education and human rights. Nationalistic education is an explicit attempt to control the minds of students to build allegiance to a culture and government. Theocratic and pan-Islamic ideas force a religious education on students. On the other hand, the basic doctrines of Islam guarantee equality in education. However, this equality is denied to women, particularly in theocratic states that base their laws on the *Shari'ah*. These problems of freedom and gender equality in education are highlighted in the following discussion of the constitutions of Islamic nations.

EQUALITY AND FREEDOM IN IRAN'S CONSTITUTION

I begin my discussion of education in Islamic constitutions with a detailed analysis of Iran's theocratic constitution. Of primary importance is the treatment of women. I then broaden this discussion by examining the constitutions of other Islamic countries, including Turkey's secular constitution.

In the Iranian constitution, as in the constitutions of most Islamic countries, concepts of equality and freedom are limited by Islamic religious dogma. The Preamble opens with a clear statement of religious purpose and with the idea of the Ummah: "The constitution of the Islamic Republic of Iran advances the cultural social, political, and economic institutions of Iranian society based on Islamic principles and norms, which represent an honest aspiration of the Islamic Ummah."[42] Similar to the Chinese constitution, the Preamble contains a long history of the struggle to establish the present government, including references to "the American conspiracy." The theocratic nature of the government is explicitly emphasized in the section of the Preamble titled, The Form of Government in Islam: "Legislation setting forth regulations for the administration of society will revolve around the Koran and the Sunnah. Accordingly, the exercise of meticulous and earnest supervision by just, pious and committed scholars of Islam is an absolute necessity."[43] Article 108 of the Constitution gives the exercise of this scholarly and religious supervision to a Guardian Council.[44] The theocratic nature of the government is further emphasized in Article 2:

Article 2 [Foundational Principles]

The Islamic Republic is a system based on belief in:

1) the One God (as stated in the phrase "There is no god except Allah"), His exclusive sovereignty and right to legislate, and the necessity of submission to His commands;

2) Divine revelation and its fundamental role in setting forth the laws.[45]

The Iran Constitution also adopts a pan-Islamic perspective when calling for the creation of a single world community and participation in revolution "at home and abroad." The Preamble states: "the Constitution will strive with other Islamic and popular movements to prepare the way for the formation of a single world community (in accordance with the Koranic verse'This your community is a single community, and I am your Lord, so worship Me' [21:92]."[46] The Preamble also commits the Iranian army to a jihad to achieve the goal of a world community:

They [the army] will be responsible not only for guarding and preserving the frontiers of the country, but also for fulfilling the ideological mission of jihad in God's way; that is, extending the sovereignty of God's law throughout the world (this is in accordance with the Koranic verse "Prepare against them whatever force you are able to muster, and strings of horses, striking fear into the enemy of god and your enemy, and others besides them" [8:60].

Obviously, given the theocratic nature of the Constitution religious strictures limit freedom, particularly freedom in education. Regarding media, the Preamble states: "The mass-communication media, radio and television, must serve the diffusion of Islamic culture ... the media ... must refrain from diffusion and propagation of destructive and anti-Islamic practices."[47] Freedom of religion is restricted in Articles 12 and 13 to Islam and the minority religions of Zoroastrian, Jewish, and Christian. No other groups are allowed to perform religious rites. Articles 24 through 27 limit freedom of the press, communication, association, and assembly by phrases such as "except when it is detrimental to the fundamental principles of Islam."[48]

While freedom is restricted by religious principles, equal educational opportunity and equality before the law are guaranteed in the Iranian Constitution. Article 3 declares as one of the goals of the Iranian government the provision of "free education and physical training for everyone at all levels, and the facilitation and expansion of higher education."[49] And Article 30 states: "The government must provide all citizens with free education up to secondary school, and must expand free higher education to the extent required by the country for attaining self-sufficiency."[50]

Missing from the Iranian Constitution is any recognition of the rights of minority cultures and languages in public schools. However, there is a separate article requiring the teaching of the Arabic language. This reflects not only the requirements for reading the original Qur'an, but also reflects the influence of Arabic nationalism. Article 16 states, "Since the language of the Koran and Islamic texts and teachings is Arabic, and since Persian literature is thoroughly permeated by this language, it must be taught after elementary level, in all classes of secondary school and in all areas of study."[51]

The major limitation on the concept of equality in the Iranian Constitution is the treatment of women as a special class of citizens. There are no statements in the Preamble or articles in the body of the Constitution that are specific to men. However, there are many that are specific to women. The Iranian Constitution justifies the treatment of women as a special class of citizen in order to maintain an Islamic family structure.

Also, the Iranian Constitution claims to be restoring women's rights by protecting them against exploitation by the international consumer market. Using a concept prevalent in Western feminism, the Constitution claims that women are treated as mere objects rather than as active participants in shaping society. The Constitution focuses on the role of women as mothers and wives. Mothers are considered key to raising a generation committed to the pan-Islamic revolution. In a specific section titled "Woman in the Constitution," the Preamble states:

> The family is the fundamental unit of society and the main center for the growth and edification of human beings.... This view of the family unit delivers woman from being regarded as an object or instrument in the service of promoting consumerism and exploitation. Not only does woman recover thereby her momentous and precious function of moth-

erhood, rearing of ideologically committed human beings, she also assumes a pioneering social role and becomes the fellow struggler of man in all vital areas of life.[52]

Article 21 of the Constitution is devoted to "Women's Rights." Article 21 lists five goals in the implementation of women's rights, ranging from creating "a favorable environment for the growth of woman's personality" to "awarding of guardianship of children to worthy mothers … in the absence of a legal guardian."[53] Central to understanding the meaning of these goals is the opening statement, "The government must ensure the rights of women in all respects, in conformity with Islamic criteria…. "[54] What is the meaning of "Islamic criteria" regarding the rights of women?

ISLAM AND WOMEN'S RIGHTS

I was giving a talk at an academic meeting when I referred to the denial of driver's licenses to women by the Saudi Arabian government as an example of the problem of balancing religious rights with universal human rights. After the meeting, I was approached by a Moslem woman who upbraided me for confusing culture with religion. She argued that the denial of driver's licenses to women was not a doctrine of Islam but a reflection of the culture of Saudi Arabia. She quite rightly pointed out that there was nothing in the *Qur'an* about driving automobiles.

The issue of separating cultural tradition from religious interpretation is pivotal in current discussions about women's rights within Islam. Internationally, Amina Wadud's *Qur'an and Woman: Rereading the Sacred Text From a Woman's Perspective* has raised the question about whether or not the traditional reading of the *Qur'an* has been from a male perspective and, as a result, has severely limited the rights of Moslem women.[55] An American Moslem scholar, Wadud's originally published her book in Malaysia (1992) and then in Indonesia (1994) and Turkey (1997). The U.S. edition appeared in 1999.

Certain passages in the *Qur'an* are critical to understanding the issues raised by Wadud and the restrictions placed on women's rights by the interpretation of the *Qur'an* made by the Iranian and other Islamic governments. For instance, at times the *Qur'an* sounds as if it is written for men, which would then give men the role of interpreting its meaning for women. Consider the following passage, which not only suggests male governance of females but also that the *Qur'an* is speaking directly to men: "Women are like fields for you; so seed them as you intend but plan the future in advance [2:223]."[56] This passage also suggests that it is the father that assumes the responsibility for planning the future of the family.

The *Qur'an* also presents the story of creation as if it were addressing only men. Also, the creation story could be interpreted to mean that women are a product of men and therefore unequal to men. "O men, fear your Lord who created you from a single cell, and from it created its mate, and from the two of them dispersed men and women in multitudes [4:1]."[57]

Amina Wadud objects to the idea that the *Qur'an* speaks directly to men and that the story of creation is interpreted to mean that women are not equal to men and have specific social functions. She argues that, "From my perspective on the *Qur'an*, every usage of the masculine plural form is intended to include males and females, *equally*, unless it includes specific indication for its exclusive application to males."[58] She points out that the creation narrative mentions nothing about cultural or intellectual differences between males and females. She contends, "At that moment [creation], Allah defines certain traits universal to all humans and not specific to one particular gender nor to any particular people from any particular place or time."[59]

The following passage *Qur'an* could be interpreted as meaning that a woman's opinion or knowledge is inferior to that of a man:

> If the borrower is deficient of mind or infirm, or unable to explain, let the guardian explain judiciously; and have two of your men to act as witnesses; but if two men are not available, then a man and two women you approve, so that in case one of them is confused the other may remind her [2:282].[60]

The *Qur'an* also provides for an unequal sharing of inherited property based on one male being worth two females. "As for the children, God decrees that the share of the male is equivalent to that of two females. If they consist of women only, and of them more than two, they will get two-thirds of the inheritance; but in case there is one, she will inherit one half [4:74]."[61]

Wadud argues that these passages must be interpreted in the cultural context of the time Allah presented the *Qur'an* to Mohamed. The passage regarding the requirement of two women and a man if two men are not available as witnesses does not mean that women are inherently less competent than men. First, she maintains that the passage indicates that only one woman is to function as a witness, while the other is to corroborate the testimony. Second, women at the time were often excluded from financial discussions and therefore might not have a clear understanding of the terms of the loan. Given this exclusion, Wadud argues, it would help to have two women consult over the loan issue. From Wadud's perspective, both passages are now obsolete in societies where women have an equal chance to participate in financial matters.[62]

Strict social roles for men and women and the right of husbands to beat wives can be inferred from the following passage. As I will discuss, the translation of the Qur'an I am using does not indicate the right of the husband to beat his wife.

> "Men are the support of women as God gives some more means than others, and because they spend of their wealth (to provide for them). So women who are virtuous are obedient to God and guard the hidden as God has guarded it. As for women you feel are averse, talk to them suasively; then leave them alone in bed (without molesting them) and go to bed with them (when they are willing) [4:34]."[63]

An interpretation and translation of the last two lines of this passage that indicates the right of the husband to beat the wife reads as follows: "So good women are qanitat [obedient], guarding in secret that which Allah has guarded. As for those from whom you fear, admonish them, banish them to beds apart, and scourge them. Then, if they obey you, seek not a way against them."[64] In the translation of the Qur'an I am using qanitat refers to obedience to God and not the husband. Wadud translates qanitat to mean "good." Wadud, along with my translation, does not believe the passage indicates the right of husbands to "scourge [beat] them." Rather, according to Wadud, Allah is intending to present a peaceful means of ending marital disharmony. With regard to the first line stating that "Men are the support of women," Wadud argues that this only refers to the male responsibility in relationship to women bearing children. In other words, men have a responsibility, including a financial responsibility, to help mothers raise their children. This passage is not intended, according to Wadud, that women should always be financially dependent on men. Wadud concludes, "those who truly believe in the Qur'an would equally wish for the woman the opportunities for growth and productivity which they demand for the man."[65]

The actions of Afghanistan's Taliban government illustrate a sharp difference to Wadud's interpretation of the Qur'an. An August 17, 2000 *New York Times* article reported, "Saying Islam unreservedly forbids women to work, Afghanistan's Taliban government today shut down bakeries run by widows, who are among the poorest of the poor here.... When they took over, the Taliban ordered all girls' schools closed and all women out of the work force."[66] The Taliban's ambassador to Pakistan, Maulvi syed Mohammed Haqqani, declared, "We do not allow women to work."[67]

Immediately after the adoption of the 1979 Iranian Constitution, women were severely limited in their ability to work outside the home. The emphasis in the Constitution was on a woman's role as a mother. However, because of a soaring population growth, according to Ann Mayer, "the regime has sharply reversed its course, relaxing restrictions on women's participation in the workforce and energetically promoting birth control."[68] Still, women represent only 14% of the labor force.[69] Women are barred from working as attorneys and judges, and from the media and entertainment industry. In addition, Iranian women are required to be obedient to a very strict interpretation of Islamic law regarding public activities. Women face harsh criminal punishments if they do not wear concealing dress in dull colors. Morality police discourage women from appearing in public with males who aren't their relatives. Women are excluded from male sporting events. Women engaged in public athletic events, such as swimming and skiing, must wear baggy and concealing clothing.[70]

EQUALITY OF EDUCATIONAL OPPORTUNITY IN IRAN

The Iranian Constitution's education provision has significantly affected the education of women in Iran. According to UNICEF's *The State of the World's Children 2000,* the literacy rate for women in 1980, one year after the ratification of the present constitution, was 40%. By 1995, the literacy rate for women had increased to 63%. For the same period, literacy for men increased from 62% to 79%. In other words, the percentage increase was greater for women than for men. During the 1990s, the attendance of women in primary and secondary schools did lag slightly behind that of men, with 83% of primary age males and 81% of primary age females attending school for the period 1990–1996. Secondary school enrollment between 1990 and 1996 was 79% for men and 69% for women.[71]

But equality of educational opportunity does not necessarily mean an equal education. Reflecting the equal opportunity to attend universities, nearly 60% of entrants in 2000 were female. Between 1990 and 2000, the number of women entering Iranian universities tripled. In medicine and the social sciences, females outnumber males.[72]

Nevertheless, there are strict religious controls over the education of women that seriously restrict any concept of educational freedom. Moslem religious leaders strictly control what female students read and the music they hear. *New York Times'* reporter Susan Sachs describes the life of Iranian university women: "Young women are required to wear the traditional black chador— the all-enveloping cloak—over long coats and tightly pinned headscarves, not only outside the dorm but inside as well. There are curfews, bans on visitors and music, and constant supervision of reading material brought into the dormitories."[73]

EQUALITY AND FREEDOM IN ISLAMIC CONSTITUTIONS

Educational provisions in Islamic constitutions are frequently circumscribed by Arab nationalism, pan-Islamic ideals, a hostility to Western imperialism, and religious and gender restrictions. Memories of the Crusades and Western colonialism are present in many of their preambles. For instance, the Preamble to the 1973 Syrian Constitution declares, "With the close of the first half of this century, the Arab people's struggle has been expanding ... to achieve liberation from direct colonialism. The Arab masses did not regard independence as their goal ... but as a means to consolidate their struggle ... against the forces of imperialism, Zionism, and exploitation."[74] The Preamble to the 1969 Libyan Constitution pledges that the Libyan people will "stand with their brothers from all parts of the Arab Nation in the struggle for the restoration of every inch of Arab land desecrated by imperialism."[75] This anti-Western flavor spills over into provisions for education. The Iraqi Constitution requires a student to be educated to be "proud of his people, aware of all his national rights, and who struggles against the capitalistic ideology, exploitation, reaction, Zionism, and imperialism for the purpose of realizing the Arab unity, liberty, and socialism."[76]

In these constitutions education is subordinated to religious goals. Article 13 of the Constitution of Saudi Arabia makes the goal of education the promotion of nationalism and religion: "Education will aim at instilling the Islamic faith in the younger generation, providing its members with knowledge and skills and preparing them to become useful members in building of their society, members who love their homeland and are proud of its history."[77] In the Saudi Arabian Constitution, citizens are required to have allegiance to the Qur'an, and human rights are subordinated to Islamic law. The Saudi Arabian Constitution states:

> Article 6: Citizens are to pay allegiance to the King in accordance with the Holy Koran and the tradition of the Prophet, in submission and obedience, in times of ease and difficulty, fortune and adversity.

> Article 26: The state protects human rights in accordance with the Islamic Shari'ah.[78]

The meaning of protection of human rights within the boundaries of the Islamic Shari'ah was exemplified by the arrest of Canadian nurse Margaret Madil by the Saudi Arabian Mutawa'een (religious police). At the time of her arrest she was shopping, wearing a traditional dress that covered her entire body. Reportedly she was thrown into the back of a taxi and ordered to sign a paper written in Arabic. She refused to sign because she couldn't read Arabic and she asked to call the local hospital where she was employed. Denied the right to call for help, Ms. Madil was whisked away by the Mutawa'een to prison, where she was accused of public drunkenness and un-Islamic behavior. She was held in prison for 2 days and released to her employer. Two weeks later, the police demanded she sign an apology to Islam.[79]

In a more frightening case, Bernadette Ramos, a Filipino hospital secretary working in Saudi Arabia, was attending a birthday party at a Pizza Hut in Riyadh. The Mutawa'een entered and asked Ramos to cover her hair. Then they told her to come with them and requested that she sign a paper written in Arabic. Unlike Madil, she signed the paper. She unknowingly confessed to prostitution. Without being allowed counsel, she was taken to a formal hearing where she was ordered imprisoned for 25 days and to receive 60 lashes. "I thought it would be fast, but it was done one lash at a time," she said. "A stout policeman gives the lashes. I cannot describe the pain I experienced."[80]

After declaring that "Islamic jurisprudence is a main source of legislation," the Syrian Constitution places the goals of education in the framework of Arab socialism and provides for a free and compulsory educational system. The Syrian Constitution states:

> Article 23: The nationalist socialist education is the basis for building the unified socialist Arab society. It seeks to strengthen moral values, to achieve the higher ideals of the Arab nation, to develop the society, and to serve the causes of humanity. The state undertakes to encourage and to protect this education.

> Article 37: Education is a right guaranteed by the state. Elementary education is compulsory and all education is free.[81]

The Libyan Constitution declares its allegiance to Arab socialism but does not link the requirements of legislation to the Islamic Shari'ah. However, in Article 6 it is stated that Libyan socialism receives, "Its inspiration ... [from] Arabic and Islamic heritage, humanitarian values and the specific conditions of the Libyan society."[82] Rather than religious restrictions on freedom of speech, the Constitution restricts according to the public interest: "Freedom of opinion is guaranteed within the limits of public interest and the principles of the Revolution."[83] Consequently, intellectual freedom in education is limited by the same concern about the public interest. In fact, education is a defined as a duty in the Libyan Constitution. Article 14 states, "Education is a right and a duty for all Libyans. It is compulsory until the end of primary school. The State guarantees this right through the establishment of schools, institutes, and universities, and of pedagogical and cultural institutions in which education is free."[84]

Declaring its steadfastness to the socialist principle of "from each according to his ability to each according to his work," the Constitution of Pakistan states, "Islam shall be the State religion of Pakistan and the Injunctions of Islam as laid down in the Holy Qur'an and Sunnah shall be the supreme law and source of guidance for legislation."[85] Freedom in education is restricted by Islamic dogma. Pakistan's Constitution states:

31. (2) The state shall endeavor, as respects the Moslems of Pakistan,

    (a) to make the teaching of the Holy Qur'an and Islamiat compulsory, to encourage and facilitate the learning of Arabic language....

    (b) to promote unity and the observance of the Islamic moral standards.... [86]

The major exception to the religious language found in most of the constitutions of Moslem countries is that of the last remnant of the Ottoman Empire, the Republic of Turkey. Article 2 of the Turkish Constitution declares, "The Republic of Turkey is a democratic, secular and social state governed by the rule of law."[87] Despite the secular nature of the Turkish republic, all freedoms and rights granted under the Constitution are restricted by Article 13, which states that "Fundamentals rights and freedoms may be restricted by law ... with the aim of safeguarding ... public order, general peace, the public interest, public morals and public health."[88] Similar to the Chinese constitution, legal interpretation of public order, interest, and morals could be used to stifle freedom of speech, press, and assembly.

For instance, Article 13 of the Turkish Constitution could be used to limit the educational freedom granted by Article 27 that, "Everyone has the right to study and teach freely, explain, and disseminate science and arts and to carry out research in these fields."[89] On the other hand, this statement of educational freedom is rarely found in national constitutions and could be used as a model.

Article 13 could also be used to control the extensive educational rights granted by the Turkish constitution. However, I believe, the educational rights granted in Article 42 could be used as a model for amendments to constitutions currently lacking educational rights, such as the United States Constitution. Article 42 opens with the declaration that "No one shall be deprived of the right of learning and education."[90] The Article states that "Primary education is compulsory for all citizens of both sexes and is free of charge in state schools."[91] Of major importance is the constitutional guarantee that all students will have the opportunity to pursue secondary and higher education and that students with special needs will receive training:

> "The state shall provide scholarships and other means of assistance to enable students of merit lacking financial means to continue their education. The state shall take necessary measures to rehabilitate those in need of special training so as to render such people useful to society."[92]

There are, I feel, some limiting aspects to Article 42, particularly the limitation placed on the use of minority languages in the schools. The Article states, "No language other than Turkish shall be taught as a mother tongue to Turkish citizens at any institutions of training or education."[93] Indeed, all language instruction in the schools must be approved by the government.

In summary, most Islamic constitutions, the major exceptions being Turkey and Libya, impose strict religious limitations on freedom of content in education. Turkey and Libya impose restrictions on the basis of the public interest and morals (Turkey) and the Revolution (Libya). Legislative actions and arbitrary administrative decisions can make these as limiting to educational freedom as the requirements of the Shari'ah. Equality of educational opportunity, particularly gender equality, is another issue I discuss when considering economic and educational statistics for Islamic nations.

THE UNIVERSAL ISLAMIC DECLARATION OF HUMAN RIGHTS AND THE CAIRO DECLARATION ON HUMAN RIGHTS IN ISLAM

"Everyone shall have the right to advocate what is right, and propagate what is good, and warn against what is wrong and evil according to the norms of Islamic Shari'ah," declares the Cairo Declaration on Human Rights in Islam.[94] The concept of freedom exemplified by the above quote is characteristic of the two most important international declarations on human rights issued by Islamic nations. The Universal Islamic Declaration of Human Rights was prepared in 1981 under the auspices of the Islamic Council, which is affiliated with the Moslem World League headquartered in Saudi Arabia. The Moslem World League is an international, nongovernmental organization. After its preparation by representatives from Saudi Arabia, Egypt, Pakistan, and other Islamic nations, the Declaration was presented to UNESCO as representing the human rights doctrines of Islamic nations. The Cairo Declaration on Human Rights in Islam was presented to the

1993 World Conference on Human Rights in Vienna as representing a consensus of the world's Moslems. It was endorsed in 1990 by the foreign ministers of the Organization of the Islamic Conference.

Both documents subordinate human rights to religious dogma. The Foreword to The Universal Islamic Declaration of Human Rights states:

> Human rights in Islam are firmly rooted in the belief that God and God alone, is the Law Giver and the Source of all human rights.... The Universal Islamic Declaration of Human Rights is based on the Qur'an and the Sunnah and has been compiled by eminent Moslem scholars, jurists and representatives of Islamic movements and thought. May God reward them all for their efforts and guide us along the right path.[95]

The Preamble to the Cairo Declaration on Human Rights in Islam declares:

> The Member States of the Organization of the Islamic Conference ... Believing that fundamental rights and universal freedoms in Islam are an integral part of the Islamic religion ... are contained in the Revealed Books of God and were sent through the last of His Prophets ... making their observance an act of worship and their neglect or violation an abominable sin, and accordingly every person is individually responsible—and the Ummah collectively responsible—for their safeguard.[96]

Given the religious nature of these documents, it is not surprising that both of them place religious restriction on freedom of thought. In Article "XII. Right to Freedom of Belief, Thought and Speech,"of the Universal Islamic Declaration of Human Rights, limitations on freedom of thought are clearly defined by references to the Shari'ah or the Law:

a) Every person has the right to express his thoughts and beliefs so long as he remains within the limits prescribed by the Law. No one, however, is entitled to disseminate falsehood or to circulate reports which may outrage public decency, or to indulge in slander, innuendo or to cast defamatory aspersions on other persons.

b) Pursuit of knowledge and search after truth is not only a right but a duty of every Moslem.

c) It is the right and duty of every Moslem to protest and strive (within the limits set out by the Law) against oppression even if it involves challenging the highest authority of the state.

d) There shall be no bar on the dissemination of information provided it does not endanger the security of the society or the state and is confined with the limits imposed by the Law.[97]

As indicated in the opening quote of this section, freedom of speech in the Cairo Declaration on Human Rights in Islam means the right to say what is right according to the Shari'ah. In addition, Article 22 of the document places religious restrictions on expression of opinions and the distribution of information:

A. Everyone shall have the right to express his opinion freely in such manner as would not be contrary to the principles of the Shari'ah....

C. Information is a vital necessity to society. It may not be exploited or misused in such a way as may violate sanctities and the dignity of Prophets, undermine moral and ethical values or disintegrate, corrupt or harm society or weaken its faith.[98]

Similar to most Islamic constitutions, both of these documents proclaim equality of educational opportunity as a human right. The Article XXI of the Universal Islamic Declaration of Human Rights states, "Every person is entitled to receive education in accordance with his natural capabilities."[99] While the Cairo Declaration on Human Rights in Islam recognizes education as a human right, it does so within a religious framework. Article 9 of the Cairo Declaration emphasizes the religious goals of Islamic education:

A. The question [sic] for knowledge is an obligation and the provision of education is a duty for society and the State. The State shall ensure the availability of ways and means to acquire education and shall guarantee educational diversity in the interest of society so as to enable man to be acquainted with the religion of Islam and facts of the Universe for the benefit of mankind.

B. Every human being has the right to receive both religious and worldly education from the various institutions of education and guidance, including the family, the school, the university, the media, etc., and in such an integrated and balanced manner as to develop his personality, strengthen his faith in God and promote his respect for the Defense of both rights and obligations.[100]

THE REALITY OF EDUCATIONAL OPPORTUNITY IN ISLAMIC NATIONS

It is clear that the constitutions of Islamic nations and international Islamic declarations of human rights recognize education as a basic right. What does this mean in practice? Is there equality of educational

TABLE 3.1

Demographic and Economic Indicators of Selected Islamic Nations

	Life Expectancy 1970	Life Expectancy 1998	GNP per capita (U.S.$) 1997	% of Central Government Expenditure Allocated to (1992–1998) Education	% of Central Government Expenditure Allocated to (1992–1998) Defense	% of Central Government Expenditure Allocated to (1992–1998) Health
Afghanistan	37	46	250	Not available	Not available	Not available
Algeria	67	73	1500	Not available	Not available	Not available
Egypt	51	67	1200	14	9	3
Iran	55	69	1780	15	8	6
Iraq	55	63	Not available	Not available	Not available	Not available
Kuwait	66	76	20190	11	23	8
Libya	52	70	5540	Not available	Not available	Not available
Morocco	52	67	1260	17	14	3
Pakistan	49	64	500	2	31	1
Saudi Arabia	52	72	7150	14	36	6
Syria	56	69	1120	10	26	4
Turkey	56	69	3130	11	8	2
World	56	64	5132	6	9	11

This table was compiled from statistical tables included in UNICEF, *The State of the World's Children 2000* (New York: UNICEF, 2000), pp. 100–107.

TABLE 3.2
Education Indicators for Selected Islamic Countries

	Adult Literacy Rate 1995 Male	Adult Literacy Rate 1995 Female	Primary School Enrollment Ratio 1990–1996 Male	Primary School Enrollment Ratio 1990–1996 Female	Secondary School Enrollment Ratio 1990–1996 Male	Secondary School Enrollment Ratio 1990–1996 Female
Afghanistan	46	16	42	15	32	11
Algeria	71	45	95	97	65	62
Egypt	64	38	86	74	80	70
Iran	79	63	83	81	79	69
Iraq	71	45	81	71	51	32
Kuwait	82	76	65	65	65	65
Libya	87	60	98	96	95	95
Morocco	58	31	81	63	44	34
Pakistan	54	24	Not available	Not available	33	17
Saudi Arabia	80	59	63	60	65	57
Syria	85	54	95	87	45	40
Turkey	92	72	98	94	67	45
World	81	65	84	81	61	54

This table was compiled from statistical tables included in UNICEF, The State of the World's Children 2000 (New York: UNICEF, 2000), pp. 96–99.

opportunity for men and women? Tables 3.1 and 3.2 provide some an-
swers to these questions.

Life expectancy can be considered a general overall measure of the
quality of life in a country. In 1998, the life expectancy in most Islamic
countries exceeded the world's average of 64 years. The major exceptions were Afghanistan, Pakistan, and Iraq. These countries represent
special conditions within the Islamic world. The economic conditions
in Afghanistan are horrendous, with a gross national product per capita (GNP) in 1997 of only $250 (U.S.). It has been torn apart by years
of war and is now under the strict control of the fundamentalist
Taliban government. The economic conditions in Pakistan are not
much better than Afghanistan, with a GNP of $500. Iraq has been un-
der U.N. sanctions since the Gulf War, and probably the lives of many of
the veterans were shortened by participation in the war.

One measure of commitment to education as a human right is the
percentage of central government expenditure allotted to education.
Available information indicates that Islamic countries are financially
supporting their commitment to education. With the world average being 6% of central government budgets allocated to education, all Islamic nations for which information is available exceed that
percentage by significant amounts, with Morocco having the largest at
17%, followed by Iran (15%), Egypt (14%), Saudi Arabia (14%), Kuwait
(11%), Turkey (11%), and Syria (10%).

The major exception to this generous provision by Islamic governments for education is Pakistan. Only 2% of Pakistan's central government budget is allotted to education. The trade-off is with military
spending. Pakistan's long-standing conflict with India has resulted in
excessive military spending. An astonishing 31% of Pakistan's budget
goes to defense spending, as compared to a world average of 9%.
Whereas other Islamic countries exceed the world average for percentage spent on defense, Pakistan's low GNP means that defense spending
in that country is a major burden for the population and certainly de-
tracts from its ability to provide universal education.

What about equality of educational opportunity for men and
women? Except for Kuwait and Turkey, the 1995 adult literacy rates
for women in Islamic countries were below the world average of 65 %.
Reflecting generations of neglect, many of the 1995 literacy rates for
women are shockingly low, with only 16% of women in Afghanistan being literate, followed by Pakistan (24%), Morocco (31%), Egypt (38%),
Algeria (45%), Iraq (45%), Syria (54%), Saudi Arabia (59%), and Iran
(63%). Certainly, the high GNP per capita in Kuwait of $20,190 might
be one explanation for its high female literacy rate of 76 %. And Turkey's secular republic might be one explanation for its 72 % female literacy rate.

When compared to male literacy rates the discrimination against women in education becomes even more evident. For the world, there is a 16 percentage point difference between the 1995 male literacy rate of 81% and female literacy rate of 65%. For all listed Islamic countries, the percentage point difference is higher, except for Kuwait and Iran, where the differences are 5% and 16%, respectively. For the other Islamic countries the percentage differences are as follows: Afghanistan (20%), Algeria (26%), Egypt (26%), Iraq (26%), Libya (17%), Morocco (27%), Pakistan (30%), Saudi Arabia (21%), Syria (29%), and Turkey (20%).

What are Islamic countries doing to overcome this gender disparity? Compared to the rest of the world, where 1990–1996 primary-school enrollment figures are 84% for men and 81% for females, or a 3 percentage point difference, the following countries are failing to close the gender gap. The percentage point differences between males and females in primary school enrollment are as follows: Afghanistan (17%), Egypt (12%), Iraq (10%), Morocco (18%), Syria (7%), and Turkey (4%). On the other hand, the gender gap differences are being closed in the following countries, where percentage point differences in primary school enrollments are: Algeria (–2%), Iran (2%), Kuwait (0%), Libya (2%),and Saudi Arabia (3%). Differences in secondary school enrollment follow a similar pattern. These differences represent a very uneven attempt to close the gender gap in education.

How do these Islamic countries compare with other regions and countries? The UNICEF report, *The State of the World's Children 2000*, does provide regional summaries and information on other countries that have historically discriminated against women, such as India and China. The region they identify as Middle East and North Africa includes most of the Islamic countries I have been discussing, except for Afghanistan and Pakistan.[101] These two countries have been the least supportive of education and therefore the regional summary for the Middle East and North Africa presents a more positive picture of Islamic educational support of education than actually exists. The region identified as Industrial Countries includes Europe and the United States.[102] Table 3.3 presents a comparison between regions and with India and China.

As indicated in Table 3.3, the Middle East and North Africa region is making a greater effort than India in closing the gender gap in education. On the other hand, China, a society that traditionally discriminated against women, far exceeds the efforts of Islamic countries in providing equality of educational opportunity for men and women. The real statement of effort in closing the gender gap and providing equality of educational opportunity is in the percentage of government expenditures allocated to education. The major effort is being made by China (19%),

TABLE 3.3

Comparison of Educational Indicators

	% of Central Government Expenditures Allocated to (1992–1998) Education	Adult Literacy Rate 1995 Male	Adult Literacy Rate 1995 Female	Net Primary School Attendance (%) 1990–1998 Male	Net Primary School Attendance (%) Female	Secondary School Enrollment Ratio 1990–1996 (Gross) Male	Secondary School Enrollment Ratio 1990–1996 (Gross) Female
Middle East and North Africa	14	71	47	85	75	64	54
Industrial Countries	4	99 (1990)	97 (1990)	97	97	105	107
China	19	89	71	95	94	74	67
India	2	64	35	75	61	59	39

This table was compiled from statistical tables included in UNICEF, *The State of the World's Children 2000* (New York: UNICEF, 2000), pp. 96–99, 100–107.

followed by the Middle East and North Africa region (14%). India's educational problems and lack of commitment to equal educational opportunity for women and scheduled castes is reflected in its small 2% allocated to education. Of course, because of the wealth of industrialized countries, only an average of 4% has to be allocated to education to achieve literacy and educational rates above the rest of the world.

CONCLUSION

For Islam, the universal right to education is justified by the religious requirement to know the *Qur'an* and not by Western natural rights doctrines. As a result, freedom of thought and expression in Islamic nations is a religious right and not a natural right. Consequently, freedom of thought and expression must conform to the requirements of Islamic law or the Shari'ah. As so eloquently stated in the Cairo Declaration on Human Rights, this means that everyone has the right to think and express what is right according to Islamic dogma.

Also, freedom of thought has a special meaning in Islam. According to the *Qur'an* it is forbidden to actually think about things that are forbidden. Throughout the *Qur'an*, the reader is warned that God knows what is in an individual's thoughts and that thinking evil is equivalent to acting in an evil manner. The motive is as important as the actual deed. The *Qur'an* states:

> God will not call you to account for that which is senseless in your oaths, but only for what is in your hearts; for God is forgiving and forbearing [2:225].[103]

> Remember that God knows what is in your hearts; so be fearful of Him, and remember that God is forgiving and forbearing [2:235].[104]

Therefore, not only is freedom of thought not encouraged in Islamic schools; it is discouraged. In fact, it is discouraged to the point of invoking the condemnation of God for evil thoughts. Freedom of expression is also discouraged, except when it reflects the teachings of God.

Is there a conflict between religious freedom and freedom of thought and expression education? Certainly, religious freedom gives Moslems the right to act according to their own religious dogma including restricting thoughts and expressions. In addition, Moslem parents should have the right to choose a religious education for their children.

The problem is that most Islamic nations, while supporting Islamic law and education, do not practice religious freedom. After reviewing the constitutions of Islamic countries, the actions of Islamic governments, and the two Islamic declarations of human rights, legal scholar

Ann Mayer concludes that religious minorities are discriminated against in Islamic countries. In addition, freedom of expression regarding differing interpretations of Islamic doctrines are not tolerated. Mayer writes, "In fact, to the extent that they deal with the question of the rights of religious minorities, they [Islamic human rights doctrines] seem to endorse premodern Shari'ah rules that call for non-Moslems to be relegated to an inferior status.... the record also establishes that Middle Eastern regimes are in some instances ready to engage in actual campaigns of religious persecution directed at non-Moslems."[105]

Therefore, the right of Moslem parents and Islamic schools to restrict freedom of thought and expression can only be considered as fulfilling the universal right to education if religious freedom is allowed by the government. The imposition by government of religious doctrines and education is a violation of the universal right to education, which is predicated on the right and encouragement of freedom of thought and expression. Choice of religious beliefs is part of the right to freedom of thought and expression. Parents should have the right to choose a religious education for their children, including an Islamic education. However, there is no freedom of choice if the government imposes religious requirements and limits religious freedom.

Pan-Islamic and Arab nationalism also restrict freedom of thought and expression in education by imposing loyalty on students. The religious concept of jihad adds fuel to this nationalism. Unfortunately, the *Qur'an* suggests a world divided between believers and infidels. In addition, there is the long history of persecution of Moslems by the West. On the other hand, the *Qur'an* forbids compulsion in religion, including the imposition of religious beliefs on others. There is nothing in the *Qur'an* that forbids peace between Islamic countries and other nations. If fact, as previously quoted, the *Qur'an* states, "Fight those in the way of God who fight you, but do not be aggressive: God does not like aggressors (2:190)."[106] Hopefully, time and a conscious effort by the West and Moslem nations will erase this historical antagonism and reduce the teaching of nationalism.

Economic and educational equality are seriously compromised by discrimination against women. Gender discrimination is a result of conservative interpretations of the *Qur'an* and the Shari'ah. Some form of economic equality is implied in the idea of Zakat, or charity, as a basic belief of Islam. As previously quoted from the *Hadith*, Islamic teachings emphasize the right of the poor to a share of other people's wealth. The idea of Ummah, or community, and Arab socialism imposes a responsibility of community members to take care of each other. The following passage from the *Qur'an* could be interpreted as both a requirement to share wealth and as a statement of economic equality for women: "Do not covet what God has favored some with more than He has some others. Men have a share in what they earn, and women have theirs in what they earn [4:32]."[107]

However, as long as religious police in countries such as Iran, Afghanistan, and Saudi Arabia impose discriminatory laws against women, economic and educational equality between genders will not occur. Turkey as a secular state provides an example of how a country in which Moslems are in the majority can provide for equality of educational opportunity for women. Admittedly, cultural practices and beliefs still hinder full equality for Turkish women. However, the Turkish Constitution and legislation does not act as a barrier to educational equality for men and women.

With regard to the rights of Moslems in countries where they are a minority, I think a valid case can be made for recognizing the right to learn Qur'anic Arabic in public schools. It is an important international language that ties together one of the world's largest cultural communities. Qur'anic Arabic could be taught in secular public schools without using religious texts.

In summary, theocracy, government imposition of religion, and nationalism are serious hindrances to freedom of thought and expression in fulfilling the requirements of the universal right to education. Discrimination against women restricts equality of educational opportunity. On the other hand, many countries, including the United States, could benefit from the inclusion of educational rights in their constitutions. In this regard, I think the Turkish Constitution could be used as a model.

4

Natural Rights and Education in the West

The idea of "natural rights" distinguishes Western approaches to human rights from Confucian and Islamic. Within the Confucian framework, human rights result from efforts to perfect society by promoting peace and human welfare. In Islam, human rights are based on the Word of God. In the West, natural rights doctrines are derived from the supposed rights of humans in a state of nature before the formation of governments. Some Christians, such as social contract theorist John Locke, used Christian interpretations of the state of nature by alluding to the Biblical story of Adam and Eve. In this framework, the development of governments or, as it was called, the forming of "social contracts," required restrictions on the rights that existed in a state of nature. Despite these restrictions, these original natural rights remain human birthrights. This argument is exemplified in the famous opening lines of Jean-Jacques Rousseau's *The Social Contract* (1762): "Man is born free; and everywhere he is in chains."[1]

Western concepts of education, freedom, and equality are, *in part*, based on natural rights theories. I emphasize the words "in part" because Western historical concepts of what it means to be human have seriously restricted the meaning of equality and freedom. Social contract theory assumes that "humans" participate in the forming of governments and societies. But are all humans equal in creating a social contract? Are women equal to men? Are Blacks equal to Whites? Are pagans equal to Christians? Are the uncivilized equal to the civilized? How can colonialism and racism be justified under principles of equality and freedom? My discussion of Western natural rights doctrines begins with how the West reconciled ideas of equality and freedom with the creation of a global empire.

WESTERN CONCEPTS OF EQUALITY AND FREEDOM

Europe and United States introduced into the global flow ideas of equality and freedom that appear incongruent with their actions as nations. As exemplified by the anti-Western statements in Chinese and Islamic constitutions, no one can deny the major impact of the West on the ideoscapes in the global flow. This was the result of the success of the Western colonial empire. By 1914, the West controlled about 84% of the world's land mass.[2] With this kind of world power, which often subjected colonized peoples to tyrannical rule, Western advocacy of equality and freedom seemed filled with hypocrisy. It was no wonder that Asian and Islamic nations questioned Western claims of being the source of human rights doctrines.

Some of these conflicting concepts of equality and freedom were part of the heritage of the Roman Empire. Others emerged from the Enlightenment period of the 17th and 18th centuries. Others appeared under the banners of global expansion in the 20th and 21st centuries, where countries such as the United States and the European Union claimed that their economic policies would spread equality and freedom around the globe. The meaning of the terms constantly changed, both in their Western context and as they traveled in the global flow.

The contradictions between Enlightenment ideas and colonial expansion can be explained in the context of European concepts of empire. It was an *not* an aberration of history that the "equality" in the American Declaration of Independence was only intended for a limited group of men. A combination of Roman ideas of civilization and the growth of Christianity resulted in many Europeans dividing the world between humans and so-called natural slaves or between Christians and pagans. As colonialism unfolded, many Europeans came to believe that equality could exist between those blessed by Western civilization and Christianity, but not with those outside Western culture.

Western traditions support educational systems that foster inequality. From the time of Plato's *Republic* to today's reliance on high-stakes tests, schools are considered a means for identifying talents and educating for unequal occupations. Plato thought education could select future philosopher-kings; Thomas Jefferson thought schools could educate a "natural aristocracy" for political leadership. In today's learning society high-stakes tests are suppose to differentiate the talented from the dull. Many Westerners believe that colonialism was justified by the superiority of the West over the rest of the world. In the minds of many, the West was born to lead and civilize the world. The role of schools, in this Western tradition of imperialism, is to find the leaders and followers, or the masters and slaves.

Limiting equality and freedom to a select group of people, particularly to nonslaves or free people, is a tradition in Western thought. Aristotle identified "natural slaves" as those lacking the ability to reason and make choices. Consequently, equality existed between those with the ability to reason and make decisions and between those who were natural slaves, but not between the two groups.[3] Aristotle's concept justified the enslavement of some people who were considered "bound by nature to a life of perpetual labor."[4]

A similar idea prevailed in the Roman Empire, where equality was linked to ideas of citizenship and civilization. All people were equal before the law if they had Roman citizenship and lived within the Roman civilization. The Roman term *civil* referred to a certain set of laws and "to civilize" originally meant to bring a legal case under a particular kind of law. "To civilize" meant educating people into Roman society. In this context, people were equal when they shared a particular civilization. Those who were Roman citizens and lived by Roman law were "by definition,'humans'; those who did not, were not."[5] Similar to Aristotle, being human meant exercising reason. Therefore, according to political views within the Roman Empire, those who were not citizens and lived outside the Roman Empire were without "reason" and therefore were natural slaves. Consequently, in the Roman Empire concepts of equality before the law and equality of civilized peoples applied to some humans while excluding large numbers of others who were considered natural slaves.

Romans and later Western colonialists were plagued with similar uncertainties about the possibility of bringing outsiders into "civilization." Most Roman and later Europeans shared a glorified belief that they belonged to the best and only true civilization. The historian of Roman law, Thomas Mommsen observed, "a familiar concept to the Romans [was] that they were not only the *first power on earth*, they were also in a sense, *the only one* [my emphasis]."[6] But could outsiders be civilized? Would it be worthwhile for Romans and later colonialists to attempt to civilize the world? The arrogance of their worldview allowed them to proclaim the expansion of their empires as the expansion of "civilization."

Dividing the world between Romans and the provincials, Cicero called provincials "barbarians" who should be ruled "because servitude in such men is established for their welfare."[7] Sometimes, barbarians were thought incapable of sharing in the benefits of civilization. On the other hand, Romans thought their civilization could be exported, while later colonialists included missionaries and secular educators in their imperial plans to spread civilization. For some, there

was a belief that once brought under the umbrella of a "civilized" empire, barbarians would over a period of time become "civilized."

Christianity added another dimension to the idea of equality and inequality. Not only were barbarians uncivilized but they were also pagan. Did the Christian God extend blessings to both Christians and
non-Christians? Could natural slaves or barbarians be converted to
Christianity, or were they eternally damned? Could missionaries save
the souls of those not born into the bosom of Christianity? Was a
non-Christian equal to a Christian in moral sentiments?

Christianity added new impetus to the expansion of empire. Increasing the arrogance of the imperial project, Christians insisted that
the Gospels and the Church were the only valid sources of religious beliefs. Imperialists could claim that they were both civilizing the world
and spreading the true religion. By the 5th century, Christianity was
thought of as co-extensive with the *Imperium romanum*. This meant
that to be human, as opposed to being a natural slave, was to be "civilized" and Christian. Historian Anthony Pagden argues, "just as the
civitas had now become conterminous with Christianity, so to be human—to be, that is, one who was "civil," and who was able to interpret
correctly the law of nature—one had now also to be Christian."[8] After
the fifteenth century, most Western colonialists rationalized the spread
of empire with the belief that they were saving a barbaric and pagan
world by spreading Christian civilization.

Spreading Christian civilization became the primary educational
project of Western colonialists. From the Americas to India and
Indochina, Western missionaries and educators carried on their evan-
gelical efforts under the banner of imperialism. Entangled in instruction about religion and Western culture were Enlightenment ideas
about freedom and equality.

EQUALITY AND FREEDOM
IN THE WESTERN ENLIGHTENMENT

Given the Western tradition of dividing humanity into groups, such as
natural slave, barbarian, and pagan, it is easy to understand how writers of the American Declaration of Independence and the U.S. Constitution would consider freedom and equality to be limited to a select
group of people. These divisions were reinforced by the two important
Enlightenment philosophers, Englishman John Locke (1632–1704)
and Frenchman Jean-Jacques Rousseau (1712–1778), who, among
other things, related equality and freedom to concepts of schooling.

The first thing to note about both philosophers is that equality and
freedom are only intended for men. Their denial of universal equality
and freedom for *all humans* made it possible for their followers to

justify slavery and conquest of so-called pagans and other non-Western peoples. In addition, the denial of Locke and Rousseau of equality and freedom for women was clearly related to their educational proposals. This opened the door to justifying inequality of educational opportunities.

Locke argued that there are two possible sources of government. One is the family modeled on the scriptural depiction of Adam and Eve. In this model, government is a father (Adam) ruling over a dependent population (Eve). The other possible origin, he suggested, was a contract created by the consent of the governed. Locke's social contract theory of government assumed equality, except for women, in the consent to be governed. However, political equality ended with consent to the political contract. In Locke's early work, the primary reason for people to consent to a contract for government was the assurance of order. Later, he made the protection of property and the public good the primary reason for people consenting to a government.[9] The most radical aspect of Locke's argument was that people had the right to overthrow the government when the government broke the social contract by not protecting property or working for the public good.[10]

Certainly, Locke's greatest contribution to concepts of equality and freedom were the right to revolution against an unjust government. Equality in consenting to government and freedom to change governments were important. However, Locke's ideas were limited in important ways. Besides the issue of gender, freedom and equality disappeared after the creation of the social contract. Locke argued that the social contract required citizens to submit themselves to the will of the state. This was a theory of popular consent without popular control. Since the ruler was bound by the original contract to maintain the public good, people could not violate the public good by breaking the law. Inequality of power could exist as long as it did not interfere with the public good. In addition, it was the obligation of the ruler to protect inequality in the ownership of property.

Locke's concept of freedom was limited by religious concerns and the public good. His idea of freedom centers on the question of "indifference." Regarding religion, Locke argued that the Bible prescribed specific prohibitions to human actions such as the committing of murder or adultery. On the other hand, Locke argued, the Bible is "indifferent" to such human acts as men being shaved or bearded, or wearing hats in church. These were areas of human action to which God—since there was no discussion in the Bible—was indifferent. Therefore, the Bible provides the laws of God to govern human action, while governance of those things to which God was indifferent was determined by human laws.[11]

Locke applied the same reasoning to government. Rulers should not interfere with freedom of speech and conscience unless there was a violation of God's laws or the public good. But the emphasis on the disruption of the public good placed a severe limitation on freedom of speech and conscience. For instance, Locke objected to toleration of some opinions and beliefs, including Roman Catholicism and atheism. He considered these doctrines to be destructive of the public good. In general, according to Locke's arguments, rulers had the right to decide the public good and therefore had the right to limit free speech and conscience.[12]

Locke's concept of freedom reflected a more general notion of Christian liberty first stated by Martin Luther. Christian liberty, according to Luther, could only occur after salvation. In this context, freedom meant the freedom to act in a Christian manner. Similar ideas were intertwined with concepts of freedom in the early republic of the United States. Freedom was considered the freedom to do good. Early pleas for public schooling focused on the idea that people could only exercise their freedom "wisely" if they were taught the proper values and learned to act according to the public good.[13]

Implicit in Locke's argument was that the ruler could limit freedom in the name of the public good and that the public good would be determined by the ruler. In other words, freedom was the right to do good according to the ruler's definition of good. Of course, citizens had the freedom to revolt against the ruler when the ruler violated the public good. But the ruler *defined* the public good. Certainly, this circle of reasoning was an obstacle to attempts to expand notions of freedom. On the other hand, Locke did place ideas into the ideoscape that would continually broaden in meaning in the global flow.

Gender differences appear in both Locke's images of rulers as fathers and in the limitation of his educational proposals to "a gentleman's son."[14] Whenever there is a discussion of women in his educational writings—and this is infrequent—it is clearly indicated that their education should be limited. For instance, Locke describes two levels of the learning of languages. For "the softer sex ... [who] show us, that ... without the least study or knowledge of grammar, [they] can ... [demonstrate] a great degree of elegancy and politeness in their language," Locke recommended rote learning without the study of grammar.[15] On the other hand, men who do the business of the world, Locke suggested, needed to learn the proper rules of grammar.

Therefore, acceptance of inequality in wealth and gender were clearly stated in Locke's educational proposals. He limited his educational proposals to children of wealthy parents. Locke stressed that children should be educated at home by tutors. Parents were warned not to send their children to school because they were colleges of vice that taught bad habits. Parents should also be on the lookout for servants passing on bad habits. Locke considered the child similar to "wax, to be moulded and fashioned as one pleases."[16] For Locke, a child's mind was a blank slate at birth. It was the interaction between the human and its environment that filled up the blank slate of the mind. "I may say," Locke wrote, "that, of all men we meet with, nine parts of ten are what they are, good or evil, useful or not, by their education."[17] Emphasizing the malleability of the child's mind, Locke commented, "I imagine the minds of children as easily turned this or that way as water itself."[18]

Equality could be made a universal concept using Locke's image of the child's mind as a blank slate at birth. In this sense, all people are born equal with their minds waiting to filled. Theoretically, from this perspective, all people could receive an equal education and at least, according to Locke's calculation, "nine parts of ten ... [of] what they are" would be equal. Of course, this would require that all children be raised in equal economic conditions. This was not part of Locke's vision. Locke assumed that children would be raised in unequal circumstances and, therefore, despite all being born as blank slates, they would grow up to be unequal.

Ultimately, the most powerful in society determine the limitations placed on Locke's ideas of equality and freedom. The most powerful determine the public good, which then determines the limits placed on freedom. Equality exists during the formation of the social contract, during overthrow of rulers that do not protect property or violate the public good, and at birth. However, the social contract protects inequality in property. In turn, inequality in property ensures that the equality of birth results in inequality later in life.

In contrast to Locke's emphasis on the role of the state in protecting property, Rousseau stressed the importance of the mutual interdependence of the people and maintained that the state represented the collective will reflected by the reciprocal interchange between people. Since the state existed to protect collective interests, Rousseau maintained, people should obey the collective will. This reasoning, similar to Locke, places important constraints on both equality and freedom.

However, Rousseau, unlike Locke, focused on inequality of wealth as a threat to freedom. This added an important dimension to Enlightenment discussions of natural rights. Similar to Locke, Rousseau argued that at the time of forming the social contract and at birth all *men* were equal and free. (As I will discuss later, Rousseau considered women unequal to men in intellectual abilities.) But unlike Locke, Rousseau argued that freedom was lost when society recognized the right to private ownership of property and allowed for its accumulation. By making this argument, Rousseau made the issue of equality relevant to the economic conditions of modern society.

The loss of equality and freedom Rousseau attributed to five stages in the development of society. In the earliest "state of nature," men are equal and all men and women are free. In the second stage, families form but there is still no concept of private property. In these first two stages, humans are naturally sympathetic and protective of one another. In the third stage, this natural sympathy disappears as humans discover the importance of mutual aid and create nations. In the fourth stage, people declare the ownership of property a personal right and begin to hoard money. This creates a society divided between the rich and poor. In the fifth stage, the struggle between the rich and poor leads to the creation of representative government, which, according to Rousseau, primarily protects the interests of the rich.[19]

Rousseau made equality a central concern, whereas Locke stressed protection of property and freedom—at least, freedom that didn't threaten the public good. However, Rousseau's idea of economic equality was seriously compromised by his acceptance of inequality between genders. For instance, he argues in his educational tract, *Emile* (1762), that women should participate in civic life through their husbands. His educational proposals for women are intended to prepare them to be extensions of their husbands' intellectual and political world. In the *Emile*, Rousseau describes, through the character of Sophie, the ideal education of women. Reflecting his desire to educate Sophie to be an extension of her husband's (Emile's) will, Rousseau wrote, "Her mind is still vacant but has been trained to learn; its well-tilled land only waiting for the grain. What a pleasing ignorance! Happy is the man destined to instruct her. She will be her husband's disciple, not his teacher. Far from wanting to impose her tastes on him, she will share his."[20] Sophie's education centers on dressing dolls, worrying about personal dress, drawing, counting, reading, and writing.

The emphasis on gender inequality and the domestic education of Sophie is central to Rousseau's desire to maintain the mutual interdependence of humans. Sophie's role is to maintain the emotional relationships of the family, while Emile participates in civic life. Rousseau believed that the emotional attachments of the family were the basis of emotional attachments to neighbors and the state. The only hope in a world of economic inequality and competition, Rousseau maintained, was the sense of human relations developed in the family. It was the role of women to exist as symbols of virtue and models of domestic relationships. In Rousseau's vision, husbands should act for wives in the affairs of the world, while wives focus on the concerns of the family.

Therefore, in what I consider an interesting twist in logic, the maintenance of unequal conditions for women was central to Rousseau's efforts to deal with inequality in wealth. In fact, Rousseau seems to accept the inevitability of economic inequality despite his belief that it is the cause of human bondage. The sympathetic relationships developed in the family were to mitigate the worst aspects of unequal wealth. For instance, Rousseau wrote in *Emile* that the student "is rich, since it is only the rich who have the need of the natural education that would fit them to live under all conditions."[21] Similar to Locke, his actual educational plans reflected an acceptance of economic inequalities.

Freedom was restricted by Rousseau's idea of the general will. When comparing Locke to Rousseau, it is difficult to determine which one places the greatest restrictions on freedom. Locke maintained that freedom should be restricted by the ruler's interpretation of the public good. The idea of interpreting the public good was rather nebulous and could have led to the justification of extremely authoritarian governments. Similarly, Rousseau's idea of the general will was vague and could have been used to justify the power of any group claiming to know the general will. The potential totalitarianism embodied in the idea of a general will was reflected in the statement in Rousseau's 1755 article "Political Economy" that "If ... we train them [citizens] early in life never to think of their individual interests except in relation to having any meaning apart from the state, they will come in course of time to identify themselves in some fashion with this grand Whole and be conscious of their membership in their fatherland."[22] Linking the role of women to the general will, Rousseau continued, "surrounded by objects that unceasingly remind them of the tender mother that fosters them ... they [children] will learn to cherish each other as brothers and wish only what the community wishes."[23] One can almost hear the later boot steps of Nazism in Rousseau's educational plan for Poland, which stated, "A child ought to look upon his fatherland as soon as his eyes open to the light, and should continue to do so till the day of his death. Every patriot sucks in the love of country with his mother's milk. This love is his whole existence."[24]

It is not my intention in highlighting the limitations placed on equality and freedom by Locke and Rousseau to negate the importance of their contribution to concepts of natural rights. My purpose is to show how the limitations placed on the concepts of equality and freedom could allow for these ideas to enter the global flow at the same time that Europeans expanded their empires and oppressed the world's peoples. These apparent contradictions help to explain the strange career of Western ideas about rights in the global flow. European colonialists could claim they were introducing the world's people to natural rights and civilization as they unfurled the banner of imperialism because they had placed limits on the meaning of equality and freedom by an acceptance of social class differences, promotion of scientific racism, and commitment to the acquisition of private property. Within this contradictory framework, Europeans could claim they were introducing others to natural rights while, at the same, they denied these very same people freedom and equality.

EQUALITY AND FREEDOM IN THE UNITED STATES

The United States is a good example of how words like *freedom* and *equality* can be extended in meaning. Originally applied to a small group, they became more inclusive as others demanded to share in the same privileges. Non-Whites and women demanded inclusion in the ideas of equality and freedom as they marched for civil rights. What did equality and freedom originally mean in the United States? Consider the American Declaration of Independence. "We hold these truths to be self-evident," the document proclaims, "that all men are created equal, that they are endowed by their Creator with certain unalienable Rights, that among these are Life, Liberty, and the pursuit of Happiness." The use of "men" in "all men are created equal" is gender specific. It did not refer to all humans. It was meant to refer to men and to a specific group of men. For the men rallying around the Declaration, it was as "self-evident" that women were different from men as it was "self-evident" that Africans and Native Americans were not equal to the English. In *The Pursuit of Equality in American History*, J. R. Pole writes:

> "If, as was almost universally believed [at the time of the writing of the Declaration], women were by their nature different from men, then although they might have equal rights, these would be rights to different social goods. When in later generations radical feminist spokeswomen claimed that the rights of women were exactly identical to those of men, they could not win the argument by quoting the Declaration of Independence and substituting their own sex for men's ... The Declaration of Independence proclaimed a universalist equalitarian rhetoric as the standard of a highly differentiated social order."[25]

The apparent hypocrisy of a group of slave owners declaring all "men" equal can be understood by defining *men* as all free-male property holders. In fact, free-male property owners were the only group provided full citizenship rights, including the right to vote, after the American Revolution. Fourteen years after the Declaration of Independence, the United States Congress specifically added skin color as a qualification for equality with the passage of the Naturalization Act of 1790 that granted naturalized citizenship only to "White persons."

"White persons" as a limitation remained a part of U.S. laws until the 1950s.[26] Consequently, self-evident equality meant equality within a group of free-White male property holders.

Similarly, freedom and liberty were given restricted meanings by colonial and U.S. leaders in the 18th and 19th centuries. Government support of slavery indicated the limitations placed on human freedom. Even for citizens with full rights, schooling was promoted to ensure that they did not misinterpret the extent of freedom being granted. Similar to Islamic doctrines, freedom was the freedom to do "right" or "good." Often the idea of right and good was linked to Christian doctrines of morality. In this framework, schools prepared students to be free by restricting their actions through the inculcation of morality and citizenship rules. At times, the public schools to educated future citizens to act according to a restricted notion of freedom that blinded them to the unfree conditions of women, slaves, Native Americans, Mexican Americans, and Asian Americans.

EQUALITY, SCIENTIFIC RACISM, AND EDUCATIONAL DISCRIMINATION

In order to avoid future problems, it is important to understand how so-called rational Enlightenment thinkers could, without being hypocritical, limit concepts of equality to White men. Understanding how this apparent contradiction was resolved in some minds helps explain how a government that proclaimed equality could support racially segregated schools and deny equal educational opportunity to minority cultures and languages. Understanding how racism and equality could be linked also, I will argue, highlights the importance of a universal concept of what it means to be human. Without a universal concept of humanity, there exists the possibility of dividing groups of people according to their possession of certain attributes. This, as I will explain in the case of Thomas Jefferson, leads to scientific racism.

As a slave owner, Thomas Jefferson was not a hypocrite when he penned the words "all men are created equal." He did not believe the enslaved Africans he owned to be fully developed "men." Blacks were not part of the self-evident truth that "all men are created equal." Jefferson's supposed proof that Blacks were not equal to Whites was based on scientific methods popular among Enlightenment thinkers. *In Notes on the State of Virginia* (1782), Jefferson's explanation of the differences between Whites and Blacks anticipated 19th- and 20th-century scientific racism with its genetic charts, test scores, and body measurements.[27]

While I might seem a little harsh in comparing an icon of equality and freedom such as Thomas Jefferson with the racial theories of Nazism, there are parallels that underscore the importance of a commitment to the idea that all humans—men and women—are in fact equal. Once, as Jefferson did, you cross the line of trying to explain differences between humans, as opposed to how humans are similar, you create the possibility of advancing theories that will support inequality. Using scientific jargon to discuss human differences makes racism sound objective.

For instance, as Jefferson tackled the difficult task of reconciling slavery with equality, he wrote in *Notes on the State of Virginia* "They [enslaved Africans] secrete less by the kidneys and more by the glands of the skin, which gives them a very strong and disagreeable odor. This greater degree of transpiration, renders them more tolerant of heat, and less so of cold than the whites. Perhaps ... a difference of structure in the pulmonary apparatus ... may have disabled them from extricating, in the act of inspiration, so much of that fluid from the outer air, or obliged them in expiration, to part with more of it. They seem to require less sleep."[28] Stripped of the scientific jargon, Jefferson was simply arguing that enslaved Africans as compared to Whites urinated less and sweated more, and could tolerated longer hours of working in the heat of the summer. In the same manner, Jefferson explained why Whites were more beautiful than Blacks:

> Whether the black of the negro resides in the reticular membrane between the skin and scarf-skin, or in the scarf-skin itself, whither it proceeds from the color of the blood, the color of the bile, or from that of some other secretion, the difference is fixed in nature, and is as real as if its seat and cause were better known to us. And is this difference of no importance? Is it not the foundation of a greater or less share of beauty in the two races?[29]

Jefferson's rhetorical answer was, "Are not the fine mixtures of red and white, the expressions of every passion by greater or less suffusions of color in the one, preferable to that eternal monotony, which reigns in the countenances, that immovable veil of black which covers the emotions of the other race?"[30]

But the real issue of equality for Jefferson and other Enlightenment thinkers was the exercise of reason and, particularly, moral reason. For Jefferson, men were equal because they were born in a state of nature with moral "common sense." Jefferson wrote to his friend Peter Carr in 1787 that the individual is "endowed with a sense of right and wrong.... This sense is as much a part of his nature as the sense of hearing, seeing, feeling; it is the true foundation of morality."[31] Sometimes, Jefferson reasoned, moral instruction can interfere with the moral common sense born of men in a state of nature. In an often-quoted statement, Jefferson wrote, "State a moral case to a ploughman and a professor. The former will decide as well, and often better than the latter, because he has not been led astray by artificial rules."[32]

In both reasoning and moral capabilities, Jefferson claimed Africans were inferior to Whites. "Comparing them by their faculties of memory, reason, and imagination," Jefferson wrote in *Notes on the State of Virginia*, "it appears to me that in memory they are equal to the whites; in reason much inferior, as I think one could scarcely be found capable of tracing and comprehending the investigations of Euclid; and that in imagination they are dull, tasteless, and anomalous."[33] Giving supposed scientific proof of their low level of reasoning, Jefferson wrote, "In general, their existence appears to participate more of sensation than reflection. To this must be ascribed their disposition to sleep when abstracted from their diversions, and unemployed in labor. An animal whose body is at rest, and who does not reflect must be disposed to sleep of course."[34] A haunting sexual image appears in Jefferson's suggestion that enslaved Africans are animals and not humans: "They are more ardent after their female; but love seems with them to be more an eager desire, than a tender delicate mixture of sentiment and sensation ... Their love is ardent, but it kindles the senses only, not the imagination."[35]

For Jefferson, the real proof that Africans were by nature inferior were the children of interracial couples. Jefferson wrote, "The improvements of the blacks in body and mind, in the first instance of their mixture with the whites, has been observed by everyone, and proves that their inferiority is not the effect merely of their condition of life."[36] And wrapped in the language of scientific racism, Jefferson hypothesized, "I advance it, therefore, as a suspicion only, that the blacks, whether originally a distinct race, or made distinct by time and circumstances, are inferior to the whites in the endowments both of body and mind. It is not against experience to suppose that different species of the same genus, or varieties of the same species, may possess different qualifications."[37]

My discussion of Jefferson is not intended to detract from the importance of the words "all men are created equal," as these words entered the global flow and they were used by people to imagine real social and economic equality. The important point is that the language of equality can at times serve as a justification for inequality. The phrase "all men are created equal" could include all humans—men and women. But this broad meaning of equality disappears as social inequalities are justified by supposed scientific arguments that attempt to prove that one group of people is by nature superior to another group.

THE DECLARATION OF THE RIGHTS OF MAN AND OF THE CITIZEN AND THE BILL OF RIGHTS

The first governmental statement of natural rights doctrines in the West was issued by the French National Assembly in 1789. The first two articles reflect the social contract theory of the origin of government with an emphasis on the role of government in protecting rights:

1. Men are born and remain free and equal in rights. Social distinctions may be founded only upon the general good.

2. The aim of all political association is the preservation of the natural and imprescriptible rights of man. These are liberty, property, security and resistance to oppression.[38]

I would like to remind the reader of Professor Onuma Yasuaki's criticism of Western claims to be the source of human rights doctrines (quoted in chap. 1) regarding the refusal of the male-dominated French Assembly to approve the Declaration of the Rights of Women.[39]

Both the Declaration of the Rights of Man and of the Citizen and the U.S. Bill of Rights (adopted in 1791) were applied to only a select group of people. The United States's 1790 Naturalization Act ensured that the Bill of Rights at the time of its adoption did not include Native Americans. And, of course, it did not protect slaves. Nor did the concepts embodied in the Declaration of the Rights of Man ever extend to slaves held in French colonies. The French did not extend natural rights to native populations in their 19th century colonies in Southeast Asia, Africa, and the Americas. Originally, these rights were only for a select group of people.

Neither of these declarations of rights included the right to education. I do not make this as a critical statement, but at the time formal education did not play a major economic role and was not considered essential for democratic participation in government. Also, it was not considered a "natural right." Now education is thought as a "human right." Certainly, formal education did not exist in a state of nature. However, the First Amendment of the U.S. Bill of Rights would later play an important role regarding laws affecting education. The First Amendment states:

> Congress shall make no law respecting an establishment of religion, or prohibiting the free exercise thereof; or abridging the freedom of speech, or of the press; or the right of the people peaceably to assemble, and to petition the Government for a redress of grievances.

As I will discuss later, this amendment has resulted in raising issues over publicly supported religious education and the meaning of free speech in schools.

It is important to note that despite the widespread recognition in the 20th and 21st centuries of education as a human right, the U.S. Constitution still lacks an amendment recognizing the right to education. As I will discuss, this fact has seriously hampered the provision of equality of educational opportunity. I think that the United States Constitution should be amended to include education as a human right.

EQUALITY OF OPPORTUNITY

Racial and gender equalities were not the only contradictions to the natural rights concept that "All men are created equal." Economic differences seemed to belie any arguments that equality existed in the United States. The resolution of this apparent problem was made by defining equality as "equality of opportunity." The ideal of equality of opportunity was expressed in the following words by John Rawls in *A Theory of Justice*: "Those who are at the same level of talent and ability, and have the same willingness to use them should have the same prospects of success regardless of their initial place in the social system, that is irrespective of the income class into which they are born."[40]

Equality of opportunity resolved the contradiction between declarations of equality and the existence of social and racial inequality. This was a concept that seemed to reconcile the existence of a society divided by social class, gender, and race with the purported belief in equality. In addition, "equality of opportunity" provided the means for explaining how freedom could result in "the unprecedented homogeneity of American custom and opinion."[41] One might assume that freedom would support nonconformity in customs and opinions. However, equality and freedom in the United States seemed to create uniformity of thought and action. How could this happen?

As historian J. R. Pole argued, the concept of equality of opportunity emerged in the 19th century as both an attempt to rationalize inequalities and to justify personal ambitions. The critical question, as Pole points out, was, "Opportunity for what?"[42] In 1793, America's so-called Schoolmaster and dictionary writer, Noah Webster answered the question, "here [as opposed to Great Britain] every man finds employment, and the road is open for the poorest citizen to amass wealth by labor or economy, and by his talent and virtue to raise himself to the highest offices of the State."[43] This idea has dominated discussions of schooling and civil rights from Webster's time to the present. Equality of opportunity simply meant the right to be rich or poor, and to be a political leader or a follower.

The beauty of equality of opportunity was that it could be used to justify a society that was unequal in wealth and power. Within this framework, everyone had an equal right to compete for wealth. Equality of opportunity did not mean economic equality, but, on the contrary, it meant a society of winners and losers. The most important thing was ensuring that everyone had an equal chance to compete. The same thing was true of political power. Everyone was to have a chance to compete for political power; however, only a few would win.

Schooling was considered the key to achieving equality of opportunity. A major argument for public schools was providing equality of opportunity. Early 19th-century school leaders, including the so-called father of American public schools, Horace Mann, argued that if everyone went to school and received the same education they would enter the labor market with an equal opportunity to compete. In this framework, school became the economic starting line for the race for riches.[44]

A powerful role for schooling was convincing losers that they had been given equality of opportunity. If one believed that schooling could provide equality of opportunity, then it didn't matter if it really existed. Poverty could be blamed on the failure of individuals to capitalize on the equality of opportunity provided by schools. People who believed the school could ensure equality of opportunity might blame themselves for failing to take advantages of life's opportunities.

It is significant that participants in the great civil rights movement in the United States in the 1950s and 1960s primarily sought equality of *educational* opportunity and equality of opportunity for women and minority groups. It was assumed that equality of educational opportunity would contribute to an equal chance to compete in the economic system. In addition, it was assumed that ending laws and legal practices that denied women and minority groups an equal right to vote and obtain political office would create equality of opportunity to gain political power. Consequently, the primary goal of civil rights in the United States was to include all groups in the quest for equality opportunity to be rich or poor, and to be powerful or powerless.[45]

The great historical irony was that groups such as Native Americans, African Americans, Mexican Americans, and Asian Americans, who had been victims of physical and cultural genocide, slavery, and terrorism, fought to join the very system that was responsible for these acts. Rather than reject the actual social and economic inequalities that resulted from the doctrine of equality of opportunity, these exploited groups demanded participation in the competition for wealth. Ironically, these formerly oppressed groups could participate in the economic exploitation of other countries as the United States government and multinational corporations preached equality of opportunity on a global scale.

EQUALITY BEFORE THE LAW

Similar to equality of opportunity, "equality before the law" can foster inequalities. Consider the consequences of Aristotle's division of humanity into human and natural slaves. While each group is equal before the law, the law is different for each group. As Christine Koggel writes, "The examination of Aristotle's own application of procedural equality in his political theory show that his identification of relevant properties for sorting people allowed equality to be satisfied when unequals were treated unequally."[46] For instance, enslaved Africans in the United States in the early 19th century were by law not allowed to be educated while no legal restrictions on education were placed on free Whites. In this situation, all enslaved Africans were treated equally by the laws and, as a separate class, free Whites were also treated equally.

In addition, the ideology of equality of opportunity might defeat attempts to achieve equality before the law. The doctrine of equality of opportunity ensures a society divided by wealth. Even when all people are supposedly treated equally by the law, inequality in wealth can result in legal disparities. Under the rule of law, those with the most money can often hire legal expertise that will ensure that laws work in their favor. An impoverished burglar with the poorest of legal help might end up in jail, while the Wall Street embezzler might win freedom by hiring teams of lawyers. Equality before the law cannot be guaranteed when there exists inequalities in wealth.

The contradiction between equality of opportunity and equality before the law is often overlooked. This contradiction seemed to go unnoticed in the United States with the passage in 1868 of the 14th Amendment to the U.S. Constitution, which promised equality before the law. The 14th Amendment appeared shortly after the emancipation of enslaved Africans and the conclusion of the U.S. Civil War. Designed to provide citizenship and ensure the equal treatment of freed African slaves, the 14th Amendment was quickly compromised by the U.S. Supreme Court's 1896 interpretation of its meaning supporting racial segregation. Section 1 of the 14th Amendment states:

> All persons born or naturalized in the United States, and subject to the jurisdiction thereof, are citizens of the United States and of the State wherein they reside. No State shall make or enforce any law which shall abridge the privileges or immunities of citizens of the United States; nor shall any State deprive any person of life, liberty, or property, without due process of law; nor deny to any person within its jurisdiction the equal protection of the laws.[47]

I want to emphasize the importance of the 14th Amendment in the global flow before discussing its early limitations. As I discuss in chapter 5, the writers of the Constitution of India used the 14th Amendment as a model to overcome segregation and discrimination of women and the Untouchable castes. Indian constitutionalists learned from the American experience that additional clauses were needed so that it could be used in a positive way to promote equality. In the concluding chapter, I use the additions made by the writers of the Constitution of India as a model for ensuring equality of educational opportunity.

In Plessy v. Ferguson, the U.S. Supreme Court upheld segregation under the doctrine of "separate but equal."[48] This decision broadened the Aristotelean idea of procedural equality. Now people could be legally classified into different racial groups and receive equal treatment within those groups as long as there was equality of treatment between groups. Under the Plessy decision, the assumption was that while segregated from Whites, freed Africans would receive the same or equal educational resources, including textbooks, buildings, teachers, and other educational materials. Of course, this never happened. Public schools attended by Blacks received less financial support than White schools. Consequently, the separate but equal doctrine resulted in separate and unequal education.[49]

Besides the separate but equal ruling, the 14th Amendment ignored those groups excluded from citizenship. The "White" was not removed from the 1790 Naturalization Act until 1952, and Native Americans were not given citizenship until 1924. The "White" qualification for naturalization ensured that Asian immigrants could not receive full protection under the laws as United States citizens.[50]

On the surface, equality before the law never really existed in the United States until after the "White" qualification was removed from naturalization laws and the separate but equal doctrine was overturned by the U.S. Supreme Court in 1954. Even then, inequality before the law still occurred because of differences in wealth. The 1954 U.S. Supreme Court decision declared segregation to be inherently unequal. This meant that the Aristotlean idea of separate procedural equality for different groups of people would be replaced with the idea that all people would be equal under the same set of laws.[51]

Of course, equality before the law requires that laws treat all people equally. For instance, a law providing more money for college guidance and science equipment might favor well-educated students over those who are illiterate and require remedial instruction. Ensuring that laws favor a particular social group depends on political power. However, political power is often correlated to wealth. Christine Koggel argues, "Power not only creates inequalities in relationships between capitalists and workers, but it is also a pervasive force in ordinary and personal relationships where differences other than class are present."[52]

Consequently, equality of opportunity by fostering economic inequalities contributes to inequality of political power. In turn, inequality of political power can result in the passage of laws that favor one group over another. Under these circumstances, procedural equality under the law might be guaranteed, but equality of the law is not. Substantive equality before the law requires equality of political power which, in turn, requires equality of resources to enact laws and plead in court. The greatest barrier to equality before the law is the doctrine of equality of opportunity and its resulting inequalities in wealth.

This contributes to a circle of inequalities in which a major consequence is inequality of educational opportunity. Inequality of political power makes it difficult for low-income families to protect their interests in education. In addition, inequality before the law makes it difficult for the poor to protect their legal interests in education. Without some intervention by the government to redistributed resources, this circle of inequality can spiral out of control in a society where there is a close tie between income and quality of education. In a society where income is related to education, inequality of educational resources could contribute to the rich getting richer and the poor getting poorer, and the rich gaining political power and legal strength while the poor are losing in both areas. And as these divisions increase, they could be ignored by claims that everyone has equality of opportunity.

EQUALITY OF EDUCATIONAL OPPORTUNITY AS A HUMAN RIGHT IN THE WEST

The United States Constitution provides no way of rectifying the problem of equal educational opportunity without the addition of an amendment guaranteeing an equal right to an education. Without any guaranteed right to education, there is no way the central government can be required to ensure equal resources for education. This was the decision of the U.S. Supreme Court in its famous 1973 decision *Rodriguez v. San Antonio Independent School District*. Since that time, state courts and legislatures throughout the United States have been engaged in struggles over providing equal financing of public school students. A good example of this struggle and its impact on students from low-income families can be found in Jean Anyon's *Ghetto Schooling: A Political Economy of Urban School Reform*.[53]

The unequal funding of education is particularly problematic in a society dominated by the ideology that schooling is the mechanism that ensures equality of opportunity. At the time of the writing of the U.S. Constitution, the ideology of equality of opportunity through schooling was not dominant. If it had been, the writers of the constitution might have added an Article providing for the right to equal education. The same thing is true of the Declaration of the Rights of Man and of the Citizen. This list of rights, without the inclusion of the right to education, remains a part of the 1958 French Constitution which declares in its Preamble, "The French people hereby solemnly proclaim their dedication to the Rights of Man and the principle of national sovereignty as defined by the Declaration of 1789.... "[54] The one important qualification to this Declaration is that it now extends to "the peoples of the Overseas Territories who, by free determination, adopt the present Constitution.... "[55] The inclusion of a constitutional article providing for the right to education has been a common practice in European countries since World War II.

As I have suggested, "natural rights" arguments do not provide a basis for making education a human right. It is only after the intercivilizational idea of "human rights" developed in the 20th century that constitutional provisions were made for the right to education. For instance, the Danish Constitution adopted in 1953 provides for free public schooling and the right to private schooling:

Section 76 [Compulsory Schooling]

All children of school age shall be entitled to free instruction in the elementary schools. Parents or guardians who themselves arrange for their children or wards receiving instruction equal to the general elementary school standard, shall not be obliged to have their children or wards taught in elementary school.

A provision for ensuring equality of educational resources can be found in the 1947 Italian Constitution. Sections 1 and 2 of Article 34 provide for free and compulsory education. Sections 3 and 4 provide some insurance for equality of educational opportunity. Unfortunately, the provisions are compromised by the ambiguous reference to the "able and deserving" and to "competitive examinations." These qualifications could favor students from families that can provide extra help in preparation for examinations by providing richer cultural experiences and tutors. The Italian Constitution states:

(3) The able and deserving, even if lacking financial resources, shall have the right to attain the highest grades of learning.

(4) The Republic shall make this right effective by means of scholarships, allowances to families, and other provisions, to be assigned through competitive examinations.[56]

The Polish Constitution includes explicit provisions for ensuring equality of educational resources without the qualifications present in the Italian Constitution. The opening of Article 70 of the Polish Constitution echoes the Universal Declaration of Human Rights by declaring, "Everyone shall have the right to education." Clause 4 of Article 7 provides an extremely strong constitutional guarantee of equality of educational opportunity:

Article 70

(4) Public authorities shall ensure universal and equal access to education for financial and organizational assistance to pupils and students. To this end, they shall establish and support systems for individual financial and organizational assistance to pupils and students.[57]

The Spanish Constitution explicitly recognizes education as a right. In addition, freedom of instruction is directly related to the right to education. Education is also directly tied to teaching about other rights and liberties. Within the European Union, the Spanish Constitution is the most extensive in explicating conditions affecting schooling. The first two clauses of Article 27 of the Spanish Constitution provide for the right to education in the context of freedom and other rights, while the fourth clause provides for free basic education:

(1) Everyone has the right to education. Freedom of instruction is recognized.

(2) The objective of education shall be the full development of the human personality in respect for the democratic principles of coexistence and the basic rights and liberties.

(4) Basic education is obligatory and free.[58]

Also, the Spanish Constitution makes explicit provisions for the very difficult issue of religious education. Clause 3 states: "The public authorities guarantee the right which will assist parents to have their children receive the religious and moral formation which is in keeping with their own convictions."[59]

The issue of religion and education is difficult. Some constitutions, such as those of the United States and France, limit, with some exceptions, financial support to secular public school systems. Both France and the United States adopted natural rights doctrines at a time when church–state relationships were being heavily criticized. For the United States, separation of church and state was a pragmatic solution to a real problem of conflict between religious groups. Now many Western constitutions openly recognize the right to a religious education. For instance, the 1949 Constitution of Germany explicitly grants the right to a religious education even in state schools. The one constitutional exception to the provision of religious education is for schools that are identified as secular. Also, the constitution explicitly protects teachers from being required to give religious instruction. One could imagine a universal right to education that allowed parents to select a religious or a specifically identified secular school. The second and third clauses of Article 7 of the German Constitution deal with religious instruction. Article 7 states:

(1) The entire schooling system stands under the supervision of the state.

(2) The persons entitled to the upbringing of a child have the right to decide whether the child shall attend religion classes.

(3) Religion classes form part of the ordinary curriculum in state schools, except for secular schools. Without prejudice to the state's right of supervision, religious instruction is given in accordance with the tenets of the religious communities. No teacher may be obliged against his will to give religious instruction.[60]

An important part of the 1947 Italian Constitution is the protection of minority languages. Language minorities have faced many battles in U.S. schools over the language of the classrooms because there is no constitutional provisions for language protection. This has been particularly problematic for Native Americans and the large U.S. Spanish-speaking population.[61] Article 6 of the Italian Constitution states, "The Republic shall safeguard linguistic minorities by means of special provisions."[62] Similar to the United States, France makes no provision for language minorities, and, in fact, Article 2 of the French Constitution states, "The language of the Republic is French."[63] Similar restrictions appear in the Spanish Constitution, with an emphasis on the duty to know Spanish. Article 3 states: "(1) Castellon is the official Spanish language of the state. All Spaniards have the duty to know it and the right to use it."[64] In Spain, recognition of minority languages is limited to autonomous communities: "The other languages of Spain will also be official in their respective autonomous communities.... "[65]

In summary, there are three noteworthy educational provisions in the preceding constitutions. First, some constitutions provide for equality of educational opportunity. The second is the lack of provisions for freedom of thought in schools, except for Spain's recognition of freedom of instruction, which does not necessarily include freedom of thought for students. And third, the two countries that were the earliest to institute natural rights doctrines, the United States and France, do not recognize education as a right. Again, I am emphasizing this because of the continued claims by some that the West is the source of human rights doctrines. Education as a right is the product of 20th-century intercivilizational discussions about human rights.

FREEDOM AND THE RIGHT TO EDUCATION

Free speech, meaning freedom of expression and communication, as a right is granted in all Western constitutions. Some constitutions also include explicit restrictions of freedom of speech similar to those of the Convention for the Protection of Human Rights and Fundamental Freedoms. Article 1 of the Swedish Constitution grants freedom of expression and communication. However, Article 13 provides elaborate provisions for limiting freedom of expression in the interest of national security, "public safety and order, the integrity of the individual, the sanctity of private life, or the prevention and prosecution of crime."[66] Also the Article specifies that, "Freedom of expression may also be restricted in economic activities."[67]

Free speech is a difficult issue in Western countries. In the U.S. Constitution there are no restrictions placed on the free speech clause of the First Amendment. Regarding education, the U.S. Constitution has been interpreted as guaranteeing free speech for students in public schools. But this interpretation was emasculated by a series of court rulings that the exercise of free speech rights could not interfere with the educational process. These decisions allow school officials to censor student newspapers, class activities, and student speeches at assemblies. The effect has been to severely restrict free speech rights in public schools.[68]

Freedom to learn is not considered a right in Western constitutions. This is an issue where national testing plays an important role in determining the content of instruction in the classroom. Teachers teach to the test. Students worry about passing high-stakes tests because they are tickets to jobs and incomes. Should students (or their parents) have the right to determine what they want to learn? Should teachers have the right to determine what they want to teach? Should constitutional provisions include freedom to learn?

FREEDOM OF CHOICE AND THE EUROPEAN UNION'S RIGHT TO EDUCATION

Freedom of choice of schooling is another issue. Most constitutions provide some provision that allows parents to choose private schooling for their children. School choice as a reflection of religious and intellectual convictions is central to the right to education recognized in the 1950 European Convention for the Protection of Human Rights and Fundamental Freedoms. This convention serves as the human rights statement for the 1992 Treaty on European Union. The 1992 Treaty simply declares in Article 6 that member nations will respect the rights granted in the 1950 European Convention.[69] Written after the issuance of the U.N.'s Universal Declaration of Human Rights, the 1950 European Convention was an initial step in the eventual creation of the European Union. Actual enforcement and supervision of human rights was attempted through the establishment of the European Court of Human Rights. Currently, the European Union has declared its intention to protect human rights among member nations and throughout the World's community.

While recognizing the right to education, the 1950 European Convention gives primary power to parents to determine the intellectual content of education. In fact, it is the only human rights statement that I have encountered that refers to parents' "philosophical convictions" as a factor in determining the type of education. Article 2 of the Convention states:

Article 2

No person shall be denied the right to education. In the exercise of any functions which it assumes in relation to education and to teaching, the State shall respect the right of parents to ensure such education and teaching in conformity with their own religious and philosophical convictions.[70]

The European constitutions that I have reviewed do provide the right for parents to send their children to private schools. I am assuming private schooling is one means for ensuring parental rights to follow their own "religious and philosophical convictions." However, the exercise of this right can be limited by the willingness of public authorities to pay for private schooling. Also, is the phrase "religious and philosophical convictions" all-inclusive? Does it include schools for racist and anarchist (I am not suggesting these are the same)?

Parental choices are limited by the restrictions placed on freedom of thought in the Convention's Article 9. Clause 1 of Article 9 provides the right to "freedom of thought, conscience and religion." Clause 2 provides the following qualifications to this right, including concerns about national security, public safety, health, and morals. These sweeping qualifications provide the government with the right to limit a large number of religious exercises and limit freedom of expression. Clause 2 states:

Freedom to manifest one's religion or beliefs shall be subject only to such limitations as are prescribed by law and are necessary in a democratic society in the interests of public safety, for the protection of public order, health or morals, or for the protection of the rights and freedoms of others.[71]

Clause 2 might satisfy those concerned that parental freedom to choose the ideological content of the children's education might lead to the teaching of "objectionable" ideas. This clause could be used to shut down racist schools and schools teaching methods for overthrowing the government. On the other hand, phrases such as "public safety" and "protection of public order" are open to a variety of interpretations. It is not difficult to imagine parents being denied the choice of a school that taught ideas that threatened the economic and political power of national elites. Should these restrictions be placed on freedom of choice?

In the United States, school choice plans are complicated by the Constitutional provision for separation of school and state. This separation has effectively closed off public funding to parents who want to send their children to a religious school. I personally do not think that the original writers of the U.S. Constitution envisioned a separation of religion and education. Certainly, the founders of the U.S. schools included religion in public school instruction. It was not until the 1960s that the U.S. Supreme Court ruled against prayer and Bible reading in public school classrooms.

Choice of a religious education raises another issue regarding freedom and education. In Islamic countries it is assumed that most education will involve religion. Separating religion from education would be wrong in the minds of most Islamic peoples and for many other religions. Should parents, at public expense, be allowed to chose a religious education for their children? Should there be specific statements in constitutions that allows for public funding of the choice to attend a religious school?

The choice of a religious school might limit the right to freedom of thought. Freedom of thought is not part of most religious education. The purpose of religious education, in most cases, is to teach a specific set of beliefs and dogma as the truth. Should the right to a religious education be denied in order to protect freedom of thought? Does freedom of thought for children mean that parents must not impose their beliefs? Should children be given the right to choose a religious school without interference from their parents? Where are the boundaries between a child's right to freedom of thought, religious rights, and parental rights?

CONCLUSION

The 20th-century human rights movement changed Western natural rights doctrines. Human rights doctrines assume that rights should promote human welfare, which has resulted in the recognition of education, health, and economic rights. Natural rights doctrines were plagued by limitations placed on the idea of equality. In traditional Western thought, equality existed within groups that were defined by gender, religion culture, and race. For most 18th and 19th century Europeans there was no contradiction between proclamations of human equality and the enslavement of Africans, the slaughter of non-Christians, the genocide of Indigenous peoples, and the establishment of colonial empires. In many European minds, it was "natural" that women were inferior to men and that certain groups of people were inferior to others. Islamic and Asian nations are justified in pointing to North America and Europe as racist. However, as I suggested, the charge of hypocrisy misses the mark. Natural rights advocates never intended equal rights for "all humans."

The idea of equality of opportunity resolves the contradiction between doctrines of equality and the existence of inequality. Equality of opportunity is now the major Western justification for schooling. Schools are to provide equality of opportunity within the economic system by providing everyone with an equal chance to compete. Of course, equality of opportunity assumes inequality, because equal competition will result in unequal rewards. Inequality of finances resulting from the competition can create inequality before the law and inequality of educational opportunity. And, as income is tied to level of education, the rich can ensure through privileged schooling that their children remain rich. The poor might remain trapped in their poverty.

In the 20th century, European constitutions reflected human rights and, consequently, made education a right. Some of these constitutions attempt to provide for equality of educational opportunity. Some have dealt with the issue of freedom of choice. However, there is still a general neglect of constitutional provisions that would ensure the right of children to an equal education and to freedom of thought. These are difficult issues because of the continuing inequalities in family wealth, government advocacy of human capital education and nationalistic education, and the requirements of religious dogma. In the next chapter, I will examine the intersection of Western constitutional ideas with Hindu civilization through British colonialism and the adoption by India of a constitutional government. Indian leaders tried to correct the shortcomings of Western concepts of equality.

5

India: Education, Human Rights, and the Global Flow

In the 19th and 20th centuries, the global flow became a swift-moving river between India and England. Even in the 21st century, the Indian diaspora continues to North America and Europe. Educational policy was a major reason for the rapid movement of ideas and people between England and India. When instituting England's educational policy in India, Thomas Macaulay, a member of the Supreme Council of India, established the policy of educating an administrative cadre of Indians in the English language and culture. This group of English-speaking Indians were to owe their allegiance to England and were to help the English rule the vast Indian territories. Predicting the use of English as the global language, Macaulay argued, "In India, English is the language spoken by the ruling class. It is spoken by the higher class of natives at the seats of government. It is likely to become the language of commerce throughout the seas of the East."[1] In addition, he believed that "a single shelf of a good European library was worth the whole native literature of India and Arabia."[2]

The exchange of ideas sometimes took strange routes. As I explain later in this chapter, many Anglicized Indians became acquainted with Hindu literature through reading it in English translations. These English translations were distributed by the International Theosophy Society, which was founded in New York and headquartered in India. The Theosophy Society promoted the study of comparative religion and advocated a world community that would be free of discrimination based on race, gender, and religion. Through the work of the Theosophy Society, many

Westerners became acquainted with Hinduism and either made pilgrimages to India or actually moved to India to live as religious supplicants. Rather then belittling Indian culture, these Westerners worshiped it.

Today, India provides a good example of the effect of the global flow on the formation of a school system dedicated to equality of educational opportunity. Writers of the 1949 Indian Constitution put into practice legal concepts learned in the exchange of ideas with England and the rest of the world. Modeled after Western constitutions, the Indian Constitution declares in its Preamble:

> WE, THE PEOPLE OF INDIA, having solemnly resolved to constitute India into a [SOVEREIGN SOCIALIST SECULAR DEMOCRATIC REPUBLIC] and to secure to all its citizens:
>
> JUSTICE, social, economic and political;
>
> LIBERTY of thought, expression, belief, faith and worship;
>
> EQUALITY of status and opportunity; and to promote among them all
>
> FRATERNITY assuring the dignity of the individual and the [unity and integrity of the Nation]
>
> IN OUR CONSTITUENT ASSEMBLY this twenty-sixth day of November, 1949, do HEREBY ADOPT, ENACT AND GIVE TO OURSELVES THIS CONSTITUTION.[3]

As a result of India's independence struggle, Mahatma Gandhi's ideas on the use of nonviolent action to force the British out of India entered the global flow. Eventually, Martin Luther King, Jr., adapted Gandhi's nonviolent methods to the struggle for civil rights in the United States. As a result, India's struggle for independence had an important effect on ending school segregation and expanding equality of educational opportunity in the United States. This interaction within the global flow between ideas of equality and freedom in India and the United States highlights how struggles against oppression are now of global significance.

ANGLICIZED LEADERSHIP AND THE STRUGGLE FOR FREEDOM AND EQUALITY

Influenced by Western ideas of equality, writers of the 1949 Indian Constitution faced a formidable obstacle in the traditional Hindu religious and social system based on unequal treatment of castes and women by legal and educational institutions. The Hindu caste system is probably the most elaborate and complex system of social division in the world.

The caste system blends religion, bodily functions, family organization, social relationships, and economic roles into an interrelated justification for economic and social inequality. In contrast to the concept of equality of opportunity, the only hope for advancement into a higher caste is in a future life. Similar to the slave system in the United States, the caste system denies education to the lowest castes. In addition, traditional Hinduism denies equal rights and education to women.

Indian National Congress was a pivotal participant in the struggle for independence, a constitution, and equality. The Congress, as Indians called it, was founded by a group of upper class Anglicized Indians in Bombay on December 28, 1885. The Congress originated from a variety of Indian associations that were part of the Indian Renaissance "which was essentially a synthesis of Hindu tradition and the Western spirit of enquiry."[4] Initially, the Congress pledged its loyalty to England and English traditions. Presiding at the first Congress meeting, W. C. Bonerjee declared, "It is under the civilizing rule of the Queen and the people of England that we meet here together, hindered by none, freely allowed to speak our minds, without the least fear and hesitation. Such a thing is possible under British rule, and under British rule only."[5]

In the 20th century, the Congress became a mass movement for independence and constitutional government under the leadership of three Western educated men—Bhimrao Ramji Ambedkar, Mahatma Gandhi, and Jawaharlal Nehru. Ambedkar received a PhD in Economics from Columbia University, a DSc from the London School of Economics, and was admitted to the British Bar. Mahatma Gandhi was educated in law at the University College, London and admitted to the British Bar in 1891. Jawaharlal Nehru attended Harrow, the exclusive British public school, and after graduation attended Cambridge University. Exemplifying the effect of the legal and cultural interactions resulting from colonialism, Indian leaders relied on the U.S. Constitution, British Common Law, and the Irish Constitution in creating India's first constitutional government.[6]

The major educational problem in India faced by these Indian leaders was the schooling of lower caste men and women. Statistics issued by the Department of Education of the Indian Government highlight the effect of inequality of educational opportunities resulting from caste and gender discrimination. Consider the comparative figures provided in Table 2.1 for the years 1961 and 1991. These figures indicate both the differences between general literacy rates and those of females and lower castes, and the changes over a 30-year period as the result of the educational efforts of the Indian government.

As indicated in Table 5.1, illiteracy is a problem in India, with only 52.21% of the population literate in 1991. Other statistics indicate that the literacy rate did increase to 62% of the population in 1997.[7] The

TABLE 5.1

Comparison of Percentage Literacy Rates By Caste and Gender 1991

Years	All India Total	All India Male	All India Female	Lower Castes Total	Lower Castes Male	Lower Castes Female
1961	34.44	24.02	12.95	10.27	16.96	3.29
1991	52.21	64.13	39.29	37.41	49.91	23.76

From data provided by "Educational Statistics," Department of Education, Government of India, April, 2000, http://www.nic.in/vseducation/htmlweb/edusta.htm, pp. 8, 20.

striking differences in literacy rates by caste are highlighted by the comparison of a literacy rate in 1991 of 52.21% for all of India, with 37.41% for the lower castes. Similar differences exist when comparing male and female literacy rates in 1991, with all Indian males at 64.13% and all Indian females at 39.29%. Most striking is the 1991 literacy rate for lower caste females of 23.76%.

The literacy rate for lower caste females did increase from 3.29% in 1961 to 23.76% in 1991. This represents an almost sevenfold increase in the literacy rate for lower caste females. This rate of increase is much higher than the change in literacy rate for all females in India, from 12.95% in 1961 to 39.29% in 1991.

Efforts to increase literacy rates for the lower castes and for women reflect the impact of Western concepts of equality, freedom, and human rights that are embodied in the 1949 Indian Constitution. The Indian Constitution and education system demonstrate how human rights ideas in the global flow are adopted and used to justify social change. Indeed, the very idea of having a national constitution is Western in origin. In addition, the Indian Constitution draws on liberal ideas about equality of opportunity and socialist ideas about economic equality.

However, the equality promised in the Indian Constitution has to be understood in the context of traditional Hindu society. Indian leaders such as Gandhi tried to use traditional institutions to ensure greater social equality. Ambedkar, often called the father of the Indian Constitution, eventually abandoned Hinduism for Buddhism in his attempts to undermine the inequalities of the Hindu caste system. While Western ideas had a symbolic and emotional impact, their actual meaning depended on the context of traditional Indian society.

India exemplifies the resiliency of traditional social practices. Today, despite government efforts to remedy the situation, caste and gender remain potent determiners of educational opportunities. The education of cultural and language minorities remains a serious problem. I will discuss these problems after first examining how traditional

Hindu laws provided a complex justification for inequality according to caste and gender, and the efforts of those committed to independence and constitutional government.

INEQUALITY BASED ON CASTE AND GENDER

Caste is central to Hinduism. The caste system constitutes social classes according to religious dogma. During a lifetime, there is no mobility between castes. After death, reincarnation can result in mobility into another caste. Furthermore, caste identifies one's position on a scale of physical and spiritual purity, which in turn determines relationships between people. Some Indian leaders have demanded the abandonment of Hinduism because it reinforces a rigid social class structure where there is no possibility of mobility between castes except after death. Others have advocated reforms that would create equality between the castes. Some have remained orthodox Hindus who believe in the traditional caste system. Despite criticisms of Hinduism's beliefs regarding castes and women, discrimination by caste and gender continues in India.

The caste system is clearly described in ancient Indian law codes, the Dharmasutras: "There are four classes [castes]: Brahmin, Ksatriya, Vaisya, and Sudra. Among these, each preceding class [caste] is superior by birth to each subsequent."[8] This superiority includes differences in ages: "A 10-year-old Brahmin and a 100-year-old Ksatriya ... stand with respect to each other as father to a son. But of the two, the Brahmin is the father!"[9] In addition, the Harijans, or Untouchables, are below these four castes. Over time, these four castes have been subdivided into over 3,000 sub-castes, which are often linked to particular occupations.

Regarding education and caste, the Dharmasutras specifically excludes certain groups from receiving formal instruction. Eligibility for education is defined in the Dharmasutras: "Those who are not Sudras [and Untouchables] and are not guilty of evil deeds may undergo initiation, undertake Vedic study, and set up the sacred fires; and their rites bear fruit."[10] Women are also not allowed to be educated. Patrick Olivelle, a translator of the Dharmasutras, writes, "women and Sudras cannot be counted among those who know the Veda, for they are explicitly forbidden to learn it."[11] The limited power of women is clearly stated in the Dharmasutras: "A wife cannot act independently in matters relating to the Law. She should never go against her husband and keep her speech, eyes, and actions under strict control."[12]

The prohibition against education of the lower castes remained strong until recent times. "Sudra and Untouchable boys," writes a recent scholar of the caste system, "were not allowed to study or even to hear the sacred texts. In fact until thirty years ago [prior to the Indian Constitution] one of the justifications for prohibiting lower castes from the Brahman streets in South India was this prohibition [against education]—they might overhear Brahmans chanting Sanscrit religious verses."[13]

Inequality before the law is a basic part of the caste system. According to the Dharmasutras, each caste should receive different punishments for the same crime. This is expressed in the Dharmasutras in an interesting statement on the economic value of each caste:

> If someone kills a Ksatriya, he should give a thousand cows to erase the enmity, a hundred if he kills a Vaisya, and ten if he kills a Sudra. In addition a bull is to be given in each as an expiation. The same applies for killing women of these classes.[14]

For Sudras and Untouchables, economic values are also determined by the caste they serve: "Sudras are to serve the other classes; the higher the class they serve, the greater their prosperity."[15]

By offering the possibility of social and economic advancement in the next life, the Dharmasutras provide a more powerful means of controlling social unrest than the ideology of equality of opportunity. The ideology of equality of opportunity relieves social tension by holding out the promise that hard work will result in economic advancement. What happens if a person fails to advance? Failure, under the doctrine of equality of opportunity, is usually explained as the lack of individual effort. But this is an unsatisfactory answer for those feeling that they worked hard and accomplished little. In this situation, frustration can lead to demands for greater economic equality than that provided by the doctrine of equality of opportunity.

In contrast, the caste system can reduce social tensions by guaranteeing that willing servitude in this life will result in economic promotion in the next life. The Dharmasutras state, "By following the righteous path people belonging to a lower class advance in their subsequent birth to the next higher class, whereas by following an unrighteous path people belonging to a higher class descend in their subsequent birth to the next lower class."[16] Therefore, a Sudra can be made to believe that working hard at serving upper castes without wanting or hoping for advancement will result improvement after rebirth. And, they must accept their present condition as the possible result of being unrighteous in a previous life. Caught between past and future lives, a true believer is freed from envy of upper castes which will help reduce economic tensions between castes and encourage an acceptance of social and economic inequalities.

Reinforcing the caste system are an elaborate set of rules governing purity and impurity. The higher the caste, it is believed, the greater the purity and the necessity of avoiding pollution from impure persons and substances. This belief ensures that the lower castes will be engaged in the most menial of labor. For instance, any waste product from a human or animal is impure. According to the caste system, the lower castes are permanently impure and therefore engage in jobs handling impure human waste. Dietary laws also parallel caste with the belief that dead animals pollute the body. Therefore, the purer castes are vegetarians with the middle castes being allowed to eat chicken or mutton and the Untouchables being able to eat pork or beef. Therefore, the concept of purity links caste with particular occupations. The Dharmasutras spells out the lawful occupations of Brahmins, Ksatriya, and Vaisya.[17] As the caste system evolved, each caste was associated with specific occupations.[18]

The occupational structure reflects the interplay between caste and purity. Writing about the contemporary effect of the caste system, Pauline Kolenda describes how the concept of purity functions in the organization of the labor market: "The Barber deals with bodily wastes—hair and nail clippings.... The Sweeper removes human filth; he eats from pots spoiled by birth and death ... he eats left-over food that has touched the mouths of others, or meat from dead animals. So degrees of defilement relate to the ranks in caste hierarchy. The Barber is less defiled than the Washerman, who, in turn, is less defiled than the Sweeper, and so on."[19] Only the lowest castes can work with impure substances, particularly waste and the products of dead animals. So in Northern India, the Sudras are goldsmiths, carpenters, blacksmiths, barbers, washer men, and water carriers, while the Untouchables are shoemakers, leather workers, and sweepers.

Within this occupational structure, the upper castes hold the most esteemed positions, which in the 19th century resulted in the British relying on these castes for the administration and control of India. The Brahmins are the priests and teachers, and the Ksatriya are the rulers, warriors, and scribes. The Dharmasutras specifically states, "Trade is not sanctioned for Brahmins."[20] Lawful occupations for Brahmins "are studying, teaching, sacrificing, officiating at sacrifices, giving gifts, receiving gifts, inheriting, and gleaning, as well as appropriating things that do not belong to anybody."[21] Ksatriya are allowed to study and are also given the tasks of "meting out punishment and warfare."[22] For the Vaisya are reserved the occupations of "agriculture, cattle herding, and trade."[23] The Vaisya are the merchants.

The concept of purity adds a powerful dimension to the caste system, particularly the belief that anything touched by a polluted person can defile those who are considered pure. This idea provides a strong religious base for creating a sense of superiority and inferiority, and social distances between castes. Within this framework, a Brahmin should not take boiled food or water from someone of a lower caste. Brahmins can take raw food from lower castes as long as it is purified by fire or cooking. Also, Brahmins can take food purified by products of the sacred cow such as clarified butter (ghi). The purity of food is directly related to the purity of the body and of the child. According to the Bengali Hindus' theory of conception, the food eaten by the parents is digested and changed into semen and uterine blood which unite in determining the purity of the child's blood. Therefore, the purity of the child is dependent on the purity of the parents. This integration of the physical purity of parents and child provides the final cement to the caste system. Within this framework, marriage should only take place within each caste.[24]

In summary, inequality in every aspect of life, from education to eating, is prescribed in the Dharmasutras. Underpinning this system of inequalities is a belief in reincarnation, and the close relationship between bodily purity and purity of actions. Viewed as an organic whole, the caste system integrates economic class and status with occupations, religion, and families. One is born a Sudra or Untouchable because of past sins that have polluted one's body. By touching the food or person of a higher caste, a Sudra or Untouchable might spread their pollution. This possible pollution justifies segregation. In addition, occupations are passed on within families that are linked to particular castes by the requirement of marrying within one's caste.

BHIMRAO RAMJI AMBEDKAR: AN UNTOUCHABLE IN SEARCH OF EQUALITY

Written in the late 1940s, the Indian Constitution was a product of a global interchange of ideas. The effect of this interchange can be found in the differing proposals of three major contributors to Indian independence and the writing of the constitution. Ambedkar, Gandhi, and Nehru arrived at differing conclusions about the future direction of India. For Ambedkar, the central issue was the abolition of the caste system and the creation of a national constitution. Eventually, Ambedkar's frustration in trying to overcome the inequalities promoted by Hinduism caused him to convert to Buddhism. For Gandhi, the central issue was modern violence, which he considered a product of a centralized state. Consequently, he advocated revamping traditional village structures to make them the source of political power. Influenced by Western socialism, Nehru placed his hope in the development of a welfare state to eliminate social and economic inequalities.

Bhimrao Ramji Ambedkar's life illustrated the cultural blending resulting from the cultural flow of the colonial and post-colonial world. Born an Untouchable, his speeches were laced with Western natural rights concepts, such as his statement, "If you ask me, my ideal would be the society based on liberty, equality and fraternity."[25] English influence over his life began at the time of his birth on April 14, 1891. Ignoring the fact that both his father and mother were Untouchables, the British military, in its efforts to build a colonial army, allowed Ambedkar's father to advance from village servant to army officer and eventually headmaster of a military school. Later in life, Ambedkar would complain about the closing of military opportunities for Untouchables by the British. He told a crowd of Untouchables in 1927, "The military offered us unique opportunities for raising our standard of life and proving our merit and intellect ... It is nothing less than a betrayal and a treachery on the part of the British to have closed the doors of the army to the Untouchables who had helped them establish the Indian Empire while their home Government was at grips with the French during the Napoleonic War."[26]

Despite his father's position in the colonial government, Ambedkar was treated by the rest of Indian society as an Untouchable. In school, he was forced to sit in a corner and his teachers, fearing pollution, refused to touch him. Once, he was asked by a teacher to solve a problem on the chalkboard. The students stored their lunch containers behind the board. Fearing that his presence would pollute their food, the other students hurriedly moved their lunches away before Ambedkar could reach and touch the chalkboard.[27] After struggling with discrimination in high school and college, he eventually became the first Untouchable to graduate from the Elphinstine College in Bombay in 1908. From there he went to New York and London to earn advanced degrees.

While in New York, Ambedkar saw parallels between the plight of the Untouchables in India and African Americans in the United States. He sympathized with the work of Booker T. Washington and the struggle for equal rights for women. Reflecting on the meaning of Washington's life for Ambedkar and other Indians involved in the struggle against the caste system, Ambedkar's Indian biographer, Dhananjy Keer wrote:

> Ambedkar's mind must have been deeply impressed with ... the life of Booker T. Washington whose death occurred in 1915. He was a great reformer and educator of the Negro race in America and was founder and President of the Tuskegee Institute which disseminated among the Negroes the doctrine of *education ... and thus broke the shackles of bondage which had crushed the Negroes for ages physically, mentally and spiritually* [my emphasis].[28]

Also, while in the United States, Ambedkar became acquainted with the 14th Amendment of the U.S. Constitution, which guaranteed equal protection of the laws. Certainly, the equal protection clause was in stark contrast to the unequal application of laws based on caste.[29]

In New York, he wrote letters home advocating equal education for women. Ambedkar placed his faith in education as a means of providing equality and reforming society. In 1911, he wrote to a friend in India, "We ... can mould the destiny of the children; and if we but follow this principle, be sure that we shall soon see better days and our progress will be greatly accelerated if male education is pursued side by side with the female education the fruits of which you can very well see verified in your own daughter."[30]

In England, he studied law and economics, and gained admission to the Bar. He returned to India in 1923 after a 15-year absence to a society still dominated by the caste system. His status in the United States and England was in sharp contrast to his treatment as an Untouchable. Upon his arrival, he could not gain accommodation at any hotel because of his Untouchable status. When he went to work for the government to pay off his college debt, other staff members threw files and papers at him thinking it sinful to give them to him directly. No drinking water was available to him because others feared being polluted. When he started teaching at Sydenham College other professors objected to him drinking water from the pot reserved for the staff.[31]

Given such treatment, it is not difficult to understand why Ambedkar drew parallels between the treatment of Untouchables and discrimination against African Americans in the United States. One can imagine Ambedkar reflecting on segregation laws in the United States that required African Americans to use separate drinking fountains and his own inability to share a common water source with his coworkers.

It is not surprising that Ambedkar demanded social equality in India before independence from Great Britain. In 1919, he wrote to the *Times of India* that independence and home rule were as much a birthright of the Untouchables as it was of the Brahmins. He argued that the first duty of the "advanced classes" was to educate Untouchables to ensure social equality.[32]

The theme of education to achieve social equality continued in his newspaper *Mook Nayak* (Leader of the Dumb), which was first published on January 31, 1920. India, he wrote in the first issue, was the home of social inequality. He portrayed Hindu society as a multileveled tower with no ladders connecting each level. People were doomed to die in the level in which they were born. The aim of the Brahmans, he argued, was to ensure their place at the top of the tower by denying education and power to those below. The depressed state of non-Brahmins, Ambedkar claimed, was a result of their lack of education and unequal political rights.[33]

Paralleling demands for racial equality in the United States, Ambedkar led a march in 1924 demanding equal access to public facilities. At issue was the right of Untouchables to take water from the Chowdar Tank. After leading a successful march, caste Hindus began physically attacking Untouchables out of fear that they would next demand equal access to Hindu temples. Twenty Untouchables were seriously wounded. After the march on the Chowdar Tank, Ambedkar demanded that the British government allow equal access to government property, including water sources.[34]

Ambedkar then demanded affirmative action to ensure that Untouchables had equal access to educational opportunities. In this context, affirmative action meant a conscious attempt by the government to provide special help to those previously denied an education. Regarding equal educational opportunities, Ambedkar argued, "Education is something which ought to be brought within the reach of every one ... If all communities are to be brought to the level of equality, then the only remedy is to adopt the principle of inequality and to give favored treatment to those who are below the level."[35]

In addition, he argued that equal educational opportunity could not be achieved if the education of Untouchables was conducted by Brahmin teachers. He felt that Brahmin teachers would treat Untouchable students worse than dogs. Therefore, he argued, equal educational opportunity required the careful selection of teachers who would be committed to equality.

In 1928, Ambedkar established the Depressed Classes Education Society to advance the cause of equal educational opportunities. One goal of the Society was to provide hostels where students could live while attending high school. The organization immediately encountered the problem of caste Hindus who either were unwilling to provide space for Untouchable students or demanded exorbitant rents. Also, many schools refused admission to Untouchable students.

Again, Ambedkar's biographer compared this educational struggle to the work of Booker T. Washington in the United States. It is not clear whether or not Ambedkar actually made this comparison. However, in the mind of at least one Indian, Dhananjy Keer, the situation was comparable. In his words:

> When the leaders of enslaved humanity rise to lift up their race, those who resort to the political side of the movement arouse hatred of slavery and fan the slaves' passion against their oppressors; but the leaders, who are of reformative zeal, bend inward and preach the doctrine of education of the head, heart and hand. Booker T. Washington ... laid more

stress on the practical education and economic development than on the right of vote.[36]

Eventually, Ambedkar abandoned the Booker T. Washington's approach in favor of political action. In 1929, he argued that education was not enough. In fact, equal educational opportunity was not possible without equal political and social power. Rejecting efforts to reform Hinduism, Ambedkar argued that the only hope for Untouchables was to emigrate to other countries or convert to other religions. In 1935, he declared that "he was born a Hindu" but would "not die a Hindu."[37] The following year, he elaborated on this announcement in an address to a gathering of Untouchables. Again, reflecting the influence of Western thinking, particularly economic ideas, he referred to the struggle between castes as a class struggle and that the only answer was the renunciation of Hinduism. "This is not a feud between rival men," he told the audience of Untouchables, "The problem of untouchability is a matter of class struggle. It is the struggle between caste Hindus and the Untouchables ... This struggle starts as soon as you start claiming equal treatment with others."[38]

Hinduism, Ambedkar warned, was the problem. "The struggle," Ambedkar emphasized, "between the Hindus and the Untouchables is a permanent phenomena. It is eternal, because the religion which has placed you at the lowest level of the society is itself eternal, according to the belief of the Hindu caste people.... You are at the lowest rung of the ladder today. You shall remain lowest forever. This means the struggle between Hindus and Untouchables shall continue forever."[39] Never before in history, Ambedkar maintained, "can we find such inequality, which is more intense than untouchability."[40]

In the end, Ambedkar argued, Untouchables should convert to another religion because Hinduism could not be reformed. The major social evil, from his perspective, was the Hindu religion. Comparing Hinduism to other religions, Ambedkar contented, "Hindus cannot destroy their castes without destroying their religion. Moslems and Christians need not destroy their religions for eradication of their castes. Rather their religions will support such movements to a great extent."[41] Declaring conversion to any other major religion as the easiest way of achieving equality, Ambedkar contended that those "those who have become Moslems, are treated by the Hindus neither as Untouchables nor as unequals. The same can be said of those who have become Christians.... If we can gain freedom by conversion, why should we shoulder the responsibility of reforming the Hindu religion?"[42]

Claiming that many Indians who were Sikhs, Moslems, and Christians were formerly Sudras and Untouchables, Ambedkar concluded his dramatically anti-Hindu speech by linking religious conversion to ideas of equality and liberty:

Conversion brings Happiness

I tell you all very specifically, religion is for man and not man for religion. To get human treatment, convert yourselves.

CONVERT - For getting organized.

CONVERT - For becoming strong.

CONVERT - For securing equality.

CONVERT - For getting liberty.

CONVERT - For that your domestic life may be happy.[43]

As Chair of the Drafting Committee for the new constitution, Ambedkar pressed for a broad range of social reforms, including the outlawing of Untouchability. Gandhi was his major opponent, as I will discuss later, in his efforts to outlaw the entire caste system. Consequently, the final draft of the Indian Constitution limited its reform of the caste system to questions of Untouchability and discrimination between castes. Although the Indian Constitution did not embody Ambedkar's dream of abolishing the caste system, it did try to eliminate the worst forms of caste, religious, and gender discrimination.

Eventually, Ambedkar followed his own advice and converted from Hinduism to Buddhism before a crowd of 800,000 in Deeksha Bhoomi, India, on October 15, 1956. At the time of his conversion, he prescribed 22 vows for conversion from Hinduism to Buddhism that combined his anti-Hindu beliefs with Western ideas of equality. Following are some of the vows reflecting this combination of ideas:

1. I shall have no faith in Brahma, Vishnu and Mahesh nor shall I worship them.

8. I shall not allow any ceremonies to be performed by Brahmins.

9. I shall believe in the equality of man.

10. I endeavor to establish equality.

19. I renounce Hinduism which is harmful for humanity and impedes the advancement and development of humanity because it is based on inequality, and adopt Buddhism as my religion.[44]

GHANDHI AND THEOSOPHY IN THE GLOBAL FLOW

Theosophy had a major impact on Ghandhi's spiritual development. The Theosophy Society promoted comparative religious studies in the United States, England, South Africa, and India. The Theosophical Society was founded in New York City in 1875 under the leadership of Madame Helena Blavatsky. Blavatsky believed that Hinduism and other religions held the key to understanding how to reach higher spiritual levels. Madame Helena Blavatsky was born in Russia in 1831 and left home at the age of 17 to travel to Central Asia, India, South America, Africa, and Eastern Europe. In the United States, she met with others who believed in spiritualism. One of those participating in the founding meeting of the Theosophy Society, Henry Olcott, wrote about the original participants, "present were several old Spiritualists, myself included, of open mind, who ... had acquired a full conviction of [the] existence [of elemental spirits] and of the power of man to subjugate them."[45]

The original principles of Theosophy contained radical ideas for the 19th-century West. One was the call for "universal brotherhood of humanity, without distinction of race creed, sex, caste, or color." This principle reflected the involvement of Western theosophists in struggles against racism and sexism. Western theosophists, such as Annie Besant, joined Indian reformers in trying to outlaw in India the worst forms of discrimination against women and promote the education of women. The second basic principle was "To encourage the comparative study of religion, philosophy, and science."[46] The Theosophy Society and its publishing press played an important role in spreading knowledge about other religions to Western countries. Most Christians and Jews dismissed religions such as Hinduism as being pagan or primitive. The Theosophy Society took these other religions seriously and advocated their close study.[47]

Theosophy had a major influence on Mahatma Gandhi. While born into a devout and strict Hindu family of the Vaisya caste on October 2, 1869, he did not read the great Hindu poem *Mahabhatrata* with its section "The Lord's Song" (*Bhagavad Gita*) until he went to England to study law in 1888. In fact, he had never read a history of India before arriving in London.[48] He was introduced by two English Theosophists to Edwin Arnold's English translation of the *Bhagavad Gita* during his second year in England.

Gandhi's reading of the English version of *Bhagavad Gita* had a profound influence on his life and provided the basis for his use of nonviolence in India's struggle for independence from England. Gandhi wrote about his first experience reading the poem in England, "The book struck me as one of priceless worth. The impression has ever since been growing on me with the result that I regard it today as the book *par excellence* for the knowledge of Truth."[49]

The words of the *Bhagavad Gita* representing Ghandhi's ideals of nonviolence and simplicity were recited shortly after his assassination on January 30, 1948, as friends and relatives sat next to his body. The following words from the work symbolized his life's quest:

> Freedom from pride and pretentiousness; non-violence, forgiveness, up-rightness, service of the Master, purity, steadfastness, self-restraint. Aversion from sense-objects, absence of conceit, realization of the painfulness and evil of birth, death, age and disease.[50]

In England, Gandhi also gained a greater appreciation of Hinduism. An appreciation, according to his reflections, which had been hampered by the work of Christian missionaries in India. Gandhi wrote, in reference to being introduced to a general work on Theosophy in England, "This book stimulated in me the desire to read books on Hinduism, and disabused me of the notion fostered by the missionaries that Hinduism was rife with superstition."[51] In addition, during his stay in England, Gandhi read the New Testament of the Bible and was impressed by the call for nonviolence. Gandhi wrote, "The Sermon on the Mount ... went straight to my heart. I compared it with the *Gita*. The verses, 'But I say unto you, that ye resist no evil: but whosoever shall smite thee on they right cheek, turn to him the other also. And if any man take away thy coat let him have thy cloke too'."[52]

Reflecting the global flow experienced by Gandhi in his first reading of the *Bhagavad Gita*, Jawaharlal Nehru read the book at the age of 11 under the guidance of his English tutor, who was a theosophist. The tutor, Ferdinand T. Brooks, was also good friends with Annie Besant, whose English translation of the *Bhagavad Gita* I am using in this book. Influenced by Besant, Nehru joined the Theosophy society at the age of 13 with Besant doing the initiation. The next year, after leaving for England to continue his education, he claimed to have lost interest in Theosophy and religion in general.[53]

Annie Besant had an important influence on Nehru's family and on social reform in India.[54] Born in 1847, she was known in England as "Red Annie" because of her activities as a militant atheist, socialist, and trade union organizer.[55] Prior to becoming a Theosophist, Besant shocked Victorian England by glorifying sexual intercourse as "perfecting the union of heart and mind."[56] In 1889, she became a Theosophist and eventually president of the International Theosophical Society from 1907 and until her death in 1933. One attractive feature of Theosophy was its declaration of gender equality.

Claiming that in an earlier life she had been born a Brahman, Annie Besant in 1893 traveled to the headquarters of the International Theosophical Society in Adyar, India. In India, she bathed in the Ganges, wore traditional Indian clothes, and translated the *Bhagavad Gita* into English. She lectured throughout India to audiences that included Nehru's family.

Besant's support of Hinduism in India demonstrates the contradictions and compromises made in the global flow of ideas. Upon arrival in India, she glorified Hindu religion by calling it "the mother of spirituality."[57] Indian supporters of women's rights quickly pointed out to her the irony of her praise of Hinduism and Hindu scriptures which denied the right of women to read religious texts. One Indian critic of Hinduism, Kaliprasanna Kavyabisharad, wrote a year after Besant's arrival, "Had Mrs. Besant read any Hindu religious books, in the original, she would not have talked loudly about the Hindu idea of woman, which is known in all its grossness even to primary students and beginners."[58]

By the end of the 1890s, Besant became an advocate of women's education and campaigned against the practice of child marriage and the discrimination resulting from the caste system. Nancy Fix Anderson wrote about this change in attitude, "Besant claimed that purifying Hinduism of such practices as child marriage and the subdivisions of castes was not an imitation of Western ways but was rather a return to the true Hinduism as it existed in ancient days."[59] As part of her promotion of women's education, she founded the Central Hindu College Girls' School in 1904. In 1913, in a series of lectures, she openly attacked orthodox Hinduism for its restrictions of women's rights. In these lectures, she told her audience of primarily Brahman women that India could not become great until men and women "walked side by side and hand in hand."[60]

In 1916, as part of her campaign for India's independence from England, she founded the Home Rule for India League. In 1917, she became the first woman president of the Indian National Congress. At this point in her career, she linked English imperialism to the denial of women's rights in India. She claimed that the English education of Indian men had created a cultural split between the sexes. When she died in 1933, Nancy Fix Anderson wrote, "the outpourings of testimonials and praise included many tributes from Indian feminists who honored her as their inspiration." As Sarojini said, "for the women of India she had done more in her time than any other single Indian woman."[61]

Theosophy and Annie Besant's life illustrate the complex weave of the global flow. Theosophy's advocacy of gender equality and the work of Besant contributed to the stress on women's rights and education in the Indian Constitution. Gandhi worked out his plan for the reform of Hinduism through the guidance of Theosophy and its emphasis on the study of comparative religion. As the first Prime Minister of India, Nehru would be guided by the message of social equality given in the Theosophy creed. In my copy of Annie Besant's translation of the Bhagavad Gita, Besant stated her belief that, "To all such souls in East and West come these divine lessons, for the path is one, though it has many names, and all souls seek the same goal, though they may not realize their unity."[62]

GANDHI: EDUCATION IN THE GLOBAL FLOW

Mahatma Gandhi blended the ideas of radical Europeans, such as Leo Tolstoy and John Ruskin, with Hindu scriptures, which he primarily studied in England and South Africa in an attempt to reform Hinduism according to the principles of equality, communitarianism, nonviolence, classlessness, and rejection of industrialism. It was this combination of Indian and European thought that paved the way for Indian independence. Gandhi's education and religious development exemplifies the intertwining of ideas in the global flow. His education in India was a product of English influence, with the medium of instruction being English. In his autobiography, he expressed disgust for being forced to play the English game of cricket at his Indian high school.

So, rather than studying Indian literature history in India, he studied it in England. Not only was Gandhi's commitment to nonviolence influenced through reading Hindu and Christian texts in England, but so was his commitment to vegetarianism. While in school in India, he joined a meat-eating reform movement designed to drive the British out of the country. The following verse by an Indian poet was popular while he was in school:

Behold the mighty Englishman

He rules the Indian small,

Because being a meat-eater

He is five cubits tall.[63]

Without his family's knowledge, he would gather with friends to eat meat. "I wished," he claimed, "to be strong and daring and wanted my countrymen also to be such, so that we might defeat the English and make India free."[64] He never told his family about this so-called reform movement, but his mother made him take a vow not to eat meat while in England. At first, he found it very difficult to maintain a vegetarian diet in England. But, after some searching, he found a London vegetarian restaurant that carried the publications of the London Vegetarian Society. Through membership in this organization, he became acquainted with a wide variety of vegetarian publications and attended a meeting of the International Vegetarian Conference. Vegetarianism, of course, became an important part of his nonviolence philosophy.

Ironically, it was the influence of Christian missionaries in South Africa that led to a greater understanding of Hinduism. Gandhi's development as a Hindu reformer was directly effected by English policies that resulted in the great Indian Diaspora. With an empire in constant demand for labor, the English had transported Indian workers to Africa and the Caribbean. After Gandhi was admitted to the English bar, he returned to India for a brief period before joining the Indian community in South Africa in 1893. As a lawyer, he was actively involved in political struggles to protect the rights of Indian residents in South Africa. During that time, he continued his study of Hindu and Christian ideas. Shortly after arriving in South Africa, he admitted to Christian lawyer, "I am a Hindu by birth. And yet I do not know much of Hinduism, and I know less of other religions. In fact I do not know where I am, and what is and what should be my belief. I intend to make a careful study of my own religion and, as far as I can, of other religions as well."[65]

Pressured to convert to Christianity, Ghandhi wondered, "And how was I to understand Christianity in its proper perspective without thoroughly knowing I should make a dispassionate study of all that came to me.... I should not think of embracing another religion before I had fully understood my own."[66] While attending church and revival meetings, Gandhi engaged in a comparative study of religion. He joined a group of South African theosophists called the Seekers Club in the study of the *Bhagavad Gita*. It was at this point in his life that the *Bhagavad Gita* became his "dictionary of daily reference."[67]

Eventually, he openly rejected Christianity for Hinduism. His complaint about Christianity was its reliance on Christ for atonement of sins and the limiting of souls to humans rather than believing that all animals have souls. From his perspective, reliance on Christ for forgiveness of sins sometimes caused people to not focus on their own obligation not to sin. Gandhi wrote, "I seek to be redeemed from sin itself, or rather from the very thought of sin."[68] In a discussion with a Christian family about the comparative merits of Christianity and Buddhism, he stated his faith that all living creatures had souls. "Does not one's heart overflow with love to think of the lamb joyously perched on his [Buddha's] shoulders? One fails to notice this love for all living beings in the life of Jesus."[69] After suggesting that the young boy of the family not eat meat out of respect for all living things, the Christian family let Gandhi know that he was no longer welcome in their household.

The study of religious ideas in the global flow, along with his political work, led him to the principles *Brahmacharya* and *Satyagraha*. *Brahmacharya* refers to the control of bodily desires, particularly sexual desires. Combined with fasting, *Brahmacharya* achieves a state of being, according to Gandhi, that is captured in the following passage from the *Bhagavad Gita*:

For a man who is fasting his senses

Outwardly, the sense-objects disappear,

Leaving the yearning behind; but when

He has seen the Highest,

Even the yearning disappears.[70]

Within the Hindu framework that purity and pollution are part of the flesh of the human, the eating of dead animals pollutes both the body and soul of the person. However, under the influence of the international vegetarian movement and Polish-born Herman Kallenbach, who he met in South Africa, Gandhi abandoned milk and cereals so that he could gain greater control over his sexual desires. Noting the influence of the international vegetarian movement, Gandhi wrote, "milk stimulated animal passions. Books on vegetarianism strengthened the idea, but so long as I did not take the *Brahmacharya* vow I could not make up my mind to forego milk."[71] He decided that the ideal diet for *Brahmacharya* was fruits and nuts. Regarding fasting, Gandhi admitted that, "As a rule Hindus allow themselves milk and fruit on a fasting day.... So now I began complete fasting, allowing myself only water."[72]

Satyagraha represented Gandhi's concept of nonviolence. While in South Africa, he offered a prize in the *Indian Opinion*, a South African Indian newspaper he helped establish, for the best suggestion of a word that was stronger than the term *passive resistance*. Gandhi felt that to the English passive resistance merely meant a technique for political struggle used by the weak and that it could be characterized by hatred. Influenced by the concept of love in Christianity and nonviolence in Hinduism, Gandhi wanted a word that would capture the meanings present in these two religions. From the contest, he selected the word *Sadagraha* (Sat = truth, Agraha = firmness). "But," he wrote, "in order to make it clearer I changed the word to Satyagraha which has since become current in Gujarati as a designation for the struggle."[73] The following passages from the *Bhagavad Gita* highlighted the importance of selfless action in Satyagraha:

Who sitteth, controlling the organs of action, but dwelling in his mind on the objects of the senses, that bewildered man is called a hypocrite.

But who controlling the senses by the mind, O Arjuna, with the organs of action without attachment, performth yoga by action, he is worthy.

Perform thou right action; for action is superior to inaction, and, inactive, even the maintenance of thy body would not be possible.[74]

Satyagraha is forceful action without anger. In this context, *Brahmacharya* frees the self from desires that cause anger. In fact, according to the *Bhagavad Gita*, desires lead to anger which leads to the destruction of reason. The goal of *Brahmacharya* is to free oneself from the world of senses and desire so that the individual can attain pure reason. The *Bhagavad Gita* states:

Man, musing on the objects of sense, conceiveth an attachment to these; from attachment ariseth desire; from desire anger cometh forth.

From anger proceedeth delusion; from delusion confused memory; from confused memory the destruction of Reason; from destruction of Reason he perishes.[75]

Consequently, Gandhi's education in the global flow set the stage for the struggle against the British in India. *Brahmacharya* and *Satyagraha* became his methods for creating a classless and stateless society.

While in South Africa, Gandhi was also influenced by the writings of John Ruskin and Leo Tolstoy. Gandhi was impressed by Ruskin's argument that the principal motive governing human life was not the pursuit of wealth but a desire to maintain human relationships. Based on this reasoning, an economy should not be organized to maximize the production of wealth but to ensure positive human relationships. Gandhi adopted this as part of his reform plan for India.[76]

Russian anarchist Leo Tolstoy shaped Gandhi's thinking about communal living. During his stay in South Africa, Gandhi started a lengthy correspondence with Tolstoy. Part of this correspondence was published by Gandhi as the *Letter to a Hindu*. Tolstoy rejected modern industrial society for a simple communal and non-authoritarian society. Agreeing with Tolstoy, Gandhi wrote in 1909, "I have grown disillusioned with Western civilization. The people whom you meet on the way seem half-crazy. They spend their days in luxury or in making a bare living ... unless its whole machinery is thrown overboard, people will destroy themselves like so many moths."[77]

With land donated by his friend Hermann Kallenbach, Gandhi founded Tolstoy Farm in 1910, where he initiated his ideas on communal living. On the Tolstoy Farm, he had the opportunity to practice his ideas about schooling. Tolstoy identified formal schooling as the main mechanism by which the modern state controlled its population. He advocated freedom and noncompulsion in education.[78] As the schoolmaster on the Tolstoy Farm, Gandhi declared "I did not believe in the existing system of education, and I had a mind to find out by experience and experiment the true system."[79] He believed that the most important part of education was spiritual. To achieve this educational goal, he decided that he must be a model for the students. He wrote, "I must be an eternal object-lesson to the boys and girls living with me. They thus became my teachers and I learnt I must be good and live straight, if only for their sakes."[80]

Swept up in the in the global flow and Indian Diaspora, Gandhi returned to India in 1915 to lead the *Satyagraha* for independence, reform Hinduism, and advocate an abandonment of industrialism for the simplicity of traditional Indian village life. Embedded in his newly formed beliefs was the goal of economic and social equality. He believed that these could be achieved through the communitarian village and the rejection of inequalities based on the caste system.

GANDHI: EQUALITY AND THE REFORM OF HINDUISM

On his return to India, Gandhi called for the abolishment untouchability by making Untouchables part of the Sudra caste. Also, he advocated equality between the castes. His vision was a nonviolent Hinduism that promoted equality and love between castes and religions, and supported a classless society. His preaching of cooperation between Hindus and Moslems resulted in his assassination by a militant-nationalist Hindu.

Prior to his experiences in Europe and South Africa, Gandhi had briefly questioned the caste system. An Untouchable was employed by the Gandhi household to clean the toilets. Gandhi was warned that if he accidentally touched the cleaner, he would have to undergo purification rituals. He complained to his mother that untouchability was not sanctioned by Hinduism and that the cleaner was not inferior. His mother simply replied that purification rites were not necessary after touching an Untouchable and that the pollution caused by the contact could be cancelled by touching a Moslem who would be free of Hindu taboos.[81]

This early questioning of Untouchability quickly evolved into rebellion against the power of the caste system. When, in 1887, he decided to go to England to study, his caste leader, the Sheth, refused to grant permission. The Sheth feared that Gandhi would be unable to maintain his religion in a foreign country. Gandhi replied that he intended to go and that his father's friend, a Brahman, raised no objections. In his autobiography, Gandhi wrote that the Sheth asked, "But will you disregard the orders of the caste?" After Gandhi replied that he intended to still go, the Sheth declared, "This boy shall be treated as an outcaste from today. Whoever helps him or sees him off at the dock shall be punishable with a fine of one rupee four annas."[82]

His banishment placed a strain on family relationships. Gandhi recalled,

> I fully respected the caste regulations about excommunication. According to these, none of my relations, including my father-in-law and mother-in-law, and even my sister and brother-in-law, could entertain me; and I would not so much as drink water at their houses. They were prepared secretly to evade the prohibition, but it went against the grain with me to do a thing in secret that I would not do in public.[83]

It was in the 1930s, during the last phases of the independence movement, that Gandhi's differences with Ambedkar became a focus of public attention. As a leader of the Congress, Gandhi envisioned a reformed Hinduism that would flourish with indigenous Indian institutions that were adapted for use in a modern state. He argued that a traditional Indian village could be the basis for a decentralized government. A pacificist, Gandhi believed that a centralized state was the logical product of violence and that nonviolence depended on decentralization. He proposed that the state be a social service organization whose power was derived from village governments. Gandhi believed, historian Granville Austin wrote, that "Resting on this village base would be a stateless, classless society where prime ministers and governments would be unnecessary."[84] In addition, Gandhi, in comparing the hand-operated spinning wheel to mechanized textile plants, objected to the impact of the industrial revolution. Possibly reflecting the impact of Western socialist ideas and the writings of Marx, Gandhi argued, "The present use of machinery tends more and more to concentrate wealth in the hands of a few, in total disregard of millions of men and women whose bread is snatched by it out of their mouths."[85]

In 1932, the British government announced a plan for a democratic India which included a separate electorate for Untouchables or, as they were now officially called, the *Scheduled Castes* and *Depressed Classes*. Gandhi immediately objected to the plan for a separate electorate because it would "vivisect and disrupt Hinduism."[86] He made the dramatic announcement that "in the event of their decision creating a separate electorate for the Depressed Classes, I must fast unto death."[87]

After the British Prime Minister Ramsay MacDonald announced the creation of a separate electorate for Moslems, Sikhs, Europeans, Christians, and Scheduled Castes, Gandhi declared his intention to fast unto death on September 20, 1932. Gandhi did not object to representation of these groups in an Indian parliament, but he believed that treating them as separate electorates would result in major divisions in Indian society and cause irreparable conflicts within Hinduism. He believed that the treatment of Untouchables as a separate group by law would undo his attempts to reform Hinduism. Gandhi wrote to MacDonald, "In the establishment of a separate electorate for the Depressed Classes I sense the injection of poison that is calculated to destroy Hinduism.... "[88]

At 11:30 on the morning of September 20th , Gandhi took his last meal and declared that while born a touchable, he was now an Untouchable by choice. He then declared the abolition of Untouchability as essential for the preservation of Hinduism:

> What I want, and what I am living for, and what I should delight in dying for, is the eradication of untouchability root and branch.... I believe that if untouchability is really rooted out, it will not only purge Hinduism of a terrible blot but its repercussions will be world-wide. My fight against untouchability is a fight against the impure in humanity.[89]

On the fourth day of the fast, Gandhi approached death's door as his blood pressure reached alarming heights, and he could no longer walk and had to be carried to the bathroom. Fearing his imminent death, British and Hindu leaders hurried to work out a compromise. The compromise had to be acceptable to both Gandhi and Ambedkar, who wanted to ensure representation of the Scheduled Castes in the future Indian parliament. A compromise plan was reached through a primary system that guaranteed representation for the Scheduled castes without creating separate electorates. The compromise ended Gandhi's fast.

Gandhi's fast focused national attention on the inequalities of the caste system. Throughout India, Hindus opened their temple doors to the Scheduled Castes, permitted them to use village wells, and touched them. Many Hindus observed Untouchability Abolition Week. According to Gandhi's biographer, "The fast could not result in the demise of untouchability, but it would never be the same again. Orthodox Hinduism was shaken."[90]

On January 30, 1948, after preparing a constitutional proposal to enhance the political power villages, Gandhi was slain by a militant Hindu while on his way to an evening prayer meeting. The assailant, Nathuram Godse, objected to Gandhi's attempts to create a unified India where Moslems and Hindus could live in peace. Rejecting nonviolence and British rule, Godse wrote that India belonged to Hindus because "they have no other place which they can call their own ... To the Hindus largely this country owes its fame and glory, its culture and art, knowledge, science and philosophy."[91]

From a historical perspective, Gandhi's major contributions were the use of nonviolent methods to force the end of British rule and his efforts to reform Hinduism by demanding equality between the castes. Later, India's first Prime Minister Jawaharlal Nehru argued that the Congress "never considered" Ghandhi's decentralization vision of society, "much less adopted it."[92] From Nehru's standpoint, the adoption of a democratic, centralized parliamentary constitution was an adoption of Western culture to Indian needs. Nehru wrote in *The Unity of India* published in 1948:

> As of old, India seeks a synthesis of the past and the present, of the old and the new. She sees the new industrial civilization marching irresistibly on; she dislikes it and mistrusts it to some extent, for it is an attack against and an upheaval of so much that is old; yet she has accepted that industrial civilization as an inevitable development. So she seeks to synthesize it with her own fundamental conceptions, to find a harmony between the inner man and his ever changing outer environment.[93]

Gandhi's ideals of nonviolence quickly entered the global flow and influenced other struggles against oppression. His biography contains a 1968 *Chicago Sun-Times* cartoon published shortly after the assassination of Martin Luther King, Jr. King is standing and looking down on Gandhi seated on the ground. Gandhi is explaining to King that, "The odd thing about assassins, Dr. King, is that they think they've killed you."[94]

"Gandhi," King wrote in his early description of the U.S. civil rights movement, *Stride Toward Freedom: The Montgomery Story*, "was probably the first person in history to lift the love ethic of Jesus above mere interaction between individuals to a powerful and effective social force on a large scale." King was convinced that nonviolent philosophy of Gandhi "was the only morally and practically sound method open to oppressed people in their struggle for freedom."[95]

Ambedkar and Gandhi can be credited with having major influence over provisions in the 1949 Constitution outlawing Untouchability and discrimination based on caste. Also, Annie Besant's legacy can be found in the outlawing of discrimination based on gender. However, the actual wording of the Constitution's Fundamental Rights section reflected a study of the United States' Constitution. In his history of the writing of the Indian Constitution, Granville Austin states, "A.K. Ayyar explained to the Rights Sub-Committee that the U.S. Constitution laid down civil rights in a general fashion and the scope of the rights had been narrowed and expanded by judgements of the Supreme Court."[96] Consequently, looking to the concepts surrounding U.S. rights in the global flow, the writers included specific limitations on concepts of equality. In addition, rights were framed according to the specific requirements of India, which included a concern about discrimination based on caste.

For instance, Article 15 of the Fundamental Rights section of the Indian Constitution specifically refers to caste and includes an important limitation:

15. Prohibition of discrimination on grounds of religion, race, caste, sex or place of birth.

   (1) The State shall not discriminate against any citizen on grounds only of religion, race, caste, sex, place of birth or any of them.

   (2) No citizen shall, on grounds only of religion, race, caste, sex, place of birth or any of them, be subject to any disability, liability, restriction or condition with regard to—

      (a) access to shops, public restaurants, hotels and places of public entertainment; or

      (b) the use of wells, tanks, bathing ghats, roads and places of public resort maintained wholly or partly out of State funds or dedicated to the use of the general public.[97]

Interestingly, these provisions parallel the civil rights efforts in the United States to end racial segregation in public accommodations and housing. The important restriction placed on this discrimination is:

   (4) Nothing in this article or in clause (2) of article 29 shall prevent the State from making any special provision for the advancement of any socially and educationally backward classes of citizens or for the scheduled Castes and the Scheduled Tribes.[98]

The reference to "clause (2) of article 29" deals specifically with education. One of the major shortcomings of the U.S. Constitution is the lack of provision for education. Article 29 (2) of the Indian Constitution states:

No citizen shall be denied admission into any educational institution maintained by the State or receiving aid out of State funds on grounds only of religion, race, caste, language or any of them.[99]

And, of course, the major triumph of Ambedkar and Gandhi is Article 17 abolishing status of being Untouchable.

17. Abolition of Untouchability: "Untouchability" is abolished and its
     practice in any form is forbidden. The enforcement of any disabil-
     ity arising out of "Untouchability" shall be an offence punishable
     in accordance with law.[100]

NEHRU

Jawaharlal Nehru embraced socialism and rejected religion for Western science and industrialism. He exerted immense influence as President of the Indian National Congress from 1946 to 1954 and as India's
first Prime Minister (1947–1964). For Nehru, the central issues were
economic equality and equality of opportunity. Within Nehru's framework, the purpose of education was industrial development and providing equal economic opportunity for all. A barrier to his dreams was
the continued power of Hinduism and the caste system.

In contrast to the rather humble origins of Ambedkar and Ghandhi,
Nehru was born on November 14, 1889, into a wealthy Brahman family
that mimicked Western styles. Writing about his father, Nehru described,
"He was attracted to Western dress and other Western ways at a time
when it was uncommon for Indians ... Full of the spirit of play and fond of
good living in every way, he found no difficulty in spending what he
earned. And gradually our ways became more and more Westernized."[101]
As a result, Nehru was raised by English governesses and tutors.

His family paid little attention to his religious education. "Of religion," he recalled, "I had very hazy notions ... Father and my older
cousins treated the question humorously and refused to take it seriously."[102] In fact, his father flaunted his scorn of Hindu religion by refusing to undergo purification rights after returning from European
visits. Similar to Gandhi's caste, the Brahman community was divided
over the issue of pollution caused by contact with foreigners. One
Brahman, Pandit Bishan Narayan, had traveled to England to obtain
admission to the Bar. On his return, orthodox Brahman considered
him an outcast despite undergoing purification rites. This resulted in a
division between foreign travelers, who were considered outcasts, and
other caste members. Nehru's father went one step further and refused, according to Nehru, "to go through any ceremony or to submit in
any way, even outwardly and formally, to a so-called purification. A
great deal of heat was generated chiefly because of father's aggressive
and rather disdainful attitude."[103]

As mentioned previously, Nehru was introduced to the *Bhagavad
Gita* by his Theosophist tutor Ferdinand T. Brooks. Brooks also introduced Nehru to English literature, particularly children and boy's literature. In one of those ironies of the global flow and an example of

cultural hegemony, Nehru's favorite books included Rudyard Kipling's Indian novels *Kim* and the *Jungle Book.*[104]

Nehru claims to have been aware of the contradiction between the Anglization of his household and British control of India. He recalled that his childhood family conversations often reflected on the insulting manners of the English towards Indians. In addition, his childhood was surrounded by the privileges granted Europeans, from special railroad compartments to reserved chairs and benches in parks. He wrote about his childhood, "I was filled with resentment against the alien rulers of my country who misbehaved in this manner, and whenever an Indian hit back I was glad."[105] At the age of 14, he recalled, "I mused of Indian freedom and Asiatic freedom from the thraldom of Europe. I dreamt of brave deeds, of how, sword in hand, I would fight for India and help in freeing her."[106]

Ironically, it was his education in England that prepared him to overthrow the yoke of English domination and profess a new direction for the development of India. At 15, he was shipped off to England to attend Harrow, the elite boarding school. Two years later, he entered Cambridge University. He admitted that his life at Cambridge was devoted to soft and pleasant experiences influenced by the ideas of sexual freedom of Havelock Ellis, Kraft Ebbing, and Oscar Wild. However, he and other Indians did form a society called the Majlis to discuss political problems in India.

It was at Cambridge that Nehru came to the conclusion that Indian nationalism was reactionary because it was a form of religious nationalism. Despite his later loyalty to Gandhi, he would also consider Gandhi's religious emphasis as reactionary. While at Cambridge, he was introduced to socialism and other radical politics. However, after returning to India in 1912 as a lawyer, he adopted a life which he characterized, using the language of Marxism, as: "My politics had been those of my class, the bourgeoisie ... represented especially [by] the handful of the upper middle class who had on the whole prospered under British rule ... [and] close relations with the British Government and the big landlord class."[107]

Nehru claims his radicalization took place in 1920, when the British colonial government ordered him to not have contact with a visiting Afghan delegation. Refusing to obey the order, Nehru suddenly was plunged into a political movement that result in his contact with India's poor. He wrote about this contact, "I was filled with shame and sorrow, shame at my own easy-going and comfortable life ... which ignored this vast multitude of semi-naked sons and daughters of India, sorrow at the degradation and overwhelming poverty of India. A new picture of India seemed to rise before me, naked, starving, crushed, and utterly miserable."[108]

Rather than caste, Nehru focused on the issue of economic class and ownership of the means of production. His path to equality became socialism. He placed British imperialism in the context of industrial development. Writing in 1928, he admitted that India was not as industrialized as other nations but, he argued, the industrialization of Europe caused European nations to seek raw materials and markets. The result was British economic imperialism, which brought India into an international system of industrialization. Consequently, he argued, Indian independence should not be thought of in terms of nationalism, but in terms of economic equality within a global economic system. "The world," he wrote, "has become internationalized. Production is international, markets are international and transport is international."[109]

Consequently, Nehru argued, political independence was not enough. What was required was a battle against capitalism. Sounding like a European Marxist, Nehru wrote, "Capitalism necessarily leads to exploitation of one man by another, one group by another. If therefore, we are opposed to this imperialism and exploitation, we must also be opposed to capitalism. The only alternative that is offered is some form of socialism."[110] According to this view, rebellion against England had to include rebellion against capitalism.

It is within this socialist framework that he attacked the caste system. "Another consequence of the socialistic view is that we must change all customs which are based on privilege and caste. We must cast out all parasites and drones, so that they who lack the good things of life may share in them."[111] He believed that the call for "Indianization" of government offices would only favor the Brahmin and upper classes. The Indian leadership was largely ignoring the mass of people in their quest to enhance their economic position through independence. "It is essential," he wrote, "that we must clearly lay down an economic programme for the masses with socialism as its ideal."[112]

For Nehru, religion stood in the way of achieving equality through socialism. He reacted with strong anti-religious sentiments to Gandhi's 1932 fast-to-death over the issue of a separate electorate for Untouchables. He believed in the use of Gandhi's non-violent methods and he recognized Gandhi's appeal to the masses. But, similar to Karl Marx, Nehru believed that religion distracted from the real sources of inequality. For instance, he argued that the British claimed the highest ethical standards based on Christianity while following a predatory policy in Asia and Africa. Protestantism, he contended, gradually accommodated "big business." Religion, from his perspective, primarily protected the monied groups. Writing about religion in India, he argued, "Almost always it seems to stand for blind belief and reaction, dogma and bigotry, superstition and exploitation, and the preservation of vested interests."[113] Turning to Western philosophers, Nehru found his answer in the writings of American educator and philosopher, John Dewey:

> A very modern definition of religion, with which the men of religion will not agree, is that of Professor John Dewey. According to him, religion is "whatever introduces genuine perspective into the piecemeal and shifting episodes of existence"; or again "any activity pursued in behalf of an ideal end against obstacles, and in spite of threats of personal loss because of conviction of its general and enduring value, is religious in quality."[114]

Nehru's secularism was combined with a belief in the power of science to improve society. In arguing that youth should focus on social inequalities, he warned, "Like the old man of the sea, religion has mounted our backs and effectively prevented all progress and advancement."[115] Nehru argued that youth should study science for the reform of society. He contended, "The universities have much to teach in the modern world and their scope of activity ever enlarges. I am myself a devotee of science and believe that the world will ultimately be saved, if it is to be saved, by the method and approach of science."[116]

Nehru's vision of a socialist society guided by the supposedly impartial hand of science required the expansion of educational opportunity. Education, from his perspective, would provide the labor force needed for industrial development. Higher education would provide the scientific labor force needed to guide society. "We say," Nehru declared, "that we require education for the purpose of achieving the national aims and social objectives of free India, and in particular, to train the right type of personnel for the speedy execution of our development plans."[117] He declared it the duty of the state to provide a free education to every child in the country.

Of primary concern, from Nehru's perspective, was equal educational opportunity for women. This was important, he argued, because women had the primary role of child care. Their education directly influenced the development of a whole generation of workers. In addition, women would be a source of labor for the development of India. Therefore, part of his plea for increasing women's educational opportunities, was opening up the occupational structure to the employment of women. "The idea that women should be kept away from most occupations," he contended, "no longer finds favor."[118]

Social class attitudes, Nehru felt, restricted the use of education for the purposes of economic development. Traditional attitudes—meaning the caste system—reinforced the idea that intellectual work was only suited for the upper classes. "I doubt," he stated, "if any other thing had done more harm to India than this particularly fantastic notion that manual labor is meant for some lower classes and that the high-class person should not move his hand and should only do what is called mental and intellectual work."[119] In reference to women's education and employment, Nehru complained, "Unfortunately, the idea has been prevailing ... that the less work one does the higher is one's status in society. Thus the person who never works at all has the highest status."[120]

Besides providing equality of opportunity and a labor force for economic development and the rule of science, education was considered a means of creating national unity. In this regard, Nehru worried that India's many languages would hinder the development of a sense of national unity. In addition, there was the problem of the English language imposed by the British. Nehru argued that, "Some people imagine that English is likely to become the *lingua franca* of India. That seems to me a fantastic conception, except in respect of a handful of upper-class intelligentsia. It has no relation to the problem of mass education and culture."[121] However, Nehru did not believe that independence from England should result in not teaching English in India. Recognizing the imperialism of the English language, Nehru argued, "English is ... undoubtedly the most widespread and important world language, and it is gaining fast on the other languages. It is likely to become more and more the medium of international intercourse and radio broadcasting."[122]

The issue of language was hotly debated during the writing of the Constitution. Hindi was decided upon as the national language. However, there was still the question of other minority languages and the use of minority languages in education. Nehru worried, "The real problem will remain: as to what policy we shall adopt in a scheme of general mass education and the cultural development of people; how shall we promote the unity of India and yet preserve the rich diversity of our inheritance?"[123]

A problem in using Hindi as the national language was that at the time of the writing of the Constitution it was not universally known in India. Consequently, a transitional period was needed to allow time for a general education program in Hindi. This transitional period gave new life to the use of English. English would be the official language for a 15-year period after the acceptance of the Constitution. The Constitution stated:

> 343. Official language of the union. (1) The official language of the Union shall be Hindi ... (2) For a period of fifteen years from the commencement of this Constitution, the English language shall continue to be used for all the official purposes of Union.... [124]

In summary, Gandhi's death and Nehru's assumption of leadership of the new nation meant that rather than trying to create a decentralized society based on a vision of traditional Hindu values, India would take the path of industrialization, scientific progress, socialism, and secularization. Western socialism guided Nehru's advocacy of equality of opportunity in an industrialized economy based on national planning. Rather than education serving Gandhi's purpose of developing a religious person and protecting a reformed Hinduism, education under Nehru would serve the goals of building an industrial society.

CONSTITUTIONAL PROVISIONS FOR EDUCATION

The secular and socialist spirit that guided Nehru and his followers is reflected in the educational provisions of the Indian Constitution. The Indian Constitution is a model for provisions regarding education. In addition, the educational provisions of the Indian Constitution recognized the importance of minority languages and cultures. In part, this is a reflection of concerns about the domination of English culture and language. Also, as part of the proclamation of independence from England, Nehru and other Indian leaders felt that education should contribute to the evolution of Indian culture and civilization. These goals are clearly expressed in the first report issued by the University Education Commission created by the Indian Government shortly after independence in 1948.

The following represent the important constitutional provisions for a free, equal, and secular education:

28. (1) No religious instruction or religious worship shall be provided in any educational institution wholly maintained out of the State funds.

45. Provision for free and compulsory education for children. The State shall endeavor to provide, within a period of ten years from the commencement of this Constitution, for free and compulsory education for all children until they complete the age of fourteen.

46. Promotion of educational and economic interests of the scheduled castes, scheduled tribes and other weaker sections. The State shall promote with special care the educational and economic interests of the weaker sections of the people, and, in particular, of the scheduled castes and the scheduled tribes, and shall protect them from social injustice and all forms of exploitation.[125]

Not only does the Indian Constitution grant the right to a free secular education, but it also provides the right for special attention to the education of disadvantaged social groups. These constitutional provisions reflect a commitment to the role of an active socialist state in archiving some level of economic equality.

A unique feature of the Indian Constitution is its protection of minority language rights. Most countries face the issue of maintaining a national language while protecting the interests of cultural and linguistic minorities. The Indian Constitution states:

> 350. Facilities for instruction in mother-tongue at primary stage. It shall be the endeavor of every State and of every local authority within the State to provide adequate facilities for instruction in the mother-tongue at the primary stage of education to children belonging to linguistic minority groups.[126]

The role of education in economic and cultural development in an independent India was outlined by the University Education Committee appointed in 1948 shortly after independence. One Indian educational scholar, J. C. Aggarwal, claimed that, "The report of the Commission is a document of great importance as it has guided the development of university education since independence."[127] Filled with references to Western philosophers such as Plato, Kant, and Newman, the Commission's report argued that the role of the university was central to economic development: "It is for the universities to create knowledge and train minds who would bring together the two—material resources and human energies. If our living standards are to be raised, radical change of spirit is essential."[128] The goal of the university system, the report argued, was to help create a new social order that would protect the principles of "democracy, justice and liberty, equality and fraternity."[129] This new social order would include the cultural unity of India.

The global vision and human rights emphasis of the Commission's report predates Western concerns with educational globalization by almost 30 years.[130] One reason for this visionary conceptualization was the reality of India's role in the world economic system that was created by the British. In addition, the report was written at the same time that India was participating in the drafting of the Universal Declaration of Human Rights. Within the framework of a global economy, the report argued that the development of Indian cultural unity must include a critical study of the past wedded to a new nationalism that recognized the existence of a global economy. The report argued, "The setting for the development of a world culture through the cross fertilization of cultures is ready. The world had become, through speed of transportation and communication and economic interdependence, a *single body* [my emphasis]."[131] In addition, the report contended that global education must be related to human rights. To overcome a nationalism based on self-righteousness and unreasoning, the report contended, students must "accept the inter-dependence as well as the individuality of all men, we must develop a sensitivity to the hopes and fears, needs and emotions of human beings everywhere. A programme of education for world citizenship should be made a part of every person's general education."[132]

THE PURSUIT OF EQUALITY IN INDIAN EDUCATION

Caste and gender discrimination remain the most difficult obstacles to achieving equal educational opportunity in India. The caste system remains alive and well though changing in urban areas. On June 17, 2000, newspapers reported the slaughter of "34 people, mostly women, children and old men from a low-caste community" in Patna, India. Dressed in black, the gunmen were, according to the police, "members of an upper-caste militia backed by rich landlords." The attack was one of eight caste-related armed attacks over the previous 6 months. Reflecting the ongoing importance of caste as a social classification in India, the victims were reported to include "26 members of the Yadav community of cattle herders, six Dalits—members of the lowest rung of India's caste hierarchy—and two people of another low caste."[133]

The continuing importance of gender and caste in defining educational opportunities is indicated in the previously discussed Table 5.1. This table does suggest some improvement, with the literacy rate for all Indian women tripling between 1961 and 1991. However, it still remained at the low level of 39.29 % as compared to the 64.13% for all males. The literacy rate for lower caste females increased almost seven times but still remained at the low level of 23.76% in 1991. The literacy rate in 1991 for lower caste males of 49.91% still remained behind the all-India percentage of 64.14.

Many reports attested to the difficulties of overcoming caste and gender discrimination in education. A 1964 report of the National Council for Women's Education points out that despite the Constitution providing *de jure* equality for women, "Nevertheless, women continue to suffer from a number of social and economic handicaps." The Council urged the reduction in the gap between male and female education.[134] A 1978 report of the University Grants Commission complained that, "access to them [colleges and universities] is selective and is mostly availed of by the top social groups, either because they can afford the costs involved or because ... existing methods of selection show a high correlation with social status."[135]

The value system of education remained dominated by the British model. English continued as the medium of instruction in elite schools. In fact, the 1978 University Grants Commission's report complained that the educational system was not developing the character needed for a cooperative socialist society but still continued to emphasize the British values of "narrow individualism, unhealthy competition to the neglect of social good."[136]

The top arts and science college selected by the magazine *India Today* in 1998 exemplifies the continued influence of the British model, the English language, and social class. The top college was St. Stephen's, Delhi, which was described this way: "Perhaps the last repository of the Oxbridge culture in India, St. Stephen's has often been accused of being a finishing school, a networking society and even a dilettante's paradise.... To successive generations of Calcutta's elite, however, one of its attributes has remained constant: it is the place where you acquire that lifelong chip on the shoulder."[137] The reputation of the college was based in part on its "English literature faculties" and student societies, such as the Shakespeare and Wodehouse societies. Mixing class and caste in its description, *India Today* stated, "There are day scholars and boarders, but in the college hierarchy 'gentlemen (and since last year, ladies) in residence' are the brahmins."[138]

The continued lack of educational equality in any form in India might be a result of the low level of government financial support. Economic indicators presented in UNICEF's *The State of the World's Children 1999: Education* specify that the percentage of the Indian's government expenditures allocated between 1990 and 1997 were 1% for health, 2% for education, and 13% for defense. The contrast between the 2% for education and 13% for defense suggests that national leaders are more concerned with their ongoing dispute with Pakistan and their place among world powers than with achieving equal educational opportunities. The full impact of India's limited support of education is highlighted in Table 5.2, which compares India's government expenditures with those in other parts of the world.

The comparisons in Table 5.2 show a dramatic lack of effort by the Indian government to fund education. The percentage allocated by the Indian national budget for education is only one third that of the rest of the world. The difference with other developing countries is shocking, with India spending about one fifth that of others (2% versus 11%). Also, India leads the way in defense spending, with the highest percentage devoted to the military. Equally shocking is the 1% of government expenditures devoted to health. Health can be considered a prerequisite for obtaining any form of equality, including equal educational opportunity.

Based on the preceding figures, I would argue that along with the continuing effect of the caste system, the lack of government spending for education has been the greatest roadblock in achieving equal educational opportunities for Scheduled Castes and women. Unless there are concrete actions to remedy centuries of discriminatory behavior, the constitutional promises to promote equality are meaningless.

TABLE 5.2

Comparison of India's Government Expenditures With Other Countries

	% of Government Expenditures for Health	% of Government Expenditures for Education	% of Government Expenditures for Defense
India	1	2	13
World	11	6	9
Industrialized Countries	13	4	9
Developing Countries	4	11	11
Least Developed Countries	5	13	4

Source: Carol Bellamy, *The State of the World's Children 1999: Education* (New York: UNICEF, 1999), pp. 115, 117.

THE CASE OF THE MISSING WOMEN

Highlighting gender inequality are the 37 million women who are statistically missing from the Indian population as estimated by economist Amartya Sen. Female infanticide and abortion of female fetuses help reduce the population of women. However, Sen argues, "The main culprit would seem to be the comparative neglect of female health and nutrition, especially during childhood. There is indeed considerable direct evidence that female children are neglected in terms of health care, hospitalization and even feeding."[139] Besides the basic issue of equality, the right to life is an important measure of freedom. Premature death severely restricts the freedom of the person to act. The Hindu bias against women promotes inequality and takes away freedom.

CONCLUSION: THE LESSONS OF INDIA

Colonized by England, India could not escape the influence of Western ideas. The global flow mixed Hindu and Western traditions. Gandhi's Satyagraha against the British became a worldwide symbol of the struggle against oppression. The struggle against Untouchability and the disparities created by the caste system used Western concepts of social class, racial, and gender inequalities. It is not difficult to understand the parallels Ambedkar made between the segregation and discrimination encountered by African Americans in the United States and the plight of the Depressed or Scheduled Castes in India.

In addition, the writers of the Indian Constitution recognized the problem of minority cultures and languages that were largely ignored by other constitutions, such as the U.S. Constitution. They might have been more sensitive to this issue because of the imposition by British colonialism of the English language and culture. Maybe the U.S. Constitution and later amendments never recognized the problem of minority cultures and languages because the United States acted as an imperial power in conquering Native Americans, Northern Mexico, and Puerto Rico. The U.S. educational system continues to struggle over the issue of language and culture.

A great deal can be learned from the Indian struggle for independence and the resulting constitution. Of particular importance is the constitutional provision for providing special efforts and funding to help traditionally subjugated groups. Writers of the Indian Constitution were aware of the limitations placed on the U.S. government by the failure of the U.S. Constitution and its later amendments to allow for subjugated groups to receive special help without violating the spirit of equality under the law. As I stated before, the Indian Constitution in its section on fundamental rights, including the right not to be discriminated against, added this important qualification:

> Nothing in this article or in clause (2) of article 29 shall prevent the State from making any special provision for the advancement of any socially and educationally backward classes of citizens or for the scheduled Castes and the Scheduled Tribes.[140]

In addition, the Constitution provides for special educational help to oppressed groups. As I quoted before, Article 46 of the Indian constitution specifically calls for the: "Promotion of educational and economic interests of the scheduled castes, scheduled tribes and other weaker sections."

These constitutional provisions recognize that equality in any form cannot be achieved unless those who have been traditionally oppressed receive extra help to bring them to the social, educational, and economic level of traditionally privileged groups. In countries such as the United States, there has been a continuing debate about whether special help for women and minority populations is a violation of the constitutional requirement of equality before the law. This debate could be ended and past inequities corrected with a similar amendment being put in the U.S. Constitution.

Is it the resiliency of Hinduism and Hindu traditions that results in the continued gap between the educational achievements of women and men, and between the Scheduled Castes and other castes? Is it impossible to create equality in a society where religion dictates social class? In part, the answer might be yes! Despite independence and a Western constitution, the majority of people might remain unaffected by these constitutionally mandated changes. The lesson, one could argue, is that in spite of the impact of the global flow and Western imperialism, local cultures are slow to change.

On the other hand, the Indian government failed to adequately fund its educational efforts. Militarism placed education in the backseat of government concerns. The writers of the constitution hoped that education could lift the masses from the bondage of the upper castes. Under slavery in the United States and the rule of the Dharmasutras, the oppressed were denied an education. Now under the rule of law, the oppressed in India are still denied an education because of the unwillingness of leaders to spend more money. Therefore, educational and constitutional reform must be accompanied by a commitment to use economic resources.

But circumstances are changing. Consider the impact of the introduction of computers. In Embalan, India, *New York Times* writer Celia Dugger describes, "the century-old temple has two doors. Through one lies tradition. People from the lowest castes and menstruating women cannot pass its threshold.... Through the second door lies the Information Age, and anyone may enter."[141] Behind the second door are two solar powered computers approved by the village elders. On these computers, 14-year-old V. Aruna is learning Word and PowerPoint. The daughter of a farmer, she expresses the hope that, "If I can get a job through this, I'll be happy. I want to work instead of sitting in the house."[142]

Although the temple is bound by Hindu tradition, the computer is not discussed in the Dharmasutras. However, the vast majority of Web sites are in English, and only 5% of the Indian population knows English. Of course, these figures present a dilemma since the goal is to maintain Hindi while overcoming the imperialism of the English language. But the upper castes learn English while attending elite schools. In addition, the continued low literacy rates for women and scheduled castes contributes to a growing gap in computer literacy.

Within this clash between Hindu tradition and the intentions of the Indian Constitution there is in fact a slowly evolving greater degree of equality before the law, equality of opportunity, and gender equality. Realistically, the evolution of these forms of equality must take place within the context of Hindu traditions. Comparison of the time line in race relations in the United States with the time line for caste relations in the India demonstrates the long period of time required to change attitudes. Slavery ended in the United States in the 1860s, while the status of Untouchable ended in the 1940s. The difference is roughly 80 years, or three to four generations. In the United States, despite continued struggles, race is still related to income, health, and educational inequalities. Therefore, based on the American experience, one could assume that caste and gender will remain major sources of inequality in India throughout the 21st century.

6

A Constitutional Provision for Educational Rights

I will conclude this book by proposing a constitutional provision for educational rights that reflects my intercivilizational analysis of educational ideas and my examination of national constitutions. I will refine some of the exemplary educational rights statements found in national constitutions so that they more clearly promote equality of educational opportunity and take into account intercivilizational conflicts. Certainly, the most challenging issue is that of religion as exemplified by the strong references to religious laws in the constitutions and statements about human rights from Islamic countries. The adherence to Islamic religious law is sharply different from the secular nature of Western, Indian, and Chinese constitutions. Also, India, the West, and Islam have different concepts of rights as compared to China and the Confucian tradition which considers rights as secondary to social duties. Of course, one could argue that Islam's emphasis on religious duties might be close to the Confucian concept of social duty. However, it is important to understand that the Confucian concept of duty is related to society and not to a metaphysical being or idea.

Also, what I have identified as the global culture of education uses human capital models that measure educational outcomes with economic indicators. To a certain extent this is also true of the West and India. While Chinese government is interested in the contribution of education to socialist modernization, it does place emphasis on the traditional Confucian concern that education should maintain the social good, or in the case of China, support a socialist society. Islamic nations tend to be more concerned about the religious well-being of society than the use of human capital methods to determine the value of education. Overall, it is important to consider the role of human capital regarding educational rights and equality of educational opportunity.

Educational rights are part of the human rights doctrines that entered the global flow after World War II. As a human right, educational rights are justified by their contribution to human welfare. In the context of Confucianism and the Chinese Constitution, rights that promote human welfare are also duties. People have a duty to work for the welfare of others and for a peaceful and harmonious society. Education is not only an individual right but also a duty because of its contribution to the good of others. Therefore,similar to the Chinese Constitution, the right to education should be stated as, "Everyone has the duty as well as the right to receive an education."

If education is considered a duty and right necessary for human welfare, then all people should receive equal benefits from this right. In other words, all people should have equal educational opportunities. The problem is creating a constitutional provision for ensuring equality of educational opportunity.

There are several dimensions to ensuring equality of educational opportunity. First is family wealth. Any constitutional provision must recognize the ability of wealthy families to purchase superior educational advantages for their children. A constitution can never compensate for all the cultural and educational advantages of growing up in a wealthy and privileged family. Even the Constitution of the People's Republic recognizes different family economic circumstances in Article 6: "The system of socialist public ownership supersedes the system of exploitation of man by man; it applies the principle of 'from each according to his ability, to each according to his work'."[1] The second issue is the child's access to adequate nutrition, shelter—particularly for street children—and medical care. These are necessary conditions for receiving an adequate education. Third, there is the issue of making higher education free to all.

At best, the constitutional right to education can only ensure equal access to educational institutions regardless of a child's economic circumstances. The Turkish Constitution provides a model for rectifying the problems of differences in wealth with its provision that, "The state shall provide scholarships and other means of assistance to enable students of merit lacking financial means to continue their education. The state shall take necessary measures to rehabilitate those in need of special training so as to render such people useful to society."[2] The one problem I have with the Turkish Constitution is the vagueness of the phrase "enable students of merit." Merit can be defined from many different perspectives. Sometimes "merit" is a reflection of social class when it is measured by culturally biased tests. Therefore, I would not use that wording.

Realistically, even with provisions for financial aid and protection of children's welfare, complete equality of educational opportunity cannot be achieved. There are so many variables, including differences in peer groups, access to cultural institutions, the culture of families, and even geographical locations, such as rural versus urban living. Therefore, the best that can be hoped for is maximizing the chance of achieving equality of educational opportunity. The following constitutional provision would help increase the chances for achieving this goal:

(A) Everyone has the duty as well as the right to receive an education.

(B) Primary, secondary, and higher education shall be free. Primary and secondary education shall be compulsory until the age of 16.

(C) The government will ensure through financial assistance, scholarships, or other means that no one is denied an education or access to an educational institution because of lack of financial resources, including resources for food, shelter, and medical care.

The educational background of the family might also play a role in preventing full exercise of the right to education. This is recognized in the Indian Constitution with regard to scheduled castes and women. In the United States similar circumstances might exist in families of former enslaved Africans who were denied an education or with other dominated groups, such as Native Americans. Therefore, there should be some constitutional provision to ensure equal educational opportunity for groups formerly discriminated against by educational systems. As stated earlier, Article 46 of the Indian Constitution declares, "The state shall promote with special care the educational and economic interests of the weaker sections of the people, and, in particular, of the scheduled castes and the scheduled tribes, and shall protect them from social injustice and all forms of exploitation." Using this article as a model, I would propose the following addition to the duty and right to education.

(D) The government will promote with special care and financial resources the educational interests of racial, ethnic, language, religious, and gender groups formerly discriminated against by the public and private educational system. The government will protect these groups from social injustice and all forms of exploitation.

As I have noted throughout this book, language rights are an important educational issue. First is the problem of educational equality when classroom instruction is presented in a language that is different from the family language of the student. In this circumstance, the student is at a disadvantage compared to pupils whose home language is the same as the language of instruction. Second is the issue of minority language rights. Destruction of a language can contribute to the destruction of a culture. Therefore, minority languages should be recognized and supported by the school. On the other hand, students from minority language families need to learn the dominant language of their country if they are going to have equal political and economic opportunities. Third is the issue presented by those demanding instruction in Qur'anic Arabic. Should public schools teach what is essentially a religious language?

Tove Skutnabb-Kangas has proposed " A Universal Covenant of Linguistic Human Rights" which states:

Everybody has the right

- to identify with their mother tongue(s) and to have this identification accepted and respected by others

- to learn the mother tongue(s) fully, orally (when physiologically possible) and in writing

- to education mainly through the medium of their mother tongue(s), and within the state-financed educational system

- to use the mother tongue in most official situations (including schools).

Other Languages

- whose mother tongue is not an official language in the country where s/he is resident ... to become bilingual (or trilingual, if s/he has 2 mother tongues) in the mother tongue(s) and (one of) the official language(s) (according to her own choice).

The Relationship Between Languages

- to any change ... [in] mother tongue ... [being] voluntary (includes knowledge of long-term consequences) ... [and] not imposed.

Profit from Education

- to profit from education, regardless of what her mother tongue is.[3]

The Indian Constitution comes closest to the spirit of this Covenant with the declaration that, "It shall be the endeavor of every State and of every local authority within the State to provide adequate facilities for instruction in the mother-tongue at the primary stage of education to children belonging to linguistic minority groups."[4]

While many constitutions recognize minority languages, there are often no provisions for ensuring that these languages will receive educational support. For instance, the Chinese Constitution declares, "The state promotes the nationwide use of Putonghua."[5] It also states, "The people of all nationalities have the freedom to use and develop their own spoken and written languages, and to preserve or reform their own ways and customs."[6] However, there is nothing in the Chinese Constitution dealing with the language to be used in the classroom, nor any suggestion that classroom instruction might be given in the mother-tongue of the student. The Italian Constitution is equally vague with its statement, "The Republic shall safeguard linguistic minorities by means of special provisions."[7] The "special provisions" are never clearly defined. To give substance to the right of minority languages to "develop" requires a more explicit statement regarding language rights in the school system.

The educational protection of minority languages is contrary to the language policies of many countries. One of the most restrictive clauses is in the Turkish Constitution, which states, "No language other than Turkish shall be taught as a mother tongue to Turkish citizens at any institutions of training or education."[8] France makes no provision for language minorities, and Article 2 of the French Constitution states, "The language of the Republic is French."[9] Skutnabb-Kangas' Covenant does recognize the importance of instruction for all students in the official or dominant language of a nation. The Covenant would require nations to recognize and support instruction in minority languages while maintaining their official languages.

However, there is a concern regarding the educational rights of minority languages when there are only a limited number of students speaking a language. This is particularly a problem in a country with a high number of immigrants. Should the government be required to provide classes in a mother tongue that is spoken by only one or two students in a community? Some requirement must be added that this right can only be exercised when there are enough students speaking the same minority language to make it economically feasible to operate classrooms in that minority language. Considering this realistic problem the Covenant can be rewritten to state:

(E) Everyone has a right to an education using the medium of their mother-tongue within a government-financed school system when the number of students requesting instruction in that mother-tongue equals the average number of students in a class-room in that government-financed school system.

Of equal importance is learning the dominant or official language of society. Therefore, an addition to the right to learn minority languages should state:

(F) Everyone has the right to learn the dominant or official language of the nation. The government-financed school system will make every effort to ensure that all students are literate in the dominant or official language of the country.

The other issue is the teaching of Qur'anic Arabic and other religiously oriented languages, such as Hebrew. The problem for some constitutional systems is the separation of church and state. The Establishment Clause of the First Amendment to the U.S. Constitution is used to bar any school instruction that might support some religion. However, the Free Exercise Clause of the First Amendment forbids the government to interfere with the free practice of religion. The problem in interpreting these two clauses is this: When does government non-support of religiously related instruction interfere with the free exercise of religion?

A corrective to the dilemma presented by the First Amendment of the U.S. Constitution is Article 18 of the Universal Declaration of Human Rights, which provides the right to have religious beliefs reflected in "teaching" while at the same time recognizing the right to change religions. Article 18 states:

Everyone has the right to freedom of thought, conscience and religion; this right includes freedom *to change* his religion or belief, and freedom, either alone or in community with others and in public or private, to manifest his religion or belief in *teaching*, practice, worship and observance.[10]

Any genuine expression of religious rights must recognize the relationship between education and religion. The right to education must recognize the importance of religious rights. Therefore, instruction in religious languages in government-financed schools is an important educational right. This does not mean that classroom instruction should be conducted in a religious language but that language instruction should be offered. However, similar to the issue of minority languages, there must be enough students requesting a class in a language. Therefore, the following language right should be added to the list of educational rights,

(G) Everyone has the right to instruction in a language used for religious purposes, such as Qur'anic Arabic or Hebrew, within a government-financed school system when the number of students requesting instruction in that language equals the average number of students in a classroom in that government-financed school system.

The discussion of religious languages opens the broader issue of religion and education. Most Islamic states subordinate laws and education to religious dogma. The reader will remember that constitutions such as that of Pakistan make specific references to the teaching of Islamic religious principles: "The state shall endeavor, as respects the Muslims of Pakistan to make the teaching of the Holy Qur'an and Islamiat compulsory ... [and] to promote unity and the observance of the Islamic moral standards.... "[11] The Universal Islamic Declaration of Human Rights declares the right to education within the context of religious precepts.

The religious rights of Islam, and other groups, should be recognized and guaranteed. But the problem is that Islamic nations often discriminate against women and other religions. Of course, a woman should have the right to willingly submit to religious practices even if they violate principles of gender equality. The question in Islamic countries is whether or not parents and children can freely choose religious-oriented schooling and whether women can freely submit to religious strictures. The example of persecuted female foreign workers in Saudi Arabia highlights the many cases when religious standards are imposed rather than being freely accepted. In other words, religious freedom should include the right to submit and right to refuse to obey religious laws.

Religious rights applied to education should mandate the right to choose a secular or religious education. Pupils should not be forced to receive a religious education, but they should also be allowed the choice of a religious education. A model for this can be found in the 1950 European Convention which incorporated into the Treaty for the European Union. Currently, the European Union includes within its jurisdiction a variety of religions, including Islam. The Convention declares, "the State shall respect the right of parents to ensure such education and teaching in conformity with their own religious and philosophical convictions."[12]

In order to combine both the right to a religious education and the right to a secular education, I would propose the following:

(H) The duty and right to an education includes the right to a secular or religious education financed by the government. No student will be forced to receive a religious education.

Religious schools often limit the right of freedom of speech and access to information in education. Islamic constitutions specifically place religious boundaries around this right. The Chinese constitution limits this right in the name of public order, safety, and interests. In fact, most constitutions place some limitations on this right. Freedom of speech also has different meanings across civilizational lines. Confucianism and the Chinese Constitution recognize freedom of speech as a political method for criticizing government officials. And the Universal Islamic Declaration of Human Rights declares that everyone has the right to say what is right.

One answer to the dilemma posed by the intercivilizational differences over freedom of speech can be found in that part of the 1950 European Convention which gives parents the right to choose an education that is in conformity with their "philosophical beliefs." While this approach does not guarantee freedom of speech and access to information within schools, which is impossible with the recognition of the right to a religious education, it does present the opportunity for ideological freedom between schools.

The idea of ideological freedom between schools poses a threat to nationalistic forms of education. Many nations consider their school systems as a means of making citizens loyal to the state and its ideological goals. For example, the Chinese Constitution proclaims the goal of education to be "building of socialist spiritual civilization" and "love of motherland."[13] The Syrian Constitution states, "nationalist socialist education is the basis for building the unified socialist Arab society."[14] These are only two of many examples that could be cited regarding the use of schooling to achieve the ideological objectives of the state.

Also problematic are the limits to be placed on the "philosophical beliefs" of the parents. Should parents have the right to demand government financing of schools that teach terrorism or the overthrow of the government? Should parents have the right to government-financed schools that teach racial hatred and advocate genocide? An answer to these questions, which are often presented as objections to full-choice plans based on philosophical differences, is that choice should be limited by the requirement that schools do not teach anything that violates the Universal Declaration of Human Rights.

School choice based on philosophical differences is also a means of combating the uniformity in educational systems being created by the global culture and economy. The relentless march to human capital education may stifle the growth and development of human thought through its high-stakes tests, its commitment to linking education to economic development, and its support of a mass consumption. In hopes of achieving labor market efficiency, high-stakes testing standardizes school knowledge.

Of course, no one should be denied the choice of participating in the schools spawned by the global economy. Perhaps comodification of most aspects of life and mass consumption are the keys to the good life. However, some civilizations, such as Hinduism, have been built on spiritual values that deny the importance of material goods. One of many lines from the Bhagavad-Gita reflecting this sentiment is, "Whoso forsaketh all desires and goeth onwards free from yearnings, selfless and without egoism—he goeth to Peace."[15]

Besides standing as a barrier to the growing uniformity of the global culture and economy, school choice based on philosophical convictions can protect minority cultures, particularly indigenous cultures, from extinction. Historically, school systems have been used in attempts at cultural genocide. The sad story of Native American education in the United States involves government removal of children from their families and placement in boarding schools where they were not allowed to use their mother tongues, wear traditional clothing, observe their customs, or practice their religions. The heavy hand of European and Japanese imperialism attempted to destroy local cultures.

Cultural rights is an important issue when trying to improve, change, or find alternatives to the uniformity of global culture. Philosophical convictions in school choice can include the right to choose an education that reflects a particular culture. This decision should include the content and methods of instruction. To achieve this objective and to support alternatives to the uniformity of global culture, I would propose the following:

(I) The duty and right to an education includes the right of parents to choose a government-financed school based on their philosophical convictions and cultural values as along as that school does not advocate or teach anything that violates rights granted in the Universal Declaration of Human Rights. The exercise of this right is dependent on enough parents making the same choice based on philosophical convictions and/or cultural values to make it financially feasible for the government to operate the school.

(J) The right of the parents to choose a government-financed school based on their philosophical convictions and/or cultural values includes the right for their philosophical convictions and/or cultural values to be reflected in the content and methods of instruction.

This proposal will be most controversial with governments that support highly nationalistic forms of education. Just as controversial will be the following proposal on school funding. As I discussed, the failure of the Indian government to achieve its literacy goals for women and scheduled castes is directly related to the small portion of the government budget allotted to education while allocating a large portion to military spending. This disproportionate spending exists in Pakistan and other countries. Since education is now considered essential for human welfare, and defense spending actually might detract from human welfare, I would propose the following:

> (K) Except in the time of war, the total government funds allocated for education should always exceed the total of government funds allocated for the military, weapons research, and other forms of defense spending.

CONCLUSION

In summary, I propose the following amendments to the world's constitutions. These amendments are based on my intercivilizational analysis of educational rights. They recognize education as a requirement for human welfare and define education as both a right and a social duty. They are designed to include concerns of world religions, particularly those of Islam. They will help provide a corrective to, or improvement on, the growing uniformity of global education. These propositions encompass the natural rights and human capital concerns of the West, the religious concerns of Islam, the spiritual and equalitarian concerns of India, and the stress on social harmony and public order in China. These propositions are not meant to satisfy all civilizational needs. But they do represent an attempt to balance the objectives of universal human rights doctrines with differing civilizational perspectives. They are founded on the belief that the improvement and stability of the world's future depends on some compromise between civilizational beliefs and human rights. In order to achieve this objective with regard to education, I submit the following constitutional amendment:

The Duty and Right to Receive an Education

> (A) Everyone has the duty as well as the right to receive an education.

> (B) Primary, secondary, and higher education shall be free. Primary and secondary education shall be compulsory until the age of 16.

> (C) The government will ensure through financial assistance, scholarships or other means that no one is denied an education or access to an educational institution because of lack of financial resources, including resources for food, shelter, and medical care.

> (D) The government will promote with special care and financial resources the educational interests of racial, ethnic, language, reli-

gious, and gender groups formerly discriminated against by the public and private educational system. The government will protect these groups from social injustice and all forms of exploitation.

(E) Everyone has a right to an education using the medium of their mother-tongue within a government-financed school system when the number of students requesting instruction in that mother-tongue equals the average number of students in a classroom in that government-financed school system.

(F) Everyone has the right to learn the dominant or official language of the nation. The government-financed school system will make every effort to ensure that all students are literate in the dominant or official language of the country.

(G) Everyone has the right to instruction in a language used for religious purposes, such as Qur'anic Arabic or Hebrew, within a government-financed school system when the number of students requesting instruction in that language equals the average number of students in a classroom in that government-financed school system.

(H) The duty and right to an education includes the right to a secular or religious education financed by the government. No student will be forced to receive a religious education.

(I) The duty and right to an education includes the right of parents to choose a government-financed school based on their philosophical convictions and cultural values as along as that school does not advocate or teach anything that violates rights granted in the Universal Declaration of Human Rights. The exercise of this right is dependent on enough parents making the same choice based on philosophical convictions and/or cultural values to make it financially feasible for the government to operate the school.

(J) The right of the parents to choose a government-financed school based on their philosophical convictions and/or cultural values includes the right for their philosophical convictions and/or cultural values to be reflected in the content and methods of instruction.

(K) Except in the time of war, the total government funds allocated for education should always exceed the total of government funds allocated for the military, weapons research, and other forms of defense spending.

Notes

Chapter I

[1]Onuma Yasuaki, "Toward an Intercivilizational Approach to Human Rights," in *The East Asian Challenge for Human Rights*, edited by Joanne Bauer and Daniel Bell (Cambridge: Cambridge University Press, 1999), p. 119.

[2]Ibid., p. 105.

[3]Ibid., p. 105.

[4]Ibid., pp. 103–124.

[5]Ibid., p. 110.

[6]The American Declaration of Independence can be found in a number of places. One on-line source is *U.S. Historical Documents Archive, http://w3.one.net/~mweiler/ushda.*

[7]"Henry, Patrick," *Microsoft® Encarta® 98 Encyclopedia.* © 1993–1997 Microsoft Corporation. All rights reserved.

[8]UNESCO, *Human Rights: Comments and Interpretations: A Symposium edited by UNESCO* (Westport, CT: Greenwood Press, 1973).

[9]Chung-Shu Lo, "Human Rights in the Chinese Tradition," Ibid., p. 186.

[10]Ibid., p. 186.

[11]Ibid. p. 188.

[12]S. V. Puntambekar, "The Hindu Concept of Human Rights," *Human Rights: Comments and Interpretations* ... , p. 197.

[13]Ibid., p. 197.

[14]Ann Elizabeth Mayer, *Islam and Human Rights: Tradition and Politics* (Boulder, CO: Westview Press, 1999), p. 26.

[15]Ibid., p. 21.

[16]Quoted in Ibid., p. 203.

[17]Paul Gordon Lauren, *The Evolution of International Human Rights: Visions Seen* (Philadelphia: University of Pennsylvania, 1998), p. 5.

[18]Ibid., p. 11.

[19]See Arjun Appadurai, *Modernity at Large: Cultural Dimensions of Globalization* (Minneapolis: University of Minnesota Press, 1996).

[20]See Arjun Appadurai, *Modernity at Large: Cultural Dimensions of Globalization* (Minneapolis: University of Minnesota Press, 1996).

[21]Ibid.

[22]Ibid., p. 36.

[23]I develop this argument in Joel Spring, *Education and the Rise of the Global Economy* (Mahwah, NJ: Lawrence Erlbaum Associates, 1998).

[24]Maenette Kape 'ahiokalani Padeken Ah Nee-Benham with Joanne Elizabeth Cooper (Eds.), *Indigenous Educational Models for Contemporary Practice: In Our Mother's Voice* (Mahwah, NJ: Lawrence Erlbaum Associates, 2000), p. xxi.

[25]Spring.

[26]National Commission on Excellence in Education, *A Nation at Risk* (Washington, DC: U.S. Government Printing Office, 1983).

[27]See Joel Spring, *The American School 1642–2000* (New York: McGraw-Hill, 2001), pp. 420–439.

[28]See Joel Spring, *Education and the Rise of the Global Economy* (Mahwah, NJ: Lawrence Erlbaum Associates, 1998), pp. 37–69.

[29]Ibid., pp. 70–91.

[30]C. Douglas Lummis, "Equality," in *The Development Dictionary: A Guide to Knowledge as Power* (New York: Zed Books, 1992), p. 45.

[31]Ibid., p. 45.

[32]Ibid., p. 45.

[33]Ibid., p. 45.

[34]"Convention on the Rights of the Child, 1989," in *Basic Documents on Human Rights Third Edition*, edited by Ian Brownlie (New York: Oxford University Press, 1994), p. 187.

[35]As an example of the controversies over the intellectual content of public school instruction, see Joel Spring, *American Education 9th Edition* (New York: McGraw-Hill, 1999), pp. 3–27.

[36]"Convention on the Rights of the Child, 1989," p. 187.

[37]"Convention Against Discrimination in Education, 1960," in *Basic Documents ...* , p. 319.

[38]Ibid., p. 320.

[39]Ibid., pp. 320–321.

Chapter 2

[1]Barry Keenan, *The Dewey Experiment in China: Educational Reform and Political Power in the Early Republic* (Cambridge: Harvard University Press, 1977), pp. 9–36.

[2]David L. Hall and Roger T. Ames, *The Democracy of the Dead: Dewey Confucius, and the Hope for Democracy in China* (Chicago: Open Court, 1999), pp. 141–144.

[3]"Constitution of the People's Republic of China (Adopted on December 4, 1982)" in *Education and Socialist Modernization: A Documentary History of Education in the People's Republic of China, 1977–1986*, edited by Shi Ming Hu and Eli Seifman (New York: AMS Press, 1987), p. 156.

[4]De Bary, Theodore, "Preface," *Confucianism and Human Rights*, edited William Theodore De Bary and Tu Wei-ming (New York: Columbia University Press, 1998), pp. ix–xvi.

[5]"Confucius Culture University Opens in East China," *Peoples' Daily* (16 May 2000), *http://www.peopledaily.com.cn/english/200005/16/eng20000516_40878.html*.

[6]"Confucius Popular on Chinese Website," (19 March 2000), *http://www.peopledaily.com.cn/english/200003/19/eng20000319R102.html*.

[7]Wei-Ming, Tu, "Introduction," *Confucian Traditions in East Asian Modernity: Moral Education and Economic Culture in Japan and the Four Mini-Dragons*, edited by Tu Wei-Ming (Cambridge: Harvard University Press, 1996), p. 7.

[8]Jonathan Mirsky, "Taiwan Stand Up," *The New York Review of Books* Vol. xlvii, No. 11 (29 June 2000), p. 37

[9]Confucius, *The Analects*, translated by D.C. Lau (New York: Penguin Books, 1979), p. 143.

[10]Irene Bloom, "Mencian Confucianism and Human Rights," in *Confucianism and Human Rights* ... , p. 96.

[11]Ibid., p. 98.

[12]Confucius, p. 86.

[13]Herbert Fingarette, *Confucius: The Secular as Sacred* (Prospect Heights, IL: Waveland Press, 1972), p. 19.

[14]D. C. Lau, "Introduction," in Confucius, *Analects* ... , p. 11.

[15]Bloom, p. 105. D.C. Lau's translation of the *Analects* represents the first two lines of this quotation as "Wealth and high station are what men desire but unless I got them in the right way I would not remain in them. Poverty and low station are what men dislike, but even if I did not get them in the right way I would not try to escape from them."

[16]Bloom, p. 102.

[17]Ibid., p. 101.

[18]Ibid., p. 102.

[19]Ibid., p. 102.

[20]Fingarette, p. 55.

[21]Fingarette, pp. 42–44.

[22]Ibid., p. 30.

[23]Confucius, p. 63.

[24]Wei-Ming, Tu, p. 9.

[25]Onuma Yasuaki, "Toward An Intercivilizational Approach to Human Rights," in *The East Asian Challenge for Human Rights*, edited by Joanne R. Bauer and Daniel A. Bell (Cambridge: Cambridge University Press, 1999), p. 107.

[26]Wm. Theodore De Bary, "Confucian Education in Premodern East Asia," in *Confucian Traditions in East Asian Modernity* ... , pp. 21–38.

[27]Confucius, *The Doctrine of the Mean*, in James Legge, *Confucius: Confucian Analects, The Great Learning & The Doctrine of the Mean: Chinese; Translation with Exegetical Notes and Dictionary of all Characters* (New York: Dover Publications, Inc., 1971), p. 413.

[28]Ibid., p. 414.

[29]Ibid., pp. 23–28.

[30]Ibid., p. 24.

[31]Ibid., p. 73.

[32]Chang Hao, "The Intellectual Heritage of the Confucian Ideal of Ching-Shih ... ," p. 76.

[33]Ibid., p. 73.

[34]Wm. Theodore De Bary, *Asian Values and Human Rights: A Confucian Communitarian Perspective* (Cambridge: Harvard University press, 1998), p. 17.

[35]Ibid., p. 20.

[36]Mencius, *The Works of Mencius*, translated by James Legge (New York: Dover Publications, 1970), pp. 249–250.

[37]Chang Hao, "The Intellectual Heritage of the Confucian Ideal of Ching-Shih," in *Confucian Traditions in East Asian Modernity* ... , p. 80.

[38]Wm. Theodore De Bary, *Asian Values and Human Rights* ... , p. 27.

[39]Confucius, p. 121.

[40]Joseph Chan, "A Confucian Perspective on Human rights for Contemporary China," in *The East Asian Challenge for Human Rights* ... , p. 228.

[41]Ibid., p. 229.

[42]Chenyang Li, *The Tao Encounters the West: Explorations in Comparative Philosophy* (Albany, NY: State University of New York Press, 1999), p. 109.

[43]Ibid., 110.

[44]Ibid., p. 112.

[45] Wm. Theodore De Bary, *Asian Values and Human Rights* ... , p. 121.

[46]Ibid., pp. 121–122.

[47]Ibid., p. 120.

[48]Constitution of the People's Republic of China ... , p. 156.

[49]Ibid., p. 156.

[50]Deng Xiaoping, "Building A Socialism With A Specifically Chinese Character, June 30, 1984," *Selected Works of Deng Xiaoping, www.peopledialy.com.cn/english/*, p. 1.

[51]Ibid., p. 1.

[52]Philip Short, *Mao: A Life* (New York: Henry Holt and Company, 1999), p. 31.

[53]Ibid., p. 33.

[54]Ibid., p. 33.

[55]"Sakuma Shozan: Reflections on My Errors, 1855," in Herbert Passin, *Society and Education in Japan* (New York: Teachers College Press, 1965), p. 202. For a general history of the attempt of Japanese leaders to balance Western learning with traditional culture see Joel Spring, *Education and the Rise of the Global Economy* (Mahwah, NJ: Lawrence Erlbaum Associates, 1998), pp. 37–70.

[56]Byron Marshall, *Learning to Be Modern: Japanese Discourse on Education* (Boulder, Colorado: Westview press, 1994), pp. 25–26.

[57]Short, p. 38.

[58]Ibid., p. 32.

[59]Peter Zarrow, "Human Rights in Twentieth-Century Chinese Thought," in *Confucianism and Human Rights* ... , pp. 209–234.

[60]Ibid., p. 216.

[61]Ibid., p. 215.

[62]Ibid., p. 216.

[63]Ibid., p. 217.

[64]Wm. Theodore De Bary, *Asian Values* ... , p. 112.

[65]Ibid., p. 113.

[66]Ibid., p. 114.

[67]Merle Goldman, "Confucian Influence on Intellectuals in the People's Republic of China," in *Confucianism and Human Rights* ... , p. 262.

[68]"Constitution of the People's Republic of China ... ," p.155.

[69]Philip Short, *Mao: A Life* (New York: Henry Holt and Company, 1999), p. 357.

[70]"Constitution of the People's Republic of China ... ," p. 156.

[71]Ibid., p. 25.

[72]Short, p. 78.

[73]Ibid., p. 94.

[74]Ibid., p. 104.

[75]Ibid., pp. 112–113.

[76]Ibid., pp. 97–98.

[77]Ibid., pp. 310–311.

[78]Mao Zedong, "Sixty Points on Working Methods—A Draft Resolution from the Office of the Center of the CCP" in *Mao Papers: Anthology and Bibliography*, edited by Jerome Ch'en (London: Oxford University Press, 1970), p. 68.

[79]Ibid., p. 68.

[80]Mao Zedong, "Directive on Re-Education of Intellectuals" in *The Maoist Educational Revolution* edited by Theodore Hsi-en Chen (New York: Praeger Publishers, 1974), p. 273.

[81]Mao Zedong, "The May the Seventh Instruction" in *Mao Papers* ... , p. 104.

[82]Ibid., p. 104.

[83]Confucius, *The Doctrine of the Mean* ... , pp. 395–396.

[84]"Decision of the Central Committee of the Chinese Communist Party Concerning the Great Proletarian Revolution," in Chen, p. 236.

[85]Short, p. 460.

[86]Ibid., p. 458.

[87]Ibid., p. 458.

[88]Ibid., p. 466.

[89]Ibid., p. 466.

[90]Goldman, p. 262.

[91]Jennifer Lee, "China's Censor Is Customer No. 1," *The New York Times on the Web* (16 August 2000), p. 3.

[92]Ibid., p. 1.

[93]"White Paper Refutes Dalai's Allegation of Tibet Culture Extinction," *People's Daily* (22 June 2000), *http://www.peopledaily.com.cn/english/20000622*, p. 1.

[94]Ibid., p. 1.

[95]"Li Ruihuan on National and Traditional Culture," *People's Daily* (10 May 2000), *http://www.peopledaily.com.cn/english/20000510*, p. 1.

[96]Ibid., p. 1.

[97]"Jiang Expounds Principles of Respect for Sovereign Equality, Human Rights," *People's Daily* (8 September May 2000), *http://www.peopledaily.com.cn/english/20000908*, p. 1.

[98]"Constitution of the People's Republic of China," *http://www.insidechina.com/constit/chcons01.php3*, p. 5.

[99]Ibid., p. 5.

[100]Ibid., p. 6.

[101]"Donald Tsang Reiterates IT Education Strategy," *People's Daily* (4 June 2000), *http://www.peopledaily.com.cn/english/200006/4*, p. 1.

[102]Ibid., p. 7.

[103]Ibid., p. 2.

[104]Ibid., p. 7.

[105]Ibid., p. 14.

[106]Ibid., p. 10.

[107]Ibid., p. 13.

[108]Ibid., 13.

[109]Ibid., p. 14.

[110]Ibid., p. 14.

[111]Amartya Sen, *Development as Freedom* (New York: Alfred A. Knopf, 1999), pp. 104–107.

[112]Ibid., p. 105.

[113]UNICEF, *The State of the World's Children 2000* (New York: UNICEF, 2000), pp. 108–109.

[114]Erik Eckholm, "For Chinese Students, Fate is a Single Exam," *The New York Times* (10 July 2000), p. A1.

[115]Ibid., p. A1.

[116]Ibid., p. A1.

[117]Ibid., A4.

[118]Ibid., A4.

[119]See Spring, pp. 37–92. In this section, I detail the Confucian traditions embodied in the current school systems in Singapore and Japan.

[120]Hall and Ames, pp. 143–145.

Chapter 3

[1]Jeffrey Goldberg, "The Education of a Holy Warrior," *The New York Times Magazine* (25 June 2000), pp. 32–37, 53,63–64,70.

[2]*Al-Qur'an* translated by Ahmed Ali (Princeton: Princeton University Press, p. 200).

[3]This translation is provided by Akhtar Emon, "A Case for Qur'anic Arabic—Arabic as a Second Language," *http://islamcity.com/Education/asl.htm,* p. 2.

[4]*Al-Qur'an*, p. 223.

[5]Akhtar Emon, p. 7.

[6]Ibid., p. 10.

[7]*The Sayings of Muhammad,* selected and translated from Arabic by Neal Robinson (Hopewell, NJ: Ecco Press, 1991), pp. 24–25.

[8]*Al-Qur'an*, p. 34.

[9]Ibid., p. 35.

[10]Ibid., p. 71.

[11]Ibid., p. 83.

[12]Goldberg, p. 35.

[13]Ibid., p. 35.

[14]*Al-Qur'an*, p. 45.

[15]Ibid., p. 45.

[16]Quoted in Ann Elizabeth Mayer, *Islam and Human Rights: Tradition and Politics* (Boulder, CO: Westview Press, 1999), p. 27.

[17]Quoted in Ibid., p. 27.

[18]Amin Maalouf, *The Crusades Through Arab Eyes* (New York: Shocken Books, 1984), pp. 19–36.

[19]Ibid., p. 39

[20]Ibid., p. 39.

[21]Ibid., p. 50.

[22]Ibid., pp. 50–51.

[23]Ibid., pp. 176–200.

[24]Ibid., p. 200.

[25]Ibid., p. 259.

[26]Ibid., p. 261.

[27]Ibid., p. 264.

[28]For this history see Amartya Sen, *Development as Freedom* (New York: Alfred Knopf, 1999), pp. 243–244.

[29]See Bassam Tibi, *Arab Nationalism: Between Islam and the Nation-State* (New York: St. Martin's Press, 1997), pp. 78–79.

[30]Ibid., p. 225.

[31]Ibid., p. 85.

[32]Ibid., p. 85.

[33]Ibid., p. 85.

[34]Ibid., p. 91.

[35]Ibid., p. 93.

[36]Ibid., p. 148.

[37]Ibid., p. 148.

[38]Ibid., p. 148.

[39]Ibid., p. 148.

[40]Ibid., p. 208.

[41]Ibid., pp. 203–208.

[42]"Iran—Constitution," http://www.uni.wuezburg.de/law/ir00000_.html, p. 1.

[43]Ibid., p. 3.

[44]Ibid., p. 20.

[45]Ibid., p.6.

[46]Ibid., p. 3.

[47]Ibid., p. 5.

[48]Ibid., pp. 9–10.

[49]Ibid., p. 6.

[50]Ibid., p. 10.

[51]Ibid., p. 8.

[52]Ibid., p. 4.

[53]Ibid., p. 9.

[54]Ibid., p. 9.

[55]Amina Wadud, *Qur'an and Woman: Rereading the Scared Text From a Woman's Perspective* (New York: Oxford University Press, 1999).

[56]*Al-Qur'an*, p. 39.

[57]Ibid., p. 73.

[58]Wadud, p. 4.

[59]Ibid., p. 26.

[60]*Al-Qur'an*, pp. 48–49.

[61]Ibid., p. 74.

[62]Wadud, pp. 85–86.

[63]*Al-Qur'an*, p. 78.

[64]Wadud, p. 74.

[65]Ibid., pp. 90–91.

[66]The Associated Press, "Citing Islamic Law, Taliban shut Bakeries That Aided Widows," *The New York Times on the Web* (17 August 2000), p. 1.

[67]Ibid., pp. 1–2.

[68]Mayer, p. 115.

[69]Susan Sachs, "In Iran, More Women Leaving Nest for University," *The New York Times on the Web* (22 July 2000), p. 3.

[70]Mayer, pp. 113–117.

[71]UNICEF, *The State of the World's Children 2000* (New York: UNICEF, 2000), p. 97.

[72]Sachs, pp. 1–2.

[73]Ibid., p. 4.

[74]"Syria Constitution," *www.uni-wuerzburg.de/law/sy00000_.html*, p. 1.

[75]"Libya-Constitution," *www.uni-wuerzburg.de/law/li00000_.html*, p. 1.

[76]"Iraq-Constitution," *www.uni-wuerzburg.de/law/iz00000_.html*, p. 3.

[77]"Saudi Arabia—Constitution," *www.uni-wuerzburg.de*, p. 2.

[78]Ibid., pp. 1,3.

[79]Ron Lajoie, "Behind the Veil," *Amnesty Now* (Summer 2000), pp. 4–7.

[80]Ibid., p. 7.

[81]"Syria—Constitution," pp. 4–5.

[82]"Libya—Constitution," p. 2.

[83]Ibid., p. 2.

[84]Ibid., p. 2.

[85]"Pakistan—Constitution," Part I, Introductory, *http://www.stanford.edu/group/pakistan/constitution*, p. 1.

[86]Ibid., p. 4.

[87]"The Constitution of the Republic of Turkey," *http://byegm.gov.tr/constitution.htm*, p. 1.

[88]Ibid., p. 3.

[89]Ibid., p. 6.

[90]Ibid., p. 10.

[91]Ibid., p. 10.

[92]Ibid., p. 10.

[93]Ibid., p. 10.

[94]"Cairo Declaration on Human Rights in Islam," in Mayer, p. 208.

[95]"The Universal Islamic Declaration of Human Rights," *http://www.alhewar.com/ISLAMICDECL.html*, pp. 1–2.

[96]"The Cairo Declaration on Human Rights in Islam," p. 203.

[97]"Universal Islamic Declaration of Human Rights," p. 7.

[98]"Cairo Declaration on Human Rights in Islam," pp. 207–208.

[99]"Universal Islamic Declaration of Human Rights," p. 10.

[100]"Cairo Declaration on Human Rights in Islam," p. 205.

[101]Included in Middle East and North Africa region are: Algeria, Bahrain, Cyprus, Djibouti, Egypt Iran Iraq, Jordan, Kuwait, Lebanon, Libya, Morocco, Oman, Qatar, Saudi Arabia, Sudan, Syria, Tunisia, United Arab Emirates, Yemen.

[102]Included in the Industrial Countries are: Andorra, Australia, Austria, Belgium, Canada, Denmark Finland, France, Germany, Greece, Holy See, Iceland, Ireland, Israel, Italy, Japan, Liechtenstein, Luxembourg, Malta, Monaco, Netherlands, New Zealand, Norway, Portugal, San Marino, Slovenia, Spain, Sweden, Switzerland, United Kingdom, United States.

[103]*Al-Qur'an*, p. 39.

[104]Ibid., p. 41.

[105]Mayer, p. 148.

[106]*Al-Qur'an*, p. 34.

[107]*Al-Qur'an*, p. 78.

Chapter 4

[1]Jean-Jacques Rousseau, *The Social Contract and Discourses* (New York: E.P. Dutton and Company, 1950), p. 3.

[2]See Daniel R. Headrick, *The Tools of Empire: Technology and European Imperialism in the Nineteenth Century* (New York: Oxford University Press, 1981), pp. 3–4.

[3]See John E. Coons and Patrick M. Brennan, *By Nature Equal: The Anatomy of a Western Insight* (Princeton: Princeton University Press, 1999), p. 35.

[4]Anthony Pagden, *Lords of All the World: Ideologies of Empire in Spain, Britain and France c.1500–c.1800* (New Haven: Yale University Press, 1995), p. 21.

[5]Ibid., p. 20.

[6]Quoted by Pagden, p. 23.

[7]Ibid., p. 20.

[8]Ibid., p. 24.

[9]Philip Abrams, "Introduction," in *John Locke, Two Tracts on Government*, edited by Philip Abrams (Cambridge, England: Cambridge University press, 1967), 63–84.

[10]John Yolton, *The Locke Reader: Selections from the Works of John Locke with a General Introduction and Commentary* (London: Cambridge University Press,), pp. 237–330.

[11]Abrams, pp. 3–115.

[12]Ibid., p. 105.

[13]See Joel Spring, *The American School 1642–1993 Third Edition* (New York: McGraw-Hill, 1994), pp. 32–97.

[14]John Locke, *Some Thoughts Concerning Education* in *John Locke on Education* (New York: Teachers College Press, 1964), p. 176.

[15]Ibid., p. 129.

[16]Ibid., p.176.

[17]Ibid., p. 20.

[18]Ibid., p. 20.

[19]See Stephen Ellenburg, *Rousseau's Political Philosophy: An Interpretation from Within* (Ithaca, NY: Cornell University Press, 1976).

[20]*The Emile of Jean-Jacques Rousseau*, translated and edited by William Boyd (New York: Teachers College Press, 1956), p. 153.

[21]Ibid., p. 20.

[22]Jean-Jacques Rousseau, "Political Economy" in *The Minor Educational Writings of Jean-Jacques Rousseau*, edited by William Boyd (London: Blackies and Son, 1910), pp. 42–43.

[23]Ibid., p. 45.

[24]Jean-Jacques Rousseau, "Considerations on the Government of Poland," in Ibid., pp. 141–142.

[25]J. R. Pole, *The Pursuit of Equality in American History: Second Edition* (Berkeley: University of California, 1993), p. 37.

[26]See Ian F. Haney Lopez, *White by Law: The Legal Construction of Race* (New York: New York University Press, 1996), pp. 1–36.

[27]For a discussion of these later forms of scientific racism see Kenan Malik, *The Meaning of Race: Race, History and Culture in Western Society* (New York: New York University Press, 1996), pp. 101–123.

[28]Thomas Jefferson, *Notes on the State of Virginia*, in *The Life and Selected Writings of Jefferson*, edited by Adrienne Koch and William Peden (New York: The Modern Library, 1944), p. 257.

[29]Ibid., p. 256.

[30]Ibid., p. 256.

[31]Thomas Jefferson, "To Peter Carr, With Enclosure," in Gordon Lee (Ed.), *Crusade Against Ignorance: Thomas Jefferson on Education* (New York: Teachers College Press, 1961), pp. 145–46.

[32]Ibid., p. 146.

[33]Thomas Jefferson, *Notes on the State of Virginia* ... , p. 257.

[34]Ibid., p. 257.

[35]Ibid., p. 257–258.

[36]Ibid., p. 259.

[37]Ibid., p. 262.

[38]The Declaration of the Rights of Man and of the Citizen can be found in a number of places. One online source is *U.S. Historical Documents Archive, http://w3.one.net/~mweiler/ushda.*

[39]Onuma Yasuaki, "Toward an Intercivilizational Approach to Human Rights," in *The East Asian Challenger for Human Rights* edited by Joanne Bauer and Daniel Bell (Cambridge: Cambridge University Press, 1999), pp. 103–124.

[40]Quoted by Koggel, p. 76.

[41]Lummis, p.43.

[42]Poole, pp. 150–151.

[43]Ibid., p. 151.

[44]See Joel Spring, *The American School 1642–1996* (New York: McGraw-Hill, 1997), pp. 79–96.

[45]See Ibid., pp. 358–385.

[46]Koggel, p. 43.

[47]"Constitution of the United States," *Microsoft® Encarta® 98 Encyclopedia.* © *1993–1997 Microsoft Corporation. All rights reserved.*

[48]"Plessy v. Ferguson," *Microsoft® Encarta® 98 Encyclopedia.* © 1993–1997 Microsoft Corporation. All rights reserved.

[49]A study of the conditions of schooling under the separate but equal doctrine can be found in James Anderson, *The Education of Blacks in the South 1860–1935* (Chapel Hill: University of North Carolina Press, 1988).

[50]For a history of citizenship laws and the struggle for equality before the law see Joel Spring, *Deculturalization and the Struggle for Equality* (New York: McGraw-Hill, 2001).

[51]See Ibid.

[52]Koggel, p. 81.

[53]Jean Anyon, *Ghetto Schooling: A Political Economy of Urban Educational Reform* (New York: Teachers College Press, 1997).

[54]"France—Constitution," *http://www.uni-wuerzburg.de/law/fr00000_.html.* , p. 1.

[55]Ibid., p. 1.

[56]"Italy—Constitution," http://www.uni-wuerzburg.de/law/it00000_.html , p. 5.

[57]"Poland—Constitution," http://www.uni-wuerzburg.de/law/p00000__.html, p. 9.

[58]"Spain—Constitution," http://www.uni-wuerzburg.de/law/sp00000__.html, p.5.

[59]Ibid., p. 5.

[60]"Germany—Constitution," http://www.uni-wuerzburg.de/law/gm00000__.html, p. 2.

[61]Spring, *The American School*, pp. 396–405.

[62]"Italy—Constitution," p. 1.

[63]"France—Constitution," p. 1.

[64]"Spain—Constitution," p. 1.

[65]Ibid., p. 1.

[66]"Sweden—Constitution," http://www.uni-wuerzburg.de/law/sw00000__.html, p. 4.

[67]Ibid.

[68]See Joel Spring, *American Education 9th Edition* (New York: McGraw-Hill, 1999), pp. 281–291.

[69]For a review of current human rights work of the European Union see "Making Human Rights a Reality," http://ue.eu.int.pesc/human_rights/en/99/main1.htm.

[70]"European Convention on Human Rights and Its Five Protocols," in *Basic Documents on Human Rights ...* , p. 342.

[71]Ibid., p. 330.

Chapter 5

[1]Joel Spring, *Education and the Rise of the Global Economy* (Mahwah NJ: Lawrence Erlbaum Associates, 1998), p. 16.

[2]Ibid., p. 16.

[3]A copy of the Indian Constitution can be found at http://alfa.nic.in/const/preamble.html.

[4]Yogesh Chadha, *Gandhi: A Life* (New York: John Wiley & Sons, 1997), p. 197.

[5]Quoted in Ibid., p. 198.

[6]For a discussion of the role of these constitutions in shaping the Indian Constitution see Granville Austin, *The Indian Constitution: Cornerstone of a Nation* (New Delhi: Oxford University Press, 1966), pp. 50–113.

[7]"Educational Statistics," Department of Education, Government of India, April, 2000, *http://www.nic.in/vseducation/htmlweb/edusta.htm*, p. 8.

[8]*Dharmasutras: The Law Codes of Apastamba, Gautama, Baudhayana, and Vasistha*, translated and edited by Patrick Olivelle (Oxford: Oxford University Press, 1999), p. 7.

[9]Ibid., p. 25.

[10]Ibid., p. 7.

[11]Ibid., p. xl.

[12]*Dharmasutras*, p. 110.

[13]Pauline Kolenda, *Caste in Contemporary India: Beyond Organic Solidarity* (Prospect Heights, IL: Waveland Press, Inc., 1985), p. 32.

[14]Ibid., p. 34.

[15]Ibid., p. 7.

[16]Ibid., p. 54.

[17]Ibid., pp. 53–54.

[18]Kolenda, pp. 40–42.

[19]Ibid., p. 65.

[20]*Dharmasutras*, p. 31.

[21]Ibid., p. 53.

[22]Ibid., p. 53.

[23]Ibid., 53.

[24]Kolenda, p. 75.

[25]See "Thus Spoke Ambedkar," http://www.angelfire.com/ak/ambedkar/BRquotes. html, p. 1.

[26]Dhananjay Keer, *Dr. Ambedkar: Life and Mission* (Bombay: A. V. Keer, 1954), p. 67.

[27]Ibid., p. 17.

[28]Ibid., p. 29.

[29]Ibid., p. 29.

[30]Ibid., p. 26.

[31]Ibid., pp. 32, 37.

[32]Ibid., p. 38.

[33]Ibid., p. 39.

[34]Ibid., pp. 66–77.

[35]Ibid., p. 80.

[36]Ibid., 121–122.

[37]"Dr. B. R. Ambedkar (1891–1956)," http://www.dalitusa.org/ambedkar.html, p. 1.

[38]B. R. Ambedkar, "Why Go for Conversion," translated from Marathi by Vasant Moon, http://www.angelfire.com/ak/ambedkar/BRwhyconversion.html, p. 2.

[39]Ibid., p. 2.

[40]Ibid., p. 4.

[41]Ibid., p. 5.

[42]Ibid., pp. 4–5.

[43]Ibid., p. 7.

[44] "22 Vows of Dr. Ambedkar," http://www.angelfire.com/ak/ambedkar/BR22vows. html.

[45]"The Esoteric World of Madame Blavatsky, chapter 6, The Founding of the Theosophical Society and the Writing of Isis Unveiled," *http//www.theosophical.org/csw6.html*, p. 1.

[46]Ibid.

[47]"The Three Fundamental Principles," http//www.theosophycompany.org/funda. html, p. 1.

[48]Mohandas K. Gandhi, *An Autobiography: The Story of My Experiments with Truth*, translated from the original Gujarati by Mahadev Desai (Boston: Beacon Press, 1957), p. 82.

[49]Gandhi, p. 67.

[50]Chadha p. 463.

[51]Gandhi, p. 68.

[52]Ibid., p. 68.

[53]Jawaharlal Nehru, *An Autobiography* (London: John Lane, *The Bodley Head*, 1936), pp. 15–16.

[54]See Austin, p. 42.

[55]Nancy Fix Anderson, "Bridging Cross-Cultural Feminism: Annie Besant and Women's Rights in England and India, 1874–1933," *Women's History Review* Volume 3, Number 4 (1994).

[56]Ibid., p. 565.

[57]Ibid., p. 566.

[58]Ibid., p. 569.

[59]Ibid., p. 571.

[60]Ibid., p. 574.

[61]Ibid., p. 576.

[62]Annie Besant, "Preface," in *The Bhagavad Gita*, translated by Annie Besant (Wheaton, IL: The Theosophical Publishing House, 1998), p. xvi.

[63]Gandhi, p. 21.

[64]Ibid., p. 21.

[65]Ibid., p. 120.

[66]Ibid., p. 121.

[67]Chadha, p. 100.

[68]Ibid., p. 124.

[69]Ibid., p. 160.

[70]Ibid., p. 332.

[71]Ibid., p. 328.

[72]Ghandhi, p. 330.

[73]Ibid., p. 319.

[74]*The Bhagavad Gita*, translated by Annie Besant ... , p. 47.

[75]Ibid., p. 41.

[76]Chadha, p. 104.

[77]Ibid., p. 159.

[78]See Joel Spring, *Wheels in the Head: Educational Philosophies of Authority, Freedom, and Culture from Socrates to Human Rights* (New York: McGraw-Hill, 1999), pp. 49–51.

[79]Gandhi, p. 333.

[80]Ibid., p. 339.

[81]Chadha, p. 10.

[82]Gandhi, p. 40.

[83]Ibid., p. 90.

[84]Ibid., p. 28.

[85]Chadha, p. 336.

[86]Ibid., p. 323.

[87]Ibid., p. 323.

[88]Ibid., p. 325.

[89]Ibid., p. 326–327.

[90]Ibid., p. 330.

[91]Ibid., p. 471.

[92]Austin, p. 39.

[93]Ibid., p. 49.

[94]Located opposite page 279 in Chadha.

[95]Martin Luther King, Jr., *Stride Toward Freedom: The Montgomery Story* (New York: Harper & Row, 1958), pp. 90–107.

[96]Austin, p. 69.

[97]Indian Constitution, op. cit.

[98]Ibid.

[99]Ibid.

[100]Ibid.

[101]Nehru, pp. 3,5.

[102]Ibid., p. 8.

[103]Ibid., p. 13.

[104]Ibid., p. 14.

[105]Ibid., p. 6.

[106]Ibid., p. 16.

[107]Ibid., p. 48.

[108]Ibid., p. 52.

[109]Jawaharlal Nehru, "Swaraj and Socialism," in *Jawaharlal Nehru: An Anthology*, edited by Sarvepalli Gopal (Delhi: Oxford University Press, 1980), p. 292.

[110]Ibid., 292.

[111]Ibid., p.292.

[112]Ibid., p. 293.

[113]Nehru, *An Autobiography*, p. 374.

[114]Ibid., p. 380.

[115]Jawaharlal Nehru,"Awakening in the Youth," in *Jawaharlal Nehru: Anthology* ... , p. 450.

[116]Jawaharlal Nehru, "The Right Path," in *Jawaharlal Nehru: Anthology* ... , p. 458.

[117]Jawaharlal Nehru, "Basic Education," in *Jawaharlal Nehru: Anthology* ... , pp. 271–272.

[118]Jawaharlal Nehru, "Women's Education," in *Jawaharlal Nehru: Anthology* ... , p. 270.

[119]Nehru, "Basic Education" ... , P. 271.

[120]Nehru, "Women's Education" ... , p. 270

[121]Jawaharlal Nehru, "English" in *Jawaharlal Nehru: Anthology* ... , p. 507.

[122]Ibid., p. 507.

[123]Jawaharlal Nehru, "The Question of Language," in *Jawaharlal Nehru: Anthology* ... , p. 508.

[124]"Constitutional Basis of Education (1950), Constitution of India" in J. C. Aggarwal, *Landmarks in the History of Modern Indian Education* (New Delhi: Vikas Publishing House, 1984), pp. 95–96.

[125]Ibid., pp. 93–94.

[126]Ibid., p. 97.

[127]J. C. Aggarwal, "Introduction," in Ibid., p. 73.

[128]"University Education Commission (1948–1949)," in Ibid., p. 75.

[129]Ibid., p. 77.

[130]See Joel Spring, *Education and the Rise of the Global Economy* (Mahwah NJ: Lawrence Erlbaum Associates, 1998).

[131]Ibid., p. 81.

[132]Ibid., p. 81.

[133]The Associated Press, "Gunmen Kill 34 in India as Caste War Plagues State." *New York Times on the Web* (17 June 2000).

[134]"Differentiation of Curricula for Boys and Girls (1964)," Ibid., p. 171.

[135]"Development of Higher Education in India: A Policy Frame (1978)," Ibid., p. 359.

[136]Ibid., p. 359.

[137]"Top 10 Colleges of India," *India Today, http://www.India-today.com.*, pp. 2–3.

[138]Ibid., p. 3.

[139]Amartya Sen, *Development as Freedom* (New York: Alfred Knopf, 1999), p. 106.

[140]Ibid.

[141]Celia Dugger, "Connecting Rural India to the World," *The New York Times on the Web* (28 May 2000), p. 1.

[142]Ibid., p. 1.

Chapter 6

[1]"China—Constitution,"*http: www.uni-wuerzburg.de/law/ch00000_.html*, p. 3.

[2]"The Constitution of the Republic of Turkey," *http://byegm.gov.tr/constitution.htm*, p. 10.

[3]See Tove Skutnabb-Kangas, *Linguistic Genocide in Education or Worldwide Diversity and Human Rights?* (Mahwah, NJ: Lawrence Erlbaum Associates, 2000), pp. 567–638.

[4]"Constitutional Basis of Education (1950), Constitution of India" in J. C. Aggarwal, *Landmarks in the History of Modern Indian Education* (New Delhi: Vikas Publishing House, 1984), p. 97.

[5]"China—Constitution," p. 6.

[6]Ibid., p. 3.

[7]"Italy—Constitution," http://www.uni-wuerzburg.de/law/it00000_.html, p. 1.

[8]"The Constitution of the Republic of Turkey," p. 10.

[9]"France—Constitution," *http://www.uni-wuerzburg.de/law/fr00000_.html*, p. 1.

[10]"The Universal Declaration of Human Rights," *www1.umn.edu/humanarts/instree/b1udhr.htm*, p. 4.

[11]"Pakistan—Constitution," Part I, Introductory, *http://www.stanford.edu/group/pakistan/constitution*, p. 4.

[12]"European Convention on Human Rights and Its Five Protocols," in *Basic Documents on Human Rights Third Edition*, edited by Ian Brownlie (New York: Oxford University Press, 1994), p. 342.

[13]"China—Constitution," p. 6.

[14]"Syria Constitution," *www.uni-wuerzburg.de/law/sy00000_.html*, pp. 4–5.

[15]*The Bhagavad-Gita: The Lord's Song*, translated by Annie Besant (Wheaton, IL: The Theosophical Publishing House, 1914), p. 44.

Index

DATE DUE

NO 30 '04		
MY 17 '06		
APR 1 0 2009		
		WITHDRAWN

DEMCO 38-296